Language and Subjectivity

Understanding the role of language within the formation of a sense
of self has been revolutionized by developments in social theory,
particularly poststructuralism. There is now a new emphasis on the
way in which subjects are vulnerable in the face of powerful discourses such as nation, gender, race and sexuality. This book is a
clear and engaging introduction to these developments and their
relevance to students of language. Using lively and often personal
examples throughout, Tim McNamara explores the role of language
within processes of subjectivity using the insights of Conversation
Analysis (CA), creating an original conceptual and methodological
bridge between the macro- and micro-dimensions of social discourse and everyday conversational interaction.

TIM MCNAMARA is Redmond Barry Distinguished Professor
Emeritus at The University of Melbourne

T0349128

KEY TOPICS IN APPLIED LINGUISTICS

Series Editors

Claire Kramsch (University of California, Berkeley)
and Zhu Hua (Birkbeck College, London)

Books in this series provide critical accounts of the most important topics in applied linguistics, conceptualized as an interdisciplinary field of research and practice dealing with practical problems of language and communication. Some topics have been the subject of applied linguistics for many years and will be re-examined in the light of new developments in the field; others are issues of growing importance that have not so far been given a sustained treatment. The topics of the series are nuanced and specialized, providing an opportunity for further reading around a particular concept. The concept examined may be theoretical or practice-oriented. Written by leading experts, the books in the series can be used on courses and in seminars, or as succinct guides to a particular topic for individual students and researchers.

Language and Subjectivity

TIM McNAMARA
The University of Melbourne

CAMBRIDGE
UNIVERSITY PRESS

CAMBRIDGE
UNIVERSITY PRESS

University Printing House, Cambridge CB2 8BS, United Kingdom

One Liberty Plaza, 20th Floor, New York, NY 10006, USA

477 Williamstown Road, Port Melbourne, VIC 3207, Australia

314–321, 3rd Floor, Plot 3, Splendor Forum, Jasola District Centre,
New Delhi - 110025, India

79 Anson Road, #06–04/06, Singapore 079906

Cambridge University Press is part of the University of Cambridge.

It furthers the University's mission by disseminating knowledge in the pursuit of
education, learning, and research at the highest international levels of excellence.

www.cambridge.org
Information on this title: www.cambridge.org/9781108475488
DOI: 10.1017/9781108639606

© Tim McNamara 2019

First published 2019

Printed and bound in Great Britain by Clays Ltd, Elcograf S.p.A.

A catalogue record for this publication is available from the British Library.

Library of Congress Cataloging-in-Publication Data
Names: McNamara, T. F. (Timothy Francis), author.
Title: Language and subjectivity / Tim McNamara.
Description: New York : Cambridge University Press, 2019. | Series: Key topics in
applied linguistics
Identifiers: LCCN 2018038843 | ISBN 9781108475488 (hardback)
Subjects: LCSH: Conversation analysis. | Subjectivity (Linguistics) | Discourse
analysis. | BISAC: LANGUAGE ARTS & DISCIPLINES / Linguistics / Sociolinguistics.
Classification: LCC P95.45 .M38 2019 | DDC 401/.41–dc23
LC record available at https://lccn.loc.gov/2018038843

ISBN 978-1-108-47548-8 Hardback
ISBN 978-1-108-46855-8 Paperback

For Lillian

Contents

Figures

Tables

Acknowledgements

This book has been a long time in the gestation. Its origins lie in friendships with individuals who have helped me understand the constitution of the subject in terms of vulnerability and marginality, both in their experience of life and ultimately in my own. Making this an object of formal intellectual exploration began in London during my MA at Birkbeck, where I was introduced to Social Identity Theory by Michel Blanc, a theoretical framing that I used in my study of the immigrant experience of Israeli Jewish families in Melbourne in the 1980s. A realization that I would need to update my understanding in the 1990s if I wanted to continue work in the area of identity was triggered by the arrival of my new colleagues at Melbourne, Brian Lynch and Alastair Pennycook, who each in their different ways pushed me to explore alternatives to current paradigms, particularly in poststructuralist thought. Attendance at the Lavender Language and Linguistics conference at the American University in Washington in the same year (1995) introduced me to the heady mix of queer theory. A month as a guest of Claire Kramsch at Berkeley in 2003 was another formative moment: I devoured texts in the bookshops and library there, drank coffee in the café where Foucault had worked, and attended a conference on racism at UC Irvine which involved a confrontation between postcolonial theorists and workers in Derridean deconstruction, with Derrida himself present.

When I returned to Melbourne, I joined a group of graduate students in other disciplines, all much younger than me, who were interested in reading in social theory. We read Fanon's *Black Skin, White Masks* and then decided that we wanted to read Derrida. None of us were philosophers, but we persisted, starting by reading the text of *Of Grammatology* aloud in the group, pausing at the end of each paragraph to check our understanding, which was often limited – and so we talked in order to try and make sense of what we had read. We managed four or five pages in a 90-minute session and did this every week for five years. It was some of the most rigorous intellectual training I have ever had.

Attendance at conferences on continental philosophy in Sydney (where we heard and met Judith Butler), California and London also pushed forward my thinking over a number of years. An important step was giving myself the task of offering an upper-level undergraduate course on Language and Identity, setting myself a set of topics to be covered which I would have to learn about in order to deliver the relevant lectures. The experience of teaching that course every other year for the last fifteen years has formed the core of the content and organization of this book.

Throughout, I have had excellent interlocutors at Melbourne: Alastair and Brian, the members of the Derrida group, Chris, Antonia, Cara and Jess, my colleague and friend Anne Freadman, and others, including Justin Clemens, Birgit Lang, Claire Maree and Chloé Diskin. I have learned a great deal from courses at the wonderful Melbourne School of Continental Philosophy and am indebted in particular to David Rathbone and Peter Banki.

I am grateful to my colleagues in the School of Languages and Linguistics at Melbourne more generally, for creating the warm and collegial intellectual environment in which I work. Hayden Blain has played a crucial role in the latter stages of the preparation of the manuscript, and I would like to express my thanks to him. And a special thanks to Cass McGufficke, who meticulously read through and made helpful suggestions on a draft of the book. I have learned, and am learning, so much from my students who have worked with me in this and related areas over many years.

Claire Kramsch has been a superb interlocutor and mentor over many years. She has also played a more immediate role recently, as co-editor of the series in which this book appears. Her challenging and penetrating comments on drafts of the manuscript have immeasurably improved it. Zhu Hua, her co-editor, has similarly given perceptive and helpful comments – I have been very lucky in having two such editors. I would also like to thank the very professional editorial team at Cambridge University Press, particularly Jacqueline French for her meticulous copy-editing work.

I am grateful to my hosts in different universities in which I have spent extended sabbaticals or other extended periods of time, in Los Angeles, London, Vienna, Stockholm, New York and Tel Aviv. These periods of reflection, talking and reading have given me the chance to develop the argument of the book, in relation to both the theorizing of subjectivity (I especially want to acknowledge David Block) and the development of my understanding of the possibilities of Conversation Analysis as a tool for poststructuralist discourse analysis (here I am indebted to Hansun Waring, Jean Wong and Catrin Norrby; my fundamental introduction to Conversation Analysis was from my dear, late friend, Sally Jacoby). Elana Shohamy, Jim Lantolf, Bernard Spolsky, Brigitta Busch, Thomas Busch and Diane Larsen-Freeman have for many years been wonderful intellectual sparring partners on these as on so many other topics.

The map of Guinea-Bissau and neighbouring countries (Figure 9.1) is reproduced with permission.

The map of the linguistic boundaries in Guinea Bissau and surrounding countries (Figure 9.2) is reproduced by permission of Mutuzikin.com.

1 The Construction of the Subject

In the last few years, football (soccer) teams from Australia have done well for the first time in the World Cup and similar international competitions; this is a notable achievement given that this code of football has not been a mainstream sport in Australia, which has its own unique football code, Australian Rules Football, as well as the international code of rugby, and it is these latter sports which attract the greatest attendances at matches. This changed in 2006, when Australia, to the surprise and delight of most Australians, made it to the quarter finals of the soccer World Cup. I have absolutely no knowledge of this particular code and have little interest in it, but I happened to be in Buenos Aires when the match which put Australia into the quarter finals was being played. On the television in my hotel room, I happened to see Harry Kewell score the crucial goal that tied the match against Croatia, which meant that the Australian team had qualified for the next round. To my amazement I found my eyes filling with tears – I was intensely proud to be an Australian. My experience felt very personal, and clearly very emotional. But what had made this moment possible? Where had this experience of national identity, my subjectivity as an Australian, come from? And what role does language play in the construction of such experiences?

This book will argue that although subjectivity is powerfully experienced as a private feeling, something lying deep inside us, its origins lie outside us, in the social world and in the discourses that circulate within it. It will draw on the work of the philosophers of poststructuralism, particularly Foucault, Derrida and Butler, to conceptualize and discuss this phenomenon. In this chapter, we explore the origins of subjectivity, our sense of ourselves as members of social categories, within the social contexts in which individuals grow up or find themselves. The chapter is more exclusively theoretical than subsequent chapters, as it introduces a number of key terms and develops the overall argument of the book. But before we begin the discussion in this chapter, we have to address the question of why we should use an awkward term like 'subjectivity' – what's wrong with the more familiar term 'identity'?

The term *identity* has been around a long time and is associated with a range of perspectives on our sense of ourselves as individual and social beings. An important strand of thought on identity draws on a philosophy of consciousness which assumes the ultimate autonomy of the individual, the idea that the individual has agency or choice over action, thought and being. This kind of thinking about identity focuses on the individual cognitive and emotional aspects of social self-awareness, and stresses human agency. From this perspective, the role of social mediation in our identities is lessened, though of course not ignored. Several other approaches to thinking about identity see it from a very different, more social perspective, and much valuable work on identity in applied linguistics has been conducted from this social perspective in the last several decades. This book, however, will introduce and focus on social approaches to identity drawing on the intellectual tradition of poststructuralism. Here, the preferred term for thinking about identity is *subjectivity*, which focuses on social mediation in identity formation in a particular way. The term draws on the work of the French philosopher Michel Foucault: subjectivity is associated with his notions of *discourse, power* and the *visibility of subjects*, which we will consider in detail in this chapter. This conceptual framework will also be drawn upon in subsequent chapters looking at subjectivity in terms of such further categories as gender and sexuality, ethnicity, race and so on. The emphasis on the location of our sense of ourselves in the social world, rather than arising internally, raises the vexed question of individual agency, given the power of discourse in shaping the subject. We will outline this issue in the current chapter, and later return to it in more detail. We will sometimes, for convenience, use the more familiar term identity interchangeably with subjectivity throughout the book, but the emphasis throughout will be on poststructuralist accounts of the subject. Later in this chapter, and elsewhere in this book, we will contrast poststructuralist approaches to subjectivity with other more modernist social approaches to identity.

1.2 SOCIAL PERSPECTIVES ON THE SUBJECT IN POSTSTRUCTURALISM

The work of the French philosopher Michel Foucault (1926–84) offers a powerful critique of the notion of the autonomous subject. The tradition of the 'autonomous subject' goes back many centuries in Western thought. Descartes (1596–1650), the philosopher of the rational subject, summed up this perspective in his famous dictum: *Cogito, ergo sum* ('I think, therefore I am'): identity resides in consciousness. The German philosopher of the Enlightenment Immanuel Kant (1724–1804) argued that the ethical subject uses reason to transcend cultural norms and to discover absolute moral truth. In this tradition of decontextualized individualism, reason is privileged over other human capacities. The nineteenth century saw the beginning of the questioning of this Enlightenment view of the rational subject. For the German philosopher Friedrich Nietzsche (1844–1900),

> Consciousness was an *effect* rather than a *cause* ... Reason is not so much a quality or attribute of the mind as the result of political or coercive struggles between various competing perspectives, in which one gains a (provisional, temporary, historical) dominance. (Grosz, 1990, p. 1)

Foucault was strongly influenced by Nietzsche's emphasis on the social and historical origins of beliefs and understanding. Three fundamental concepts in Foucault are central to his thought: *Discourse, Subjectivity / The subject,* and *Power/Knowledge.*

Let us first examine the term *Discourse.* Stuart Hall defines this as follows: 'A group of statements which provide a language for talking about – a way of representing the knowledge about – a particular topic at a particular historical moment' (Hall, 1997, p. 44). The word 'statements' here does not refer to specifically worded utterances, but to propositions, ideas or concepts; a received way of thinking about or talking about a subject or topic; 'what people say' about a topic – including what 'experts' say. In discourse, reality is represented – talked about, understood, reasoned about – in a particular way at a particular time. In this sense, discourses define the 'objects' of our knowledge – but more: they *produce* those very objects. The emphasis is not on 'objective' knowledge of the world but on people's representations of the world which, in the case of 'knowledge' about groups of people (one's own group or those of others) may bear little relationship to other people's perceptions of the same groups. In particular, outsiders and insiders may have very different representations of a group. This will be very important when we come to examine discourses determining our perceptions of ethnic and racial groups other than our own – the 'knowledge' that is available from the discourse in the way the group is represented may be far from the lived experience of the group itself.

Note in passing that it is important not to confuse the use of the term discourse in Foucault's work with the use of the term discourse familiar within linguistics, particularly within pragmatics. James Gee (2015) distinguishes Foucault's use, which he calls 'big D Discourse' (grammatically both a non-count and countable noun, so that we can speak of discourses in the plural), from 'small d discourse' in linguistics, the study of the use of language in context (a non-count noun). While discourse analysis of the type familiar in linguistics will be an indispensable tool for studying the role of 'big D Discourse' in the construction of subjectivity, as we shall see in later chapters, it is in principle independent of the study of discourses in the Foucauldian sense.

The reference to history in Hall's definition of discourse is also important. Discourses change over historical time and reveal abrupt shifts and discontinuities. Foucault did not believe in any simple linear notion of human progress; given that he was writing in the period of a century which had seen appalling examples of brutality and violence in the colonial project, and most starkly in the Holocaust, perpetrated by the supposedly most 'advanced' civilizations in the world, his scepticism about 'progress' is hardly surprising. Instead, he sees arbitrary and sometimes abrupt shifts in ways of talking about and thinking about aspects of reality, particularly social reality: discourses change and new discourses emerge. In a series of lectures and books, Foucault traced the emergence of various discourses historically. The 'archaeology' of a number of important discourses of modernity is examined: the discourse of *madness* in *Folie et déraison* (*Madness and Civilization*) (Foucault, 1967), the discourse of *medicine* in *Naissance de la clinique* (*Birth of the Clinic*) (Foucault, 1973), the discourse of *punishment* in *Surveiller et punir* (*Discipline and Punish*) (Foucault, 1977) and the discourse of *sexuality* in *Histoire de la sexualité* (*The History of Sexuality*) (Foucault, 1978).

We can illustrate what Foucault means by discourse, its contingency and its historical shifts, by looking at discourses of *nation*, with which this chapter began. We will also see the role played by language and the discipline of linguistics itself in the changing character of this discourse.

1.3 LANGUAGE AND DISCOURSES OF THE NATION

In a justly famous discussion, Anderson (1991) defines nations as 'imagined communities': '[A nation] is an imagined political community – and imagined as both inherently limited and sovereign' (p. 6). The community is 'imagined', according to Anderson, in the sense that 'members will never know most of their fellow-members, yet in the minds of each lives the image of their communion'. I remember how moved I was *as an Australian* when Cathy Freeman, an Australian Aboriginal athlete, won a gold medal at the 2000 Sydney Olympics (I have never met her, or anyone who knows her). The community of the nation is 'limited' in that it has boundaries, and its membership, the fellow-members with whom a person feels an affinity, is limited to those within the boundaries. Nations have borders; I would not have been so moved if an indigenous person from another country had won the medal. As a person from within the same nation's borders, an imagined association with Cathy Freeman existed. The community of the nation is also 'sovereign', in that the location of sovereignty in earlier periods in transnational dynastic realms was destroyed by the forces of revolution and enlightenment, and the nation-state became sovereign. Anderson also points out that regardless of actual inequality within nations and the exploitation of some members by others (Aboriginal Australians are among the most socially disadvantaged), the nation is always conceived as a deep, horizontal comradeship: stark, even grotesque, differences in the living conditions of members of the community are elided. Anderson notes poignantly that 'millions have been prepared to die for this limited imagining' in going to fight for their country.

Language, and the academic study of language (known prior to the twentieth century as philology), played a fundamental role in the emergence of discourses of the nation and nationalism. Prior to the modern era, the vernacular languages were largely spoken, and in written form were the preserve of scholars; they lacked the status and the functionality to take on the role of the languages of nation-states, a role which they were subsequently to play. In pre-modern times, the imagined community, and hence the focus of identification, was not the nation but the transnational empire (the Holy Roman Empire) or transnational religious community (Islam, Christendom). The latter communities were imaginable through the medium of a sacred language and a written script (Latin, Pali, Arabic, Chinese). In Europe, the Protestant Reformation saw the publication of sacred texts in vernacular languages to make them more accessible to ordinary people; this also coincided with the emergence of printing. Twenty million books had been printed by 1500; this figure had grown tenfold, to 200 million, by 1600. The variety of the vernacular chosen for the translation of texts and their subsequent publication and widespread distribution gave it an elevated status and led to a great stability and consistency in the form of the language. Moreover, those who read the published texts could now imagine themselves as having something in common with other readers of the same language, thus offering the possibility of identification well beyond local geographical and dialect boundaries. In this way, print languages laid the basis for national consciousness.

The nineteenth century saw the emergence of strong national identities and nationalist movements in many countries in Europe. Anderson argues that as other nations, inspired by the French Revolutionary idea that sovereignty lies in the nation, rather than in the ruler, copied the blueprint of nation from the French Revolution, the national print languages played a central ideological and political role in these developments. In addition, linguistic research played a key role: the creation of dictionaries and grammars, and historical research, led to a change in the status of vernacular languages at the expense of older languages.

By the end of the eighteenth century, German romanticism was articulating the idea of a powerful connection between a language shared among speakers and the political entity of the nation. Among the first to voice the ideology of the mother tongue and its role in national identity was the German philosopher Johann Gottfried von Herder (1744–1803), who wrote in 1783, in his *Briefe zu Beförderung der Humanität*:

> Has a nationality anything dearer than the speech of its fathers? In its
> speech resides its whole thought domain, its tradition, history,
> religion and basis of life, all its heart and soul. To deprive a people of
> its speech is to deprive it of its one eternal good ... with language is
> created the heart of a people. Every people ... has its national culture
> as well as its language (*jedes Volk ... hat seine Nationalbildung wie seine
> Sprache*) (Cited in Fishman, 1972, p. 143)

A further articulation of the ideology of the mother tongue is found a generation later in the work of Johann Gottlieb Fichte (1762–1814), in his *Reden an die deutsche Nation* (*Addresses to the German Nation*) of 1807/ 8, following the defeat of Prussian forces by Napoleon's army at the battle of Jena in 1806 (Fichte, 1808/1922). In the first formulation of the concept of the ethnic nation, Fichte claimed that language founded the national idea: it is from 'the natural generating strength of language' that the nation is formed. A third formulation of the ideology of the mother tongue and its link to the nation is found in the work of Wilhelm von Humboldt (1767–1835). For him, too, language was seen as defining national identity. In his great work *On Language: On the Diversity of Human Language Construction and its Influence on the Mental Development of the Human Species* (1836/1999), Humboldt argued that the purpose of the comparative study of languages (comparative philology) is to show that 'language is connected with the shaping of the nation's mental power'. The 'mental individuality of a people and the shape of its language are so intimately fused with one another' that though we 'may separate intellectuality and language, no such division in fact exists'. Whatever the source of language, Humboldt concludes that language is the 'outer appearance of the spirit of a people'. Humboldt also felt that as languages differed in complexity, so the intellectual capacity of the people who spoke them would differ, with some languages being more advanced than others. We can see here the slippery slope between the idea of the nation as founded on language and language as defining a people's character, and its innate superiority. Christopher Hutton, in his book *Linguistics and the Third Reich*, argues that 'The Herder-Humboldt vision of language was an integral part of linguistics under National Socialism' (Hutton, 1999, p. 287), where the discourse of nation, language and people had lethal consequences.

1.4 DISCOURSE AND SUBJECTIVITY: FOUCAULT'S DISCIPLINE AND PUNISH

In the discourses Foucault examined, similar shifts in conceptualization are identified. Foucault's *Discipline and Punish* (1977) traces the emergence of a new, 'modern' discourse on punishment in the course of the eighteenth century. Prior to that time, punishment was primarily physical, and often extreme. The book opens with a gruesome account of the punishment of an attempted regicide in eighteenth-century France. As the crime involved an attack on the body of the king, and hence on the body of the state itself – the king embodied the state – so it was felt appropriate that the punishment should involve the body of the criminal; and given the severity of the crime, so the physical punishment should be severe – tearing of limbs from the body, inflicting extreme injury and so on. A similar type of punishment was meted out on Túpac Amaru, the Inca leader of a long insurrection against the colonial rule of Spain in Peru; when he was finally defeated, his punishment involved similarly extreme measures (Pigna, 2005). In the course of the eighteenth century, a change in thinking about crime and punishment occurred, which saw a retreat from such punishments, which were now seen as barbaric and cruel. The modern discourse which replaced the old saw the goal of punishment as the reform of prisoners by shaping their consciousness; as Foucault puts it, it was the soul of the offender, not the body, which was the target of punishment. Part of the changed system of punishment involved the principle of surveillance. Here Foucault refers to the new designs for model prisons proposed at the end of the eighteenth century by the British utilitarian, Jeremy Bentham. The principle of these new prisons was that control of prisoners should be achieved by keeping them under perpetual surveillance by the prison authorities, in other words by making them permanently 'visible'. How could this be achieved without a tremendous cost in terms of the employment of guards? Bentham found a solution by suggesting that the prison be designed in such a way that it operated as a panopticon – that all the cells should be visible to the warder from a single point. This involved, for example, building circular prisons, with the cells facing a common central point, from where a guard could look into any of the cells at will (the walls of the cells on the side facing the warder would consist of bars only, allowing a view into the cells). Other designs were possible: for example, at Port Arthur in Tasmania, Australia, a model prison had individual cells along a corridor along which a warder could walk, with slits in the heavy wooden cell doors through which he could see the prisoner inside if he wished. Even in the chapel, the prisoners were constantly visible: placed in individual cell-like pews, which permitted them to look out at the preacher, but not at anything else, they could not see the prisoners on either side of them. The system in model prisons was very efficient in terms of the level of staffing required for the surveillance to be effective: at any moment, a warder if he so desired could see into a cell. Not that all cells were actually looked at all the time; the point was to introduce uncertainty in the prisoner's mind as to whether he/ she was being observed at that moment or not. The result of this system was that all the prisoners were permanently conscious that at any moment they might be being observed, that their behaviour was visible; this consciousness of their visibility was enough to discipline their behaviour and make them docile. The prisoners internalized the sense of being observed even when they were not. Model prisons were built at Pentonville in London and in other parts of the world, including the United States and Australia.[1] The goal of the system was, in Foucault's words (1977, p. 187),

> to induce in the inmate a state of conscious and permanent visibility that assures the automatic functioning of power ...
>
> Disciplinary power ... is exercised through its invisibility; at the same time it imposes on those whom it subjects a principle of compulsory visibility. In discipline, it is the subjects who have to be seen. Their visibility assures the hold of the power that is exercised over them.

Foucault noted that other modern institutions, for example educational systems and bureaucracies, imitated the techniques of discipline of the prison; in them direct visual surveillance is paralleled by observation, but also replaced or supplemented by examination and record-keeping: 'The examination is the technique by which power ... holds [its subjects] in a mechanism of objectification' (Foucault, 1977, p. 187).

The consciousness induced in such systems is the key to Foucault's notion of subjectivity. It is a consciousness of being seen, of our visibility, of our appearance to others. This consciousness internalizes in us the sense of the power of the other as fundamental to our sense of ourselves. A kind of alienation of consciousness, a subjective sense of ourselves originating from without, is central to Foucault's idea of the subject. This is one of the double meanings of the word 'subject' in Foucault's work: the sense of being *subject to* a form of social power.

1.5 DISCOURSE AND THE RECOGNITION OF THE SUBJECT

The figure of literal social surveillance in the panopticon is extended in Foucault's discussion to explain the operation of *discourse* as achieving the same effect of visibility: it produces subjects. Discourses construct the terms in which each of us is seen, because discourses offer us ways of seeing each other as belonging or not belonging to the social categories which are the very subject of the discourse. Discourses offer terms of recognition of Self and Other – the terms in which we are socially visible to each other – visible as particular types of subject.

[1] The prison at Port Arthur in Tasmania was remarkably effective at 'reforming' previously violent and intractable prisoners but was subsequently abandoned, as the system induced madness in many of the prisoners, so that an asylum had to be built to house them, thus reversing the savings that the new system had initially achieved.

This is because discourses are frequently *about* subjects. Here the word 'subject' means a recognisable *type* of individual – recognizable by his or her membership of a social category with its associated assumed attitudes, behaviour, appearance, values, and, important in the context of this book, language use. Typically, discourses have as their subject matter or topic a stigmatized social category; the discourse in fact constructs the stigma in defining what is wrong about an individual in such a category. Foucault shows how stigmatized types of subject are central to the discourses whose archaeology he traces – 'the criminal', 'the hysteric', 'the homosexual', 'the madman'. A characteristic of such discourses is that the subjects so defined are seen as abnormal, 'Other', not 'proper'. Discourses thus have the function of offering social vision in terms of social exclusion. In contemporary discourses, various kinds of 'Other' are defined – in nationalist discourses, each nation will have one or more 'Others' to its own national identity; in discourses of race and ethnicity, there are a range of stigmatized race or ethnic Others, varying with social context. In relation to discourses of gender, Simone de Beauvoir famously defined woman as the Other (de Beauvoir, 1949/2010).

Discourses such as these create what are called 'subject positions', that is, possibilities for subjectivity, possibilities for being recognized as a certain kind of subject. The French Marxist theorist Louis Althusser (1918–90) addressed the issue of how we come to 'recognize' our 'selves' using a concept he calls 'interpellation'. Following Marxist tradition, he prefers to use the term ideology instead of discourse and suggests that ideology, like discourse, creates subjects. He gives a famous example of what this is like:

> I shall then suggest that ideology 'acts' or 'functions' in such a way that it 'recruits' subjects among the individuals ..., or 'transforms' the individuals into subjects ... by that very precise operation which I have called interpellation or hailing, and which can be imagined along the lines of the most commonplace everyday police (or other) hailing: 'Hey, you there!'
>
> Assuming that the theoretical scene I have imagined takes place in the street, the hailed individual will turn round. By this mere one-hundred-and-eighty-degree physical conversion, he becomes a subject. (Althusser, 1971, p. 174)

While this literal example is powerful as an image, how can discourses circulating more diffusely in social interaction be said to call subjects into being? What is the equivalent of the 'hailing' or interpellation in Althusser's example? We encounter the terms of the discourses salient in the social contexts in which we live in daily interaction. Such experiences are particularly powerful when we are recognized as Other through explicit or implicit racist, homophobic, xenophobic or sexist language in conversation: it is as if we stumble over a tripwire – we become aware of discursively constructed subject positions.[2] Researchers have investigated this phenomenon in everyday experience. Essed (1990; 1991) refers to it as the study of 'everyday racism' (see Chapter 4, below). Here is an example from an interview with a 21-year-old female black student in her third year of BA studies in South Africa, whose experience of rejection on race grounds by a fellow student was a moment of interpellation, of being called into social being as a subject in terms of race:

> I was attending a [subject] lecture and it's always full and I was ... I was amongst the last pupils to come into the hall because I had been attending another one. By the time I got there, it was almost full. I came there and just sat in the nearest seat and next to me was this guy, you know he looked the AWB[3] type. I just looked at him and I just sat and thought it's alright. To my surprise he moved. He just looked up and walked and ended up sitting somewhere else. He didn't say anything ... (Louw-Potgieter, 1989, p. 317)

Living in a new society or social context, for example as an immigrant, typically involves coming up against previously unfamiliar discourses which articulate relevant subject positions. The newcomer is likely to encounter such discourses in casual conversation and in everyday encounters, and in the reports of the experiences of those in similar categories; a kind of social learning takes place. We will consider an example of this, Jewish people's experience of everyday anti-Semitism, in a later chapter. People subject to persecution in their own societies on account of their social group membership (for example, Hazaras in Afghanistan) may seek protection in another society under the international refugee convention. On arrival in the receiving countries such as Western Europe or Australia, they are likely to encounter discourses involving the negative subject position of 'asylum seeker' in public discourse and in private conversation. Similarly, immigrants from traditional religious communities will encounter, possibly for the first time, contemporary Western secular discourses around homosexuality which may represent the subject position 'homosexual' in terms

---

[2] A Jewish friend has an unpublished poem with the line: 'I stumble on the trip-wire of your anti-Semitism ... '

[3] The Afrikaner Weerstandsbeweging or Afrikaner Resistance Movement is a racially based political organization whose goal is the creation of an independent Afrikaner republic in part of South Africa.

starkly different from the discourses of sexuality circulating in their own societies of origin. Encounters with such multiple new discourses are likely to have complex and conflicting impacts on the newcomer's subjectivity.

Language can play a key role in the recognition of subjects. Firstly, discourses circulate and are reproduced in language; both written texts, for example in the media or in literature, in captions, advertisements, signs and notices, and spoken texts, again in the media, but also in conversation, talks, sermons and so on will reflect prevailing discourses and the subject positions represented in them. Secondly, the moment of self-recognition as Other may be an incident involving exposure to such texts, for example in exposure to racist, sexist and homophobic remarks: subjects are 'called into being' in such moments, as we saw in the above example. Thirdly, speech (e.g. accent) may also be a cue to the recognition of subjects. That is, features of speech may actually constitute a topic within discourse about subjects: discourses may hold that certain kinds of subjects speak in a certain way. Consider discourses around native and non-native speakers of a language. Considerable energy has gone into establishing that the boundary between native and non-native speech is indelible: no matter how fluent a non-native speaker may be, they can never have the capacity of a native speaker. The caricature Hungarian phonetician, Professor Zoltan Karpathy, in the musical *My Fair Lady*, is reported to say of Eliza Doolittle's impeccable Received Pronunciation: 'Her English is too good,' he said, 'It clearly indicates that she is foreign.' As it happens, he is wrong in this case, but the vigilance he shows in detecting the social significance of features of speech is a fundamental aspect of human social interaction.

1.6 THE PSYCHE OF THE SUBJECT

So far, we have seen that the possibilities for subjectivity are constructed within discourse and that this represents a fundamental questioning of the autonomous subject. A different but equally dramatic questioning of the rational subject is represented by the work of Sigmund Freud (1856–1939): '*Contra* Descartes, Freud posits a subject that is radically *incapable* of knowing itself' (Grosz, 1990, p. 13). In Freud's model of the personality, the conscious (*ich* or ego) is distinguished from the Unconscious (*es*, id). And it is the Unconscious which is the driver of the individual's decisions and actions; the conscious is no longer seen as being in control. As the feminist poststructuralist Elizabeth Grosz (1990, pp. 1–2) puts it:

> Consciousness and its self-certainty may be the end-products of unconscious psychical 'defences' – denial, disavowal, resistance. That is, consciousness is identified with a certain mode of self-deception . . .
> The subject cannot know the . . . unconscious structures on which it relies and over which it may have little or no effect. Even where an individual functions as an agent of these structures, in no sense can he or she be considered to control them.

For Freud, says Grosz (p. 10),

> The unconscious is not a submerged consciousness, a rational system that is somehow invisible; it is an entirely <u>other</u> form of reason, logic, and pleasure, one not reducible to those available to consciousness. It undermines the subject's conscious aspirations by its symptomatic intrusions in behaviour which are uncontrolled by, and may even be unknown to, consciousness.

Freud himself was aware of the radical implications of his work in displacing the notion of the rational subject. He famously stated 'The ego is not master in its own house' (Freud, 1917/1955, p. 142) and saw the displacement of the ego (consciousness) as the centre of the universe as a revolution like the Copernican revolution in cosmology.

Freud saw social relations as the context in which the structure of the personality is formed, particularly relations within the family: the child's relations with its parents and caregivers. While Freud wrote famous texts interpreting the significance of his theories for understanding culture and society at large, unlike Foucault he did not see the society at large as forming the possibilities for subjectivity in the way that Foucault does. The question of the relationship of the Freudian perspective and the position of other theorists for whom social relations are paramount has been a major focus of theorizing in recent years, particularly in the work of feminist poststructuralist philosophers such as Judith Butler and Elizabeth Grosz among many others, who were interested in offering an account of the formation of gendered identity in patriarchal societies. A key point of reference in these discussions has been the work of the French psychoanalyst and theorist Jacques Lacan, who incorporated both a discussion of culture and a theory of language into his account of the unconscious.

For Foucault, psychoanalysis is purely a discourse; and as such it creates the subject (of the discourse). For this reason, he does not need to take the unconscious into account independently of the operation of discourse in the formation of subject, as the subject is an effect of power. There is thus a conflict between the views of Foucault on the one hand and Freud/Lacan on the other on the formation of the subject. Judith Butler explores this conflict, and asks 'what is the relation of power to the psyche (desire)'? She writes (Butler, 1997, p. 2): '[For Foucault] the subject is initiated through a primary submission to power ... The entire domain of the psyche remain[s] largely unremarked in his theory ... It makes sense to ask: What is the psychic form that power takes?' Her answer is that the psyche, though it exceeds the operation of power in a certain sense, is nevertheless not in itself capable of agency to effectively resist power.

1.7 'NORMAL' AND 'ABNORMAL' SUBJECTS IN DISCOURSE

We have argued that discourses construct the possibility of the recognition of subjects. Discourses, we have said, typically involve representations of 'normal' and 'abnormal' subjects. We have focused so far on what it is like to encounter oneself as an 'abnormal' subject, the Other of a discourse defining the character of the Other. However, discourses not only provide the terms within which the subjectivity of the stigmatized Other is proposed but also define by default the subjectivity of the 'normal' Self, as 'not-Other', by providing, usually implicitly, a 'Self' subject position in relation to the stigmatized Other. In this way, dominant subject positions are as much a construction of discourse as the stigmatized Other is. Subjectivity involves identification with one or other of the subject positions available within discourse. Subjects come into being only insofar as they exist as recognizable positions within discourse: the subject does not exist prior to discourse.

This is actually a strong claim, with very strong theoretical implications for how we conceive of subjectivity, and the possibility of agency outside of discourse. Foucault (1980, p. 98) writes:

> The individual is not to be conceived as a sort of elementary nucleus, a primitive atom, a multiple and inert material on which power comes to fasten or against which it happens to strike, and in so doing subdues or crushes individuals. In fact, it is already one of the prime effects of power that certain bodies, certain gestures, certain discourses, certain desires, come to be identified and constituted as individuals.
> The individual, that is, is not the vis-à-vis of power; it is one of its prime effects.

Accordingly, the subject sees him/herself in the terms that the discourse makes possible. This goes not only for the stigmatized subjects of discourse but also for the selves constituted as not-Other. Stuart Hall puts it this way: 'Above all, identities are constructed through, not outside, difference ... It is only through the relation to the Other, the relation to what it is not ... that the 'positive' meaning of any term – and thus its 'identity' – can be constructed' (Hall, 1996, pp. 4–5). The Self which is, as it were, protected by the dominant discourse will be less visible than the Other who is the subject of the discourse. For example, the emergence of a discourse about sexuality implicitly defines 'normal' sexuality as well as 'abnormal' sexuality. Discourses represent power precisely because they define terms in which we are socially visible: discourses engender in subjects 'a state of conscious and permanent visibility that assures the automatic functioning of power' (Foucault, 1977, p. 187). Discourses make subjects visible, make them recognizable – not in the literal, visual sense, as experienced in the model prison, but by extension or metaphorically, making subjects available to consciousness. As discourses circulate widely in society, this consciousness is more or less universally present; society itself acts as a panopticon, in which the visibility of the subject is key. And there is a further point here: while in the prison, the visibility applies to individuals who are subject to the disciplinary practices of the prison, that is, the prisoners, while the warders are invisible and are not themselves subject to this practice, in discourse everyone is subject to the consciousness of the subject categories that it articulates. This is because, as the articulation of the abnormal subject in discourse implies a normal subject by contrast, the discourse articulates two subject positions, normal and abnormal, not one, and thus consciousness of one's subjectivity as normal or abnormal is engendered in discourse. Everyone is subject to this discourse, and everyone's subjectivity is constructed within it. What, then, of invisibility? Certainly, the backgrounding of the 'normal' subject position, given that it is implied rather than expressly stated, means that the normal subject position tends to be the taken-for-granted, assumed, 'natural', unthought position. In that sense it is far more likely to be less overtly clear to those whose subjectivity is constructed in those terms ('not homosexual', for example). The power exercised through discourse is then impersonal, not the power of a cabal; Foucault is not presenting a conspiracy of power. The distribution of consciousness made available within discourse means that the power of the discourse permeates every level of society; it circulates down to the finest capillary level, and the power centre, as it were, is blank, is empty. This is what makes it so hard to challenge the power of discourse: there is nothing or no one to challenge, or everything and everyone. Of course certain interests may be served by the operation of discourse, and in that sense it is political, but the operation of power is not through the expected mechanisms of government, the police, the army and the courts – it is everywhere and potentially in every interaction.

The feminist philosopher and queer theorist Judith Butler discusses this issue in relation to the subjectivity instilled within discourses of gender. She points out that the experience of our subjectivity feels inner and private, and that normally we are not conscious of its origins in discourse, that is, that it is created socially. She says that this is instrumental in maintaining the status quo, as the disciplinary practice of gender becomes hard to identify:

> If the 'cause' of desire, gesture and act can be localized within the 'self' of the actor, then the political regulatory and disciplinary practices which produce that ostensibly coherent gender are effectively displaced from view. The displacement of a political and discursive origin of gender identity onto a psychological 'core' precludes an analysis of the political constitution of the gendered subject. (Butler, 1990, p. 174)

Foucault's view of his own philosophical project aims to undo this invisibility. He states its aims as follows: 'To study the constitution of the subject as an object for himself; the formation of the procedures by which the subject is led to observe himself, analyse himself, interpret himself, recognize himself as a domain of possible knowledge' (Foucault, 1998, p. 461). Foucault's articulation of the link between knowledge or consciousness and power is one of the major contributions of his thought. He uses the expression 'regime of truth' to refer to the way in which beliefs about what is true as expressed in discourse constitute a regime of power. We will see in later chapters how this is evident in discourses of sexuality, gender, ethnicity and so on.

1.8   ITERABILITY AND THE PROBLEM OF AGENCY IN SUBJECTIVITY

The discussion in the previous sections, on the construction of subjectivity within discourse, and the involvement of the psyche, raises the question of what scope for agency the subject might have. We have observed that agency is involved in a paradox: if, according to Foucault, agency is an effect of power, then agency is made possible within discourse, not outside of discourse. That is, there is no possibility of agency outside discourse. Ahearn (2001, p. 112) thus gives the following definition of agency: 'The *socioculturally mediated* capacity to act' (my italics). The effects of sociocultural mediation on our capacity to act are thus ambiguous: on the one hand, sociocultural mediation is *enabling* (it creates the conditions of possibility of acting); on the other hand, sociocultural mediation acts as a *constraint*. In the words of Lalu (2000, p. 51), 'Agency is constituted by the norms, practices, institutions, and discourse through which it is made available.'

This approach to understanding agency which we find in the work of Foucault and Butler, a capacity for action that historically specific relations of subordination enable and create, contrasts with popular ideas of agency in much applied linguistics research, including that inspired by feminism, which seeks to emphasize the political and moral autonomy of the subject in the face of power. That is, agency in this literature is a synonym for resistance to relations of domination. This notion of 'agency as resistance' is characterized as a 'misguided approach' by Ahearn because it locates the operation of power outside the subject; for Foucault and Butler, power forms the subject, the subject is a very function of power. Mahmood (2005, p. 20) explains the contrast in these two positions in the following way:

> To begin with, Butler questions what she calls an 'emancipatory model of agency,' one that presumes that all humans qua humans are 'endowed with a will, a freedom, and an intentionality' whose workings are 'thwarted by relations of power that are considered external to the subject' (Benhabib et al. 1995, 136). In its place, Butler locates the possibility of agency within structures of power (rather than outside of it).

The feminist writer Abu-Lughod (1990, pp. 41–2) explains in what way she came to understand Butler's position:

> In some of my earlier work, as in that of others, there is perhaps a tendency to romanticize resistance, to read all forms of resistance as signs of ineffectiveness of systems of power and of the resilience and creativity of the human spirit in its refusal to be dominated. By reading resistance in this way, we collapse distinctions between forms of resistance and foreclose certain questions about the workings of power.

The problem of agency, then, is an essential correlate of the poststructuralist understanding of the subject. As Mahmood (2005, p. 13) puts it:

A more radical strain of poststructuralist theory has situated its
critique of autonomy within a larger challenge posed to the illusory
character of the rationalist, self-authorizing, transcendental subject
pre-supposed by Enlightenment thought in general, and the liberal
tradition in particular.

This debate on the nature of agency – as resistance to power and
subordination on the one hand, or as capacity for action that is precisely made possible by power and subordination on the other – is at
the heart of a well-known 'controversy' in applied linguistics
(Seidlhofer, 2003) which usefully illustrates the difference between
poststructuralist and more modernist social approaches to identity.
Bonny Norton (Norton Pierce 1995; Norton 2000), in a famous and
influential study, used a sophisticated social theoretical framework
(informed to some extent by poststructuralism) for the study of the
relationship of language and identity among five immigrant women
in ESL classes in Canada. She used diary studies, group discussions,
interviews, before and after questionnaires, and home visits to understand in depth the lives of these women as they went about the task of
learning English. Norton emphasizes the plurality of the women's
subjectivities, as immigrants, as workers, as mothers. These different
facets of their social identities became salient or were deployed in
different contexts. Drawing on the economic metaphors for describing the language market in Bourdieu (1977; 1991), Norton introduces
the notion of 'investment' as a more insightful way of characterizing
what is more traditionally called 'motivation' to learn a language.
The notion of investment allows for fuller investigation of the social
context of motivation and represents a major advance on the barren
distinction between 'integrative' and 'instrumental' motivation, so
empty of social context. One of the women who is the subject of
a case study in this work is Martina. Martina is Czech and arrived in
Canada aged 37 with her husband and three children (aged 17, 14, 11).
Martina's subjectivities as immigrant, mother, language learner,
worker and wife are examined in the varying contexts in which they
become salient. For example, Norton argues that Martina persevered
with speaking in situations when 'silenced' as an immigrant (in interaction with her landlord) and worker (in interaction with fellow workers) because of her investment in her identity as mother.

Price (1996), in a critique of Norton's 1995 paper, criticizes her
argument on the grounds that it in fact maintains the individual/social
distinction which is the target of critique in poststructuralism. He
shows that Norton has a simple view of agency as resistance ('the
subject has human agency': Norton Peirce 1995, p. 15) when she states

that 'the subject positions a subject takes up within a particular discourse are open to argument' by the subject (p. 15). Price argues that all of Martina's 'choices' are constrained within discourse, and this is missing in Norton's interpretative account.

Given the power of discourse in determining, in fact enabling, our 'choices', what possible sites of disruption of the operation of power in discourse present themselves? A number of writers have emphasized the potential of local practices as sites of disruption. For example, the sociologist De Certeau (1925–86), in his book *The Practice of Everyday Life* (1984), explores the ways in which ordinary people use tactics to survive by subverting dominant forms of power. Judith Butler, drawing on ideas of the French poststructuralist philosopher Jacques Derrida, argues that the effect of power, distributed as it is in interactions between individuals subjecting one another in the terms that discourses offer, does not happen automatically but is repeatedly ('iteratively') re-inscribed in interaction, which paradoxically creates a space where the operation of power may misfire and provide an opening for a kind of agency. Thus, for Butler (1999, p. xxiv), 'the iterability of performativity is a theory of agency'.

Lucy (2004, p. 59) explains the Derridean notion of iterability as follows:

> For a thing to be what 'it' is, it must be able to be repeated. Every sunset is a sunset in itself *and* an example of sunsets in general. Tonight's sunset will be followed by another sunset tomorrow, and while each of these will have its singularity, they will also both be the same. In a sense, tonight's sunset will be repeated tomorrow night, but in the very fact of being tomorrow night's sunset it will not be exactly the same as it was tonight. Every repetition, then, produces a difference. This structure of sameness-and-difference conditions every singularity, which can always be repeated. The important point to notice here is that repetition is never pure; it always leads to alteration. To repeat something is to alter it, to make a difference.

This rather difficult notion is going to be central to the argument of the book. In the latter half of this book, we will argue that the analysis of discourse in face-to-face interaction, and in particular Conversation Analysis, allows us to make visible both the joint re-inscription of power, in the unfolding, iterated moves of the participants in interaction, and the potential for disruption (and hence the possibility of agency) in this very iterability. But this is a complex story, and we need to establish some further groundwork before we get to that part of the argument of the book.

1.9 CONCLUSION

In this chapter, we have introduced some key notions that will be developed further in subsequent chapters. We have introduced the notion of big D Discourse and given an example of how discourses of the nation have evolved, and the role of language and the study of language within them. We have seen how discourses circulate in social spaces, constructing possibilities for the way in which we see others and are seen by them. This process of everyday mutual surveillance, of recognizing and being recognized in terms made available within discourses, is taken up again in the chapters on gender (Chapter 2), racism in colonial contexts (Chapter 3), in the experience of everyday racism (Chapter 4), and in the final chapter. We have introduced the term subjectivity and seen that there is a pun in the term: the individual is the *subject of* discourses circulating in society at any given time, a topic of conventional social awareness within discourse, and hence *subject to* social forces, that is, governed by the power inscribed within discourse. Finally, given the way in which power, through discourse, penetrates the filaments of everyday life in this way, we have considered how the notion of agency is problematized in this overwhelming context. Paradoxically, the very notion of the infinite iterability of power may give a space for agency at the micro-level, an intriguing possibility which will be discussed in great detail in the second half of this book.

1.10 SUGGESTIONS FOR FURTHER READING

Poststructuralism does not always make for easy reading for applied linguists, as it assumes reference points and argumentative styles from philosophy that may not be available to the reader. A concise introduction to poststructuralism in the work of Foucault, Derrida and Butler, its relevance to applied linguistics and its contrast with modernist approaches, is available in McNamara (2012). An accessible overall guide to subjectivity in contemporary social theory is Nick Mansfield's *Subjectivity* (2000), with chapters on many of the writers referred to in this book. The most accessible of Foucault's books is *Discipline and Punish* (1977), although his lectures are gradually appearing in English, and these give a more audience-friendly account of themes which are discussed in a more condensed way in his classic texts. A good example is *Abnormal* (Foucault 2003), his lectures from 1974–5. An excellent introduction to feminist poststructuralism is

Grosz (1990), and classic texts by Butler include *Gender Trouble* (1990) and *The Psychic Life of Power* (1997). Anderson (1991) is a must-read on the history of discourses of the nation. The exchanges between Norton and Price are most easily accessed in Seidlhofer (2003). Bauman (2004) and Kapuściński (2008) offer thoughtful short discussions of topics central to this book.

2   Discourses of Gender and Sexuality

2.1   INTRODUCTION: 'TALKING LIKE A MAN'

In the American film *Gran Torino* (2008), Clint Eastwood plays Walt Kowalski, a retired Polish-American assembly-line worker in Detroit who is resentful of the changed character of his old white working-class neighbourhood, which now has a significant community of Hmong refugees from Laos and their American-born children. A Hmong family lives next door. Despite his racist feelings, Walt develops a protective mentoring friendship with Thao, the teenage son of the family, and decides to help him get a job in construction. But first, Walt tells Thao, 'I have to man you up a little bit' so that he seems the kind of person who would fit 'naturally' into the specific male culture of the construction site. Walt takes Thao to visit his Italian-American barber, Martin, so that Thao can learn 'how guys talk', and tells him, 'Listen to the way Martin and I batter it back and forth.' This is the exchange as Walt enters Martin's shop:

MARTIN	Perfect – a Polack *and* a Chink
WALT	How y'doin' Martin, you crazy Italian prick?
MARTIN	Walt, you cheap bastard, I shoulda known you'd come in, I was havin' such a pleasant day
WALT	Whadya do, jew some poor blind guy out of his money? Give him the wrong change?
MARTIN	Who's the Nip?
WALT	Oh he's a pussy kid from next door ... I'm just tryin' to man him up a little bit
WALT [TURNING TO THAO]	Y'see kid? Now that's how guys talk to one another ...

In this community, men's sociality is marked by racist banter and mocking insults. Thao is invited to imitate this style, but his first attempt gets it hopelessly wrong, coming over as aggressive and seriously insulting. The older men then go on to give further advice to Thao about how to talk 'like a man':

WALT	You could talk about a construction job you just came from and bitch about your girlfriend and your car
MARTIN	Um … 'Sonofabitch I just got my brakes fixed and those sons of bitches really nailed me I mean they screwed me right in the ass'
WALT	Yeah … you can bitch about your boss making you work overtime when it's bowling night
MARTIN	Right or um 'My old lady bitches for two goddam hours about how uh they don't take expired coupons at the grocery store and the minute I turn on the fuckin' game *she* starts cryin' how we never talk'
WALT	You see? … It ain't rocket science, for Chrissake

'Guys' talk', in other words, is also marked by homophobia and misogyny, and is on a set of predictable topics such as work, cars and the trouble with women. Thao, after further 'manning up' practice, faces a crucial test of whether he can pass scrutiny as a suitable 'man' when Walt takes him to meet his friend Tim Kennedy, a construction supervisor, who can offer him a job if he makes the right impression. The conversation, effectively an informal job interview, begins awkwardly: when Walt introduces Thao, Kennedy at first struggles to 'recognize' him as the kind of 'man' that is expected in this environment.

WALT	OK, this is the kid I was telling you about. Thao, this is Tim Kennedy, the super on this job.
TIM	So what have we got here, Walt?
WALT	Well he knows construction and he's a smart kid. He'll do anything you need him for.
TIM	You sure?
WALT	Yeah.
TIM	You er speak English?
THAO	Yes sir.
TIM	Were you born here?
THAO	You bet.
TIM	I see that Walt drove you here. You got a vehicle?
THAO	Not at the moment. Taking the bus for now.
TIM	The bus. Jesus Christ, you don't have a car?

Thao is not 'visibly' or 'recognizably' masculine in the white working-class world where he is seeking employment on a building site. He is not white; he has a 'difficult' non-English name, which Kennedy later struggles to pronounce. Kennedy worries that he might not even be an English speaker at all ('Can you speak English?') and is alarmed when Thao discloses that he doesn't drive and needs to take the bus to get to work. Thao manages to retrieve the situation by 'talking like a man' about car trouble and the cost of repairs, with colourful homophobic references:

KENNEDY   Jesus Christ, you don't have a car?
THAO   My head gasket cracked and the goddamn prick at the shop
           wants to bend me over for twenty one hundred
KENNEDY   Oh please I just replaced the tranny on my Tahoe and the sons
           of bitches fucked me hard – just under thirty two hundred
THAO   Goddamn thieves – it ain't right
KENNEDY   You got that right ... ok um come on in on Monday and uh
           we'll find something for you to do

The fact that Thao has mastered the art of 'speaking like a man' means that for Kennedy, Thao is visibly, recognizably the kind of 'man' who will fit in as a construction worker, and he gets the job.

These scenes from the film illustrate the way in which in order to survive inspection as the kind of man these men can feel comfortable with, Thao must be familiar with and competent in the language and behaviour dictated by discourses of masculinity circulating within Walt's world. Language use is part of these discourses; Walt and Martin use a linguistic display to teach Thao what it is to be a 'man' in that world. Becoming a 'man' involves mastery of a certain kind of language use, marked by style, topics and themes, as a public display of the knowledge that the discourse enjoins. Discourse constructs subjectivities which are acceptable – or rather, not unacceptable, not 'a pussy kid', the kind of unfortunate who is 'bent over' and 'screwed right in the ass'.

In this chapter, we will examine the role of language within discourses of gender and sexuality. To begin, then, what evidence is there to support the beliefs of Walt and Martin that there are distinct ways of speaking for men and women, and that discourses dictate that to be recognizable as an adequate or proper 'man' or 'woman', you need to be able to speak appropriately?

2.2   DO MEN AND WOMEN COMMUNICATE DIFFERENTLY?

Men are not the only ones who need to master 'gender-appropriate' speech; women have traditionally been subject to considerable advice on ways of speaking (Cameron, 1995), but the advice is very different from that given to men. Early twentieth-century advice books on elocution for women, for example, suggested that women should avoid gossip, keep their voices low, avoid stating an opinion and pay attention to 'correct' pronunciation. A particularly worrying issue a century ago was the effect of women dropping the 'g' in words ending in '-ing':

This is, unfortunately, not confined solely to the uneducated classes, and people are to be met with on every hand who consider it 'good form' to say 'Mornin'' for 'Good-morning', and so on through all their conversation, never once realising that beauty of form is just as necessary in speech as in other arts ... To chip or mar a statue would be considered an act of vandalism, and yet we systematically maltreat words, which, after all, are the only means we have of clothing our thoughts. ('The art of elocution', 1912)

Damousi (2010), in discussing nineteenth-century discourses on the relationship of language to gender in women, states: 'One of the key attributes of femininity was a woman's voice, both the sound of it (timbre and pitch) and the way in which she spoke' (p. 101). She quotes from a magazine article from 1905 by the novelist Henry James: 'A lady should speak like a lady ... Her speech must be to the liking of those whose ear has been cultivated and has thus become sensitive. She affronts this sensibility at her peril' (James, 1999, p. 62).

2.3 LANGUAGE AND GENDER DOMINANCE

It was precisely such advice and the discourses generating them that became the target of work by feminist linguists in the early 1970s, as part of second-wave feminism. The Berkeley linguist Robin Lakoff wrote a highly influential book, *Language and Woman's Place* (Lakoff, 1975), on the speech of women, arguing that women's language is a result of the powerlessness of women within the hierarchical nature of gender relations, and that as a result women's speech style shows uncertainty and powerlessness (in contrast to the confident assertiveness of men). Moreover, for Lakoff, women's speech behaviour not only signified but also reproduced the oppression of women: in Lakoff's view, as Wolfson (1989, p. 173) puts it, 'speaking like a lady keeps a lady in her place'. Lakoff claimed that several features of women's speech indicated the submissive role they adopted in relation to their conversational partners. According to Lakoff, women typically used hedges (for example *well, y'know, kinda*) to convey uncertainty even when the speaker's actual feelings were quite certain; used tag questions and rising intonation even in statements, again to suggest tentativeness and a concern to secure the agreement of the interlocutor; women's speech was marked by euphemism and tactful wording; and women did not interrupt. We can think of Lakoff's work as initiating a particular discourse on men's and women's language, with linguistic research both informed by this discourse and informing it.

Lakoff's claims were not in fact based on data from empirical research, but simply on her own intuitions. Yet they struck a chord with many readers. Later researchers explored the issues she had raised empirically and discovered certain difficulties with Lakoff's account. For example, Janet Holmes (1986) did a careful analysis of the use of 'you know' in the speech of men and women. She found that the phrase had several quite independent functions, such as when a person is searching for a more precise phrase; after a false start in an utterance; to clarify the content of a previous utterance; as an appeal for validation; or to refer to shared knowledge. A close examination of the use of 'you know' for each of these functions failed to show the claimed greater use of this phrase by women: sometimes there was no difference, sometimes men were found to use the function more than women. Similarly, Deborah Tannen (1989) studied interruptions in the speech of men and women and showed that they are difficult to distinguish from overlaps in conversation, where overlaps can be supportive. Consider this example from interaction in a language testing context, a study examining the potential impact of the gender of the examiner/interlocutor in an oral interview test, the IELTS test (Brown, 2005; Brown and McNamara, 2004). Clearly, if men and women do have differing interactional styles, then this is likely to create different opportunities for the candidate to speak and interact, and these may have implications for the score the candidate gets, resulting in potentially unfair assessment. The following shows a female interviewer, Jean, with a male candidate, Lim (Brown, 2005, p. 191):

```
J           Wha- what's the distribution of income what I mean by that is that .hh are
            there some very poor people and some very rich or a lot of middle class
            people (.) how- how is it based.
L           e:r middle class (.) I think middle class er
J      →    a lot of [middle class?
L      →             [a lot of middle class.
J           okay are there some very poor? (.) or [m-
L      →                                          [poor erm [I (.) I don't think so it
            [just (.) a small [amount (.) of them very poor
J      →    [no            [oh right .hh and what about very rich (.) are there
            some very rich people?
L           yah [>quite a lot of very<
J      →        [yeah so: SO: quite a big middle class (.) [mainly. (.) probably a =
L      →                                                   [yeah middle (.) °middle =
J      →    = [bit like Australia? [you know a large middle [class? .hhh okay =
L      →    = [class°              [yeah                    [middle class
J           = .hh [(.) ^what about if somebody erm (1.0) somebody <is poor and =
```

The data shows multiple examples of overlap, indicated by a square bracket ([) at the beginning of the overlapping section of the aligned utterances in each case. Towards the end of the exchange, Jean seems to interrupt Lim's utterances ('yeah so: SO: quite a big middle class' and 'bit like Australia?'), a supposedly 'typically male' behaviour, but these can alternatively be seen as intended to be supportive or facilitative of the exchange. After all, Jean is an experienced language teacher and interviewer, who is used to encouraging and supporting the speech of learners and test takers. (This extract and related extracts from Brown's work are discussed further in Chapter 6.)

A study by O'Barr and Atkins (1980) supported the idea that 'female' interactional behaviour was a function of powerlessness. The study involved male and female witnesses giving evidence in court, and found similar hesitancy, hedging and tentativeness in the speech of some of the witnesses, but not in that of others. However, the divide was not between male and female; rather the observed variation was associated with the degree of status of the individual in court and his/her familiarity with court procedures, unrelated to gender. Expert *female* witnesses showed fewer of the features Lakoff had described as indices of women's powerlessness, while inexperienced witnesses of either gender showed abundant use of these features.

Another study seemed to strongly support Lakoff's position about the association of interactional features in conversation with a gendered power hierarchy. Pamela Fishman (1978) argued that women consistently work to ensure the uptake of topics introduced into conversations by their male interlocutors, while the men make no such effort with the women's topics, many of which therefore do not 'fly'. Fishman uses the colourful phrase 'conversational shitwork' to describe the unequal interactive effort of men and women in the conversational data she studied.

2.4 LANGUAGE AND GENDER DIFFERENCE

In the succeeding decades of the 1980s and 1990s, however, a new discourse around male–female differences in conversational interaction emerged. This discourse had two aspects: on the one hand, a confirmation of the findings of the earlier period of research that the communication styles of men and women differed; but this time giving a different comparative account of the interactional style of women to suggest not only its legitimacy but indeed its superiority to that of men. Far from women's speech being evidence of, or even an instrument of, women's oppression, it was an expression of the positive qualities of women's value systems, in contrast to those of men. The 'difference' approach shared with the 'dominance' approach of Lakoff and others a pro-feminist stance, and asserted the distinctiveness of the speech of men and women, but differed from it in celebrating, rather than deploring, the characteristics seen to be typical of women's speech. In turn it was subsequently widely criticized for its neglect of power and dominance relations (for example by Eckert and McConnell-Ginet, 1992 and by Cameron, 1995).

The 'difference' approach was popularized in Deborah Tannen's best-selling book *'You Just Don't Understand': Men and Women in Conversation* (1990). In this analysis, male–female communication was conceptualized as a form of cross-cultural communication. Studies of children socialized within segregated same-sex peer groups appeared to show that boys and girls acquired differing verbal and non-verbal skills. For example, Sheldon (1990) made a study of the management of conflictual talk by preschool children in which the boys were found to be direct and confrontational, whereas girls were more likely to use their language skills to negotiate and mediate. For Tannen, as a result of these differences, which endure into adulthood, male–female communication is like other forms of cross-cultural communication, marked by misunderstandings and misinterpretations.

A variant on the differences approach appeared in the work of the British feminist linguist, Jennifer Coates. In detailed empirical studies of the speech of men and women in all-male and all-female groups, Coates (1986; 1997a; 1997b) found a number of differences. For example, she found that in female conversational groups it was relatively unusual for a woman to 'hold the floor'; more typically all the women participated equally, with frequent overlap and simultaneous speech, and joint construction of utterances. This was found to be in contrast to the style typical of men's groups, in which there was little sharing of the floor and little overlap; monologues and displays of expertise, both discouraged in women's speech, were regularly observed. There were differences in topics, too: while men were found to avoid self-disclosure, preferring talk on impersonal topics, women in contrast preferred to talk about people and feelings, not about objects (remember the advice to Thao in *Gran Torino*: 'You could talk about a construction job you just came from, and bitch about your girlfriend and your car'). Overall, the goal of women's talk was seen as the establishment and maintenance of good relations, while with men what was valued was the exchange of information. This is no doubt an idealized portrait of women's speech: Turner (2002), in her study of the socialization into writing of children in the first year of schooling, while finding stark differences in the interactional styles of boys and girls in separate groups of girl learners and boy learners, highlighted the destructive and manipulative aspects of the behaviour of the girls to one another.

Partly as a result of the popularization of the research of linguists such as Tannen and Coates, there consolidated a kind of public consensus – a discourse – about differences in the communication styles of men and women, summarized by Cameron (2007) as follows: men and women have different goals in communication: while men want to 'get things done' in conversation and are motivated by competitiveness and the need to achieve status, women's goals are about relationships with others, and are hence more cooperative; moreover, women, for whom communication is more important than it is for men, talk more, and more skilfully; and increasingly it was suggested that these differences are biological in origin (Moir & Jessel, 1992; Blum, 1997; Moir & Moir, 2000; Pinker, 2002; Baron-Cohen, 2003). This in turn meant that if the differences were hard-wired, it would be difficult to change them, even if this were considered desirable.

The discourse of difference in turn was disputed, particularly in the work of Deborah Cameron. Cameron first disputed the facts of the matter, arguing that empirical research did not support the difference position:

> The idea that men and women 'speak different languages' has itself become a dogma, treated not as a hypothesis to be investigated or as a claim to be adjudicated, but as an unquestioned article of faith . . . our faith in it is misplaced. . . . the evidence does not lead where most people think it does. If we examine the findings of more than 30 years of research on language, communication and the sexes, we will discover that they tell a different, and more complicated, story.
> . . . The idea that men and women differ fundamentally in the way they use language to communicate is a myth in the everyday sense: a widespread but false belief. (Cameron, 2007, p. 3)

Cameron cited a meta-analysis conducted by Hyde (2005) investigating the issue of the claimed differences in features of speech between men and women of the sort claimed by Coates, which concluded that whatever differences exist were minor even where they were real.

Studies such as that of Coates, according to Cameron, underplayed the similarities in the speech of men and women, which overlap far more than they differ, and underestimated the extent of variation among individuals of both genders.

But there is more than just a disagreement about the facts or about the empirical evidence for differences in gendered styles of communication here. Cameron's position is ultimately based on a fundamental critique of the assumptions of earlier language and gender research from the perspective of poststructuralism. Before we consider this critique, however, we need to consider the role of discourses of sexuality in discourses of gender.

2.5   DISCOURSES OF SEXUALITY IN DISCOURSES OF GENDER

Discourses of gender and sexuality go hand in hand: an important strategy in discourses defining abnormal (and hence normal) gendered identity is to make 'proper' gender isomorphic with 'proper' sexuality. This means that a principal way in which a man or woman can be not a 'proper' man or woman is to be homosexual. The homosexual is excluded from the category 'man' or 'woman'. This is apparent in the discourses of masculinity in *Gran Torino*: there is a strong othering of the (passive) homosexual in phrases such as 'they screwed me right in the ass', 'the prick at the shop wants to bend me over for twenty one hundred', 'the sons of bitches fucked me hard', all representing the ultimate humiliation for a 'man', of being the passive or receptive sexual partner – the underlying misogyny is also clear.

During the late eighteenth and through the nineteenth century, the pathologization of homosexuality, its conceptualization as a medical condition, was a feature of a discourse on sexuality emerging in medicine, psychiatry and jurisprudence (Foucault, 1978). Central to this discourse was the strategy of exclusion of homosexuals from the categories 'man' and 'woman'. This was because it was assumed that desire itself was heterosexual; the only possible desire was that of a man for a woman, and a woman for a man. How, then, could the phenomenon of male desire for another man be explained? It must be that homosexual men were 'subjectively female' and, moreover, that the target of their desire must be heterosexual men (on the grounds that a subjectively female homosexual would be incapable of desiring another subjectively female person). Similarly, lesbians were seen as 'psychologically masculine', and the target of their desire could only be heterosexual women. Cameron and Kulick (2003) show how this discourse of sexuality underlay research in the period from the 1920s to the 1940s on the language of homosexuals, the findings of which in turn fed into and supported the discourse. A recurring assumption in this research was that homosexual speech would display evidence to support the idea that male homosexuals were really subjectively female and lesbians subjectively male. Accordingly, it was soon discovered that in the male homosexual subculture of the time homosexual men sometimes used feminine pronouns to refer to homosexual men: 'look at her!' rather than 'look at him!' Homosexual men of that generation were found to give each other feminized nicknames: 'Miss Kitty', 'Pixie' and so on. These linguistic practices were seen as expressive of homosexuality per se.

The assumptions about sexuality and gender in the discourse of this early period were exploited for very different purposes during the period following the beginning of the movement known as gay liberation in the late 1960s and early 1970s. This strategy of reversal is described in general terms by Foucault (1978, p. 101):

> [The appearance of the discourse on homosexuality] ... also made possible the formation of a 'reverse' discourse: homosexuality began to speak on its own behalf, to demand that its legitimacy or 'naturality' be acknowledged, often in the same vocabulary, using the same categories by which it was medically disqualified.

Pride in the distinctiveness of the speech of homosexuals was one feature of this period, with studies of gay slang emphasizing both its historicity (Baker, 2002) and its positive qualities of humour and creativity. Gay and lesbian speech was claimed to be not only different but better: it showed the kind of positive qualities that Coates identified in her comparison of the speech of men and women – lesbian discourse was 'collaborative and supportive' and the discourse of gay men was egalitarian and cooperative in the same way. If homosexuality involved a kind of 'gender crossing', as the earlier discourse suggested, then this could be accepted and valued, rather than stigmatized. Gay men were happy to distance themselves from the 'masculine' speech of heterosexual men with all its limitations. In this period of 'identity politics', the terms within which 'them' and 'us' were defined within discourses on sexuality were accepted and reversed, but the exploitation of the categories for new ends in a sense depended on maintaining them.

2.6 POSTSTRUCTURALIST APPROACHES: GENDER AS PERFORMATIVITY

In the period since 1990, a challenge to earlier discourses of both gender and sexuality and a critique of the essentializing of subjectivity in 'identity politics' have emerged in the areas of feminist poststructuralism and queer theory. Following Foucault, the key strategy of poststructuralist thought is the possibility of stepping outside of binary terms constructed within discourses of gender and sexuality by emphasizing the instability of the gender (and sexuality) categories in prevailing discourses, and the way in which they are not exclusive of one another. In what follows, we will first give a concrete example of this instability in the transcript of a television interview on the issue of the presence of openly homosexual men in a traditionally heterosexual masculine domain, men's sport. We will then consider poststructuralist approaches to theorizing gender and sexuality as performed identities, with an example from gay male communication. We will conclude by considering a landmark study of a type of men's talk which seems to flout gender norms, and its interpretation in poststructuralist terms.

'What Would that Do to a Man': Homosexuals in a 'Man's' Domain

The idea that 'proper' masculinity excludes homosexuality is a prominent theme in the following text, but the text also illustrates the instability of a category which depends on this exclusion. The text is the transcript of a television interview with a well-known Australian football player, Jason Akermanis. Australian football, a distinctive type of football bearing little resemblance to soccer, rugby or American football, is the most popular football code in Australia, with a huge following; its leading players are celebrity figures in Australian life. Towards the end of his career, Akermanis took a job as a commentator on a populist radio station known for its conservative social views and wrote a column in a popular newspaper. His declaration there that gay footballers playing in the Australian Football League (AFL) should 'stay in the closet' caused considerable controversy. In the following, he is being interviewed by television host Karl Stefanovic to explain his views.

```
01   JA:   Well they can come out of the closet
            and we're happy for them to do that
            I think it's a safe environment we have in the AFL
            but I'm not sure
05          that (.) other players would be ready for it
            ah I know I played with a (.) a gay footballer in the twos
```


          I talk about in Mayne in Queensland (.)
          and (.) looking back in hindsight
          I really should have (.) gone and spoken to him
10   and just had a bit of a chat
          just to sort of clear any kind of (.) problems
          that I may have had
          because really (.)
          he was a terrific guy
15   and he was very tough and courageous
          uh here we are all these years later
          and I think there's been
          a a little bit of a a gay <u>hunting</u> going on
          where we're trying to get people to come out
20   and I'm not sure that's very (.) safe and healthy
          for the competition either
          if you are what you do in your private life
          th.. is <u>your</u> business
          we don't care
25   we're here to play football
          and footballers seem to be at the um peak of masculinity
          which of course then uh makes homo<u>phobia</u> almost at its peak
          so we as footballers need to be more open if there is
          and accept people if they <u>would</u> come out
30   but at the moment I'm not sure
          that while you're playing it would be a safe thing
     KS: Wha wha what do you mean by
          it wou wouldn't be a safe thing
          uh what would happen (.) Aker
35 JA: Oh I just don't think I don't think the –
          some people within it uh
          would be very accepting of (.) particular people like that
          not that there – I think some footballers think
          there's something wrong with people
40   uh they have some kind of disease
          but I – I don't think that of course
          I think uh they are just normal people
          trying to play football
          trying to make a living
45   but (.) <u>right now</u> they would be
     KS: so when you say so when you say
          just so that we can clarify
          Aker just so that we can clarify here
          you're saying you're saying that (yep)
50   um you don't think they would be ready (.)
          uh uh uh in in uh in essence what you are saying
          is that you're (.) not ready is that right
     JA: me no I'm ready I'm <u>fine</u> with it all
          but I'm my I some of my
55   the <u>homo</u>eroticism around football clubs

```
        that would be an interesting thing Carlos
        uh wha-what workplace would you be able to see twenty men uh
        nude all the time even if you wanted to
        and all of a sudden you know when you're slapping blokes on
60      the bum and just having a bit of fun
        (.) what would that do to a man in there
        when you actually work out
        oh wait a second (.) wait a second
        I don't know if I can handle that guy
65      and and there needs to be (.) a lot more done of course
        because the participation numbers is very high (.) for (...)
        sport
   KS:  Aker Aker Aker you're the one that has the problem here
        no-one else
   JA:  that's right that's right it looks like that
70      but I'm just bringing the attention of people
        so you can work through it and deal with it
        me I've got no issues Carlos (.)
        no m issues at all
```

It is interesting to note in this interview how Akermanis cites differing, sometimes contradictory discourses around homosexuality. On the one hand, there is the official position of the Australian Football League (AFL) which campaigns against homophobia in the code and is committed to tolerance. Akermanis, as a leading AFL player, cites and endorses this policy, even to the point of using the term 'homophobia' itself, a term encoding contemporary critiques of earlier prejudiced attitudes:

```
they can come out of the closet
and we're happy for them to do that
I think it's a safe environment we have in the AFL

we as footballers need to be more open [...]
and accept people if they would come out

there needs to be (.) a lot more done of course
because the participation numbers is very high (.) for (...) sport

if you are what you do in your private life
th.. is your business
we don't care
we're here to play football

I think uh they are just normal people
trying to play football
trying to make a living
```

On the other hand, within these statements there is a clear positioning of the homosexual footballer as Other, through the use of the contrasting pronouns 'we' (the AFL, which is presumed to be heterosexual), and 'they', the gay footballers. Elsewhere, more explicitly, Akermanis cites homophobic opinions and reactions from which he is careful at times to distance himself (although the interviewer challenges his sincerity):

```
I don't think the -
some people within it uh
would be very accepting of (.) particular people like that
not that there - I think some footballers think
there's something wrong with people
uh they have some kind of disease

(.) what would that do to a man in there
when you actually work out
oh wait a second (.) wait a second
I don't know if I can handle that guy
```

What is at stake here is masculinity itself. Masculinity is mapped onto heterosexuality and is seen as necessarily excluding homosexuality:

```
Footballers seem to be at the um peak of masculinity
which of course then uh makes homophobia almost at its peak
```

But there is a problem with this strategy of opposition and exclusion of the homosexual. For the Other to be excluded, it must be identifiable. How is the dangerous homosexual Other to be recognized? The problem is that the cues to recognition as masculine, and as homosexual, are shared, and hence can lead to confusion. A homosexual footballer whom Akermanis had as a team-mate in a lower level competition ('in the twos') earlier in his career in Queensland showed 'classic' signs of masculinity:

```
he was a terrific guy
and he was very tough and courageous
```

Even more confusingly, heterosexual footballers engage in physical intimacy in the locker-room in ways that might be mistaken for homosexual intimacy, so that a potential crisis of subjectivity is precipitated by the sudden awareness of what it would mean if one of the participants were 'actually' a homosexual:

```
uh wha-what workplace would you be able to see twenty men uh
nude all the time even if you wanted to
and all of a sudden you know when you're slapping blokes on
the bum and just having a bit of fun
```

```
(.) what would that do to a man in there
when you actually work out
oh wait a second (.) wait a second
I don't know if I can handle that guy
```

The recognition problem, in other words, is that the signs by which one knows who is who in this game of Self and Other turn out to be ambiguous. The personal characteristics and behaviour of the supposedly opposed categories are in fact shared, leading to confusion and insecurity. This is presumably why Akermanis thinks gay footballers should stay in the closet, to preserve an admittedly illusory *status quo ante* – prior, that is, to the confusing new world with its academic talk of 'homophobia' and 'homoeroticism'.

2.7 GENDER AND SEXUALITY AS PERFORMANCE

The instability of gender and sexuality categories apparent in the extract just discussed is the primary focus of poststructuralist theorists. A key notion here is that sexuality and gender, rather than being 'given' or 'natural' social categories, are in fact socially constructed, and hence liable to disruption. It may be helpful here to return to the notions of subjectivity and surveillance in the work of Foucault, introduced in Chapter 1. We saw there how social control is exercised by an awareness of how we are seen. The visibility of our behaviour, appearance, gestures and language means that they are permanently available for evaluation in terms that are the subject of discourses circulating in society at any time – discourses about what it means to be a 'proper' or 'normal' man, a 'proper' or 'normal' woman, discourses which define the 'normal' by default by focusing on the definition of the abnormal. In order to be 'recognized' as 'normal', we need to continually demonstrate our conformity to the norms of gender and sexuality. We do so by unconsciously orchestrating features of our speech, gestures, appearance and behaviour so that they can bear scrutiny under the conditions of social surveillance. In this sense we produce prescribed social identities by repeatedly displaying behaviours, speech and so on that we have learned will be approved. The approval does not come explicitly; rather it is a kind of negative approval – the approval which comes from not being noticed as different or 'abnormal', with all the stigma and social penalties attached to that. We are truly like the prisoners in Bentham's panopticon.

The notion of gender as produced is particularly associated with the work of the Berkeley philosopher and queer theorist Judith Butler, whose work we will consider shortly. But it is foreshadowed in a study of the performed character of gendered identity in early work in the branch of sociology known as ethnomethodology by its founder, Harold Garfinkel (1967). At the time, gender reassignment surgery had recently been legalized in California, on condition that the person presenting for such surgery be subject to an assessment by a psychiatrist. Garfinkel made a study of one such candidate for surgery, Agnes, who had been born a biological male and who presented for surgery at the age of 19. Garfinkel had access to tape-recorded interviews with Agnes, dealing with her life, her future and her fears in relation to 'passing' as a woman. Agnes's problem was to be recognizable and visible as a woman; in order to do so, she had had to make a study of the minute features of women's behaviour, speech, gestures, bodily habitus and so on, and consciously imitate them. Garfinkel realized that Agnes had become an expert observer of female behaviour, an ethnographer of gender, as she was required to do deliberately and consciously what women do unconsciously: to *perform* their subjectivity as women in order to be recognized as such. In Garfinkel's (1967, p. 181) words:

> Agnes's methodological practices [demonstrate] ... that normally sexed persons are cultural events ... whose character as visible orders of practical activities consist[s] of members' recognition and production practices. We learned from Agnes, who treated sexed persons as cultural events that members make happen, that members' practices alone produce the observable-tellable normal sexuality of persons.

Thus, for Garfinkel gender is 'observable' and hence 'tellable', that is, recognizable ('tell' here is to be understood in the sense of 'recognize' or 'know': 'you can tell she's a woman by the way she walks and talks'); gender is recognizable by things that individuals are seen to do. Gender, in other words, is a 'visible' social order. It requires members of communities within which particular discourses of gender circulate to produce the signs by which their gender is recognizable in terms which make sense in that community – Garfinkel calls these productive activities 'practices'. Note that communities will differ significantly across cultures and historical periods in the ways in which very differing practices are associated with the production of gender. Another sociologist puts it this way: 'It is surprising to realize the extent to which gender differentiation consists of a filigree of small scale, socially organized behaviours which are unceasingly iterated' (Heritage, 1984, p. 197). Or as Deborah Cameron (1995, p. 16) puts it, 'who you are ... taken to be ... depends on how you act'. Transsexuals know this very well and may undergo systematic voice coaching so that they can produce the gender-appropriate vocal quality.

The best-known discussion of gender as performed is in the work of the philosopher Judith Butler (1990). Butler draws on work on linguistic pragmatics by the Oxford philosopher J. L. Austin as the basis for her argument that our inner sense of ourselves as gendered beings is achieved through iterative performance of gender-appropriate actions.

Austin (1962) drew attention to the special class of utterances whereby, when spoken in the appropriate circumstances, certain social actions are actually performed – utterances such as 'I now pronounce you husband and wife' performing the action of marrying, 'I'm warning you, don't go in there' performing the action of warning, 'I thank you for your kind attention' performing the action of thanking, 'I christen this ship *The Daydream*' performing the action of launching a ship, and so on. Austin (1962, pp. 5–6) states:

> In these examples it seems clear that to utter the sentence (in, of course, the appropriate circumstances) is not to describe my doing of what I should be said in so uttering to be doing or to state that I am doing it: it is to do it ...
>
> What are we to call a sentence or an utterance of this type? I propose to call it a performative sentence or a performative utterance, or, for short, 'a performative' ... The name is derived, of course, from 'perform', the usual verb with the noun 'action': it indicates that the issuing of the utterance is the performing of an action – it is not normally thought of as just saying something.

It is not only such ritualistic phrases, often marked by explicit wording naming the act performed, which are performative: all utterances in context are performative. We can distinguish semantic and pragmatic (or performative) levels of the meaning of an utterance. For example, take the utterance 'The door is open.' Semantically, the sentence contains the word 'door' (as opposed to 'window', 'book', etc.) which is said to be 'open' (not 'closed', not 'ajar', not 'locked', etc.); the verb is in the present tense; it is 'the' door, not 'a' door. This is what the sentence 'means' in a dictionary and grammar book sense. But what does the person who utters this sentence mean by it? Depending on the context it could be performing a number of possible social acts: invitation ('come in'), a warning or threat ('get out'), a complaint ('you've left the door open'), an explanation ('that's why the room is cold') and so on. Pragmatic competence involves the capacity to recognize what Austin called the 'illocutionary force' of an utterance. All utterances have an illocutionary force, and so all utterances are performative: a social action is accomplished in each utterance.

2.8 BUTLER AND PERFORMATIVITY

Butler (1990) extends this notion to identify a further, larger-scale performative effect. She argues that gender is a social effect which is the result of performance: that is, that features of our speech, our bearing ('habitus'), our appearance are socially 'read' as performing our gendered subjectivity, as Agnes understood. In Foucault's terms, discourses of gender prescribe the terms within which 'normal' and 'abnormal' gendered behaviour will be recognizable; the subject then ceaselessly, iteratively, presents her/himself as intelligibly gendered by attending (usually unconsciously) to features which will render the gendered self-recognizable. In Anglo-Saxon cultures it may be compatible with normal notions of women's gendered behaviour for two women to walk arm-in-arm in public; but it is not compatible with the gendered behaviour of men to do so – or rather it is marked in another discourse, as suggesting a likely reading of homosexuality in the men (we have seen the role of homosexuality in constructions of masculinity).

We have already seen that we are subject to the power of discourse in that we are constantly open to scrutiny by others among whom particular discourses of 'normal' gendered behaviour circulate. We are subject to surveillance on a permanent basis and must enact our gendered selves so that they are visible and recognizable in terms of the understanding of gender available in the discourses to which we are subject in our particular cultural setting. What Butler observes is that this repetition of gendered performance creates a sense in us of how 'natural' it is to behave in such a way, to the extent that we feel that it is an expression of some inner gendered essential self. Butler argues however, that this sense of our 'inner nature' as men or women (or of our inner sexual nature) is actually created by the repetition (iteration) of actions that are performed in accordance with the constraints of discourses of gender (or sexuality). This then results in the conventional belief that our inner (gendered, sexual) nature is given, and that our actions are the external manifestation or expression of something 'inner'; instead, for Butler, our gendered and sexual identities are performed in accordance with external constraints. As she writes:

> Acts, gestures and desire produce the effect of an internal core or substance ... Such acts, gestures, enactments ... are performative in the sense that the essence or identity that they otherwise purport to express are fabrications manufactured and sustained through corporeal signs and other discursive means. (Butler, 1990, p. 136)

Note that language is a central cultural practice involved here. Moreover, if gender identity is the product of socially sanctioned actions yet results in a sense of inner self which is experienced as private and individual, then the origins of gendered subjectivity in social values and social ideologies remain invisible and unconscious, as we saw in Chapter 1. The aim of Butler's work is to destabilize and make obvious the social construction of gendered and sexual subjectivity. One implication of this is that instead of using social categories as the basis for organizing (as in the movement of 'gay liberation', for example), the very categories themselves are subverted. Queer theory values social practices which undermine the taken-for-granted 'naturalness' of social categories to reveal their 'performed' and conventional nature. Practices of conscious performance such as that of the transsexual Agnes have this potential; 'drag' performances within gay culture are identified as another site for such subversive practices. Within linguistic research, there followed from Butler's work a renewed interest in the significance of 'camp' homosexual talk, with its feminized naming and deictic practices, as an example of such subversion. In this view, 'camp' talk provides a set of resources to achieve disruptive effects of paradox, inversion, linguistic playfulness and parody (Cameron & Kulick, 2003).

How convincing is this? Consider the following example of chat room data from a popular gay male website (www.gay.com). Glosses and comments are added to explicate the bolded elements in each turn. The 'handles' (nicknames) of some of the members of the site reference sexuality and masculinity: 'oz_matey' uses the popular spelling for the short version of 'Australia' ('Oz') and the Australian greeting term traditionally used among men ('mate'); 'knackers' is a colloquial term for testicles. The turns are good examples of 'camp' banter, with frequent teasing using sexual insults and playful feminization of naming, and an exaggerated, theatrical style of interaction.

Member	Turn	Comment
tarquin	Goodnight all .... Sino, if **Miss Chelsea** comes	feminized title
	back, please give the **sad sac**	sac = scrotum; 'sad sac' is hence a teasing, punning put down
	my **least warm regards** :)	teasing inversion of a compliment
oz_matey	ms **Special K**	alternative title, suggesting that the person is a drug user (Special K is the name of a party drug)
knackers8	**good1** oz	'good one' – complimenting the teasing in the prior turn
oz_matey	**why** thank you :)	exaggerated acknowledgement of compliment; mocking the style of a Southern belle
*Tamb_*	Good Evening **Ms oz_ matey**	feminized title; ironic as the handle 'oz matey' trades on stereotypical Australian masculinity
oz_matey	**pfft**_Tamb	exaggerated rejecting gesture
*Tamb_*	**Mwah,**	exaggerated 'pouting' gesture
	now don't get **jealous precious**	'precious' – speech characteristic of a pantomime Dame – heightened by semi-rhyme of 'jealous/precious'
	You have to earn the respect to refer to me in the feminine:)	mock reference to feminized title as showing respect

We can read this text in multiple ways. The feminized play-acting seems to me to border on misogyny: the querying of masculinity in the feminized vocatives, the theatrical performing of speech and interactional styles stereotypically associated with women, is used in insulting play. This seems to me symbolic of the anxiety of men excluded by mainstream discourse from the category 'man'; does this mean they must then be classified as 'women'? Hardly, as the emphasis on masculinity in the handles shows. The fact that the 'feminine' is playfully embraced or turned against other members indicates that the men occupy a gendered no man's land (no pun intended!). The instability of gendered categories is certainly at play in these men's talk, but the hint of misogyny suggests an allegiance to the very gendered hierarchy from which these men have been excluded.

Table 2.1 *Some gender-related pronouns in Japanese*

	M&F	M	F
1st person	watashi	boku	atashi
		ore	
		jibun (reflexive)	
2nd person	anta	omee	-

Some studies of the speech of homosexuals focusing on gender-discordant pronominal use are more convincing examples of the creatively destabilizing potential of homosexual speech. Abe (2004) studied the use of first and second person pronouns in the speech of lesbians in lesbian bars in Shinjuku, a well-known gay and lesbian area of Tokyo. English, like many languages, does not distinguish the gender of the referent in the first and second persons: we have no specific pronouns meaning 'I, male' or 'I, female' or 'you, male' or 'you, female' (unlike in the third person, where we refer to 'he, that male person' and 'she, that female person'). Japanese, like many languages, does offer choices for indicating the gender of the referent in the first and second persons, some of which are shown in Table 2.1. Abe showed that while the lesbians in her study sometimes used the form marked as male to refer to themselves and each other, this was not automatic but involved complex, strategic use of the pronouns as a linguistic resource for projecting identity. Some of the speakers she studied avoided pronouns associated with traditional femininity but were also reluctant to use the most clearly marked masculine forms; instead they used less marked masculine forms and varied their choices according to the nature of their relationship with their interlocutors.

2.9 LANGUAGE, GENDER AND SEXUALITY: POSTSTRUCTURALIST APPROACHES

A classic locus illustrating the potential of poststructuralist approaches to gendered speech is Cameron's (1997) study of men's same-gender talk in a dorm at a US university. Several of the young men in the dorm are discussing and making fun of a gay classmate. The men's language use in this study forms a striking contrast with Coates's (1997a) findings, discussed above: the men display precisely those features which Coates argues characterize women's speech. They talk about a person, not about things, and conversation topics include talking about details of clothing (including fabrics and styles) and bodily appearance; there is frequent latching and simultaneous speech; and the main point of the conversation is not to exchange information but to affirm solidarity. Here is the extract that Cameron discusses (1997, pp. 53–4):

```
Bryan     uh you know that really gay guy in our Age of Revolution class
          who sits in front of us? he wore shorts again, by the way, it's like 42
          degrees out he wore shorts again [laughter] [Ed: That guy] it's like a speedo,
          he wears a speedo to class (.) he's got incredibly skinny legs [Ed: It's
          worse] you know=
Ed                           =you know like those shorts women volleyball players wear? It's
          like those (.) it's l[ike
Bryan                         [you know what's even more ridicu[lous? when
Ed                                                            [French cut spandex]
Bryan     you wear those shorts and like a parka on….
          (5 lines omitted)
Bryan     he's either got some condition that he's got to like have his legs exposed at
          all times or else he's got really good legs=
Ed                                              =he's probably he'[s like
Carl                                                             [he really likes
Bryan     =he
Ed        =he's like at home combing his leg hairs=
Carl                              his legs=
Bryan     he doesn't have any leg hair though=     [yes and oh
Ed                                    =he real[ly likes his legs=
Al                                                          =very long very
          white & very skinny
Bryan                      those ridiculous Reeboks that are always (indecipherable)
          and goofy white socks that are always striped=     [tube socks
Ed                                              =that's [right
          he's the antithesis of man
```

'He's the antithesis of man' – thus illustrating again the primary strategy of homophobia, the exclusion of homosexuals from the category 'man'; the homosexual is the Other of 'man', 'the antithesis of man' in a very real sense. In that sense, the men's talk is actually performative of masculinity, in the sense that masculinity is equated with heterosexuality. What the example shows, claims Cameron, is that ways of talking do not flow 'naturally' or inexorably from membership in social categories in an a priori way, although ways of talking may characterize the subjectivity of members of social categories in that members distinguish themselves from others by conforming their verbal behaviour to the norms mandated within discourse. But they are capable of speaking and interacting in ways that deviate from these norms in the appropriate circumstances – as here, in distinguishing themselves not from women, but from the homosexual male.

Perhaps surprisingly, most studies of language and sexuality have focused on sexual identity, rather than on sexual desire more generally. The emphasis has been on markers of minority sexual identity, that is, the distinctiveness of gay/lesbian speech. There have been relatively fewer studies of the language of heterosexuality, with notable exceptions, such as the well-known study of refusals in 'date rape' (Kitzinger & Frith, 1999) using the tools of Conversation Analysis. But looked at another way, the preoccupation with the minority identity, with the homosexual Other, is a way of defining the 'normal' heterosexual self, and the 'normally' gendered self – we have seen how masculinity is defined in opposition to homosexuality, and the putative 'unfeminine' characteristics of some lesbians have the same function. In other words, research on the Other is in fact research on the Self, for it is in terms of the Other that the Self is defined. As poststructuralist theorists argue, this means that the oppositions between Self and Other which are so characteristic of discourses of gender and sexuality are illusory, as the Other is crucial to definitions of the Self. Studies of men who sometimes have sex with men for example within the migration context (Baynham, 2017), but who do not identify as gay, have the potential to explore the paradoxes in these supposed oppositions. We will take this issue up again in the next chapter, in the construction of the Other in colonial settings.

2.10   CONCLUSION: PERFORMANCE AND PERFORMATIVITY

In the example of Agnes, like the situation with Thao, the performance of the expected characteristics of 'normally' gendered subjectivity is conscious and deliberate. But in the Hmong cultural context in which Thao was socialized, his masculinity would have been 'normal' and unquestioned, and his signalling of it conventionally would have been routine. It is important here to distinguish between performance and performativity, though they are each associated with the verb 'to perform'. Performance refers to behaviour, the act of displaying the signs which are interpreted within discourses of gender. Performativity refers to the interpretation of those performances within social discourses – how those behaviours are read. The relationship between these two things is something which we will explore in detail in the second half of this book. How can the details of performance be studied in the light of an understanding of its meaning in terms of discourse, for example gendered discourse? The key here, as we will see, is the idea that our gendered subjectivity needs to be iteratively, repeatedly signalled in real time, again and again, over and over. This implies that actions at the micro-level are crucial in the achievement of performed subjectivities. We will propose Conversation Analysis as a methodology for the study of this iterability in face-to-face interaction, and will use examples of gendered discourse (among others) to illustrate the argument. But before we move onto the micro-level, we need a more developed understanding of the macro-level, of discourses in Foucault's terms. In the next two chapters, we will explore processes of recognition within racist discourses.

2.11 SUGGESTIONS FOR FURTHER READING

There is a vast literature on language and gender, with dedicated journals, conferences and research organizations. Classic works are Lakoff (1975), Coates (1986) and Tannen (1990). Lakoff's work was reissued with commentaries in 2004 (Lakoff, 2004). Deborah Cameron's writing on language and gender is distinctive both for its incisiveness and for its articulation of poststructuralist perspectives on the topic. Cogent summaries of developments in the field can be found in Cameron (2007; 2010). Cameron and Kulick (2003) remains the best introduction to the topic of language and sexuality, while Baker (2008) and Milani (2018) bring together the issues of gender and sexuality. The classic text on linguistic pragmatics is Levinson (1983). The classic text by Butler on performativity is *Gender Trouble* (1990). Kitzinger (2005), Land and Kitzinger (2005, 2008), Speer (2011) and Speer and Green (2007) represent recent work on gender and sexuality in interaction (see Chapters 6 and 7 below).

3 Recognition and the Colonial Other

3.1 INTRODUCTION

Years ago, as young Australians having recently arrived in London, a friend and I were looking for accommodation. At that time, as today, it was common in London for young people to share houses and flats, with accommodation both scarce and expensive. Rooms in share houses were advertised in the daily newspapers, and you phoned to make an appointment to view the room and meet the others who were living there, in an informal interview. My friend, who, as an Australian, spoke English with an Australian accent, was amused by the reaction she got when she telephoned the young English woman who had placed the advertisement. My friend was informed that there was no point in arranging a meeting as 'we have a policy of not accepting colonials. We think you'd be happier among your own kind.' A 'colonial'? Our 'own kind'? Neither of us had thought of ourselves in those terms prior to this encounter. We came to realize as we lived in London that 'colonials' was a category applicable to people from other English-speaking countries – Australians, Canadians, New Zealanders and, even, the Revolutionary War notwithstanding, Americans! The old British Empire, it seemed, was not entirely dead. We were 'called into being' (Althusser, 1971) by being nominated in that way; and subsequently, we grew to share a fellow-feeling with others who were seen in this way. We had all learned that we might be seen as 'colonials', with the implications of that in the London of the time; we also, to a certain extent, grew to recognize ourselves in those terms. In this case the categorization and its consequences were relatively harmless (apart from perhaps making it slightly harder to get accommodation) because we were the 'beneficiaries' of a kind of racism that distinguished between 'white' and 'coloured' colonials. The Nigerian poet Wole Soyinka, in his poem

'Telephone Conversation', describes the alternative experience for a non-white colonial in a parallel conversation, a person seeking accommodation in London (Soyinka, 1963). In the poem, his accent has not 'given away' the fact that the caller seeking the room is African: everything seems fine in terms of the rent and where the flat is located; and the landlady (to whom he is speaking) does not live at that address, but elsewhere, so his privacy is protected. The only thing left is for him to arrange a meeting to inspect the property and for her to meet him. A sixth sense though tells him that he may be wasting his time, and hers, if she is prejudiced against his colour and his race. So he discloses that he is African. Silence follows, apart from the sound of the middle-class landlady drawing in smoke from what he assumes is an expensive brand of cigarette. Finally, to his astonishment, she asks him the exact shade of his skin colour – presumably, if he is not 'very' black, then she can 'make an exception' to her rule of 'No coloureds'. (This rule was a common practice in Britain at the time, until it was outlawed by the Race Relations Act of 1965.)

Here the category invoked by the British woman is not 'colonial' so much as race or colour. The experience of being so categorized (particularly in the context of a search for accommodation) comes as something of a shock, although also as absurd – the rest of the Soyinka poem involves a sharply satirical reflection back to the woman of the 'colour' category she is using. It is also a learning experience: one's expectations, and ultimately one's sense of oneself as a social being, will have been significantly altered. What is important here is that a person is seen by others in terms of particular categories, that is, is 'recognized' as an example of a relevant social category – relevant to the observer, and thus, willy-nilly, to the one so recognized. This experience of encountering *new* social categories in terms of which we are 'recognized' by others is more common when we change social contexts, in which social categories exist with which we may be previously unfamiliar.

In this chapter, we will consider the way in which the experience of being recognized is a key factor in the emergence and maintenance of subjectivity; we will illustrate this by considering the role of language in constructing the experience of racism in colonial settings. We have seen in the work of Foucault in earlier chapters that discourses typically construct a 'normal' Self in relation to an 'abnormal' Other. In this chapter we will explore the relation between Self and Other further. The chapter begins with a discussion of the influential theory of the emergence of self-consciousness through processes of recognition as Other in the work of the German philosopher Hegel. It will then introduce three theorists of racism in whose work the construction and experience of the colonial Other is central: Frantz Fanon, Edward Said and Jacques Derrida. In each case, the focus of their work on language in the context of French colonialism will be highlighted. The historical origin, the mutability and the persistence of the character of categorizations relevant to colonial settings will become apparent. The chapter concludes with a discussion of the complexity of the outcomes of the processes of recognition we have considered, and the way in which the binary 'Self' and 'Other' is problematized as a result.

3.2 HEGEL AND RECOGNITION

In a famous passage in his book *The Phenomenology of Spirit* (1807), the German philosopher G. W. F. Hegel (1770–1831) discusses how processes of recognition by others play a role in awareness of the self. He proposes that it is the natural instinct of an individual consciousness to see itself as the centre of its world, and to subsume everything in the world to this consciousness. However, when this individual consciousness first encounters another consciousness, they each become newly aware of themselves through their awareness that the other is aware of them. Hegel argues that the awareness in the two individuals of the existence of the other triggers a struggle for power, in which one individual will attempt to dominate the other. Let us assume that one individual wins the struggle and is master. The irony is that even though the master appears to have prevailed, its mastery is dependent on the recognition of this mastery by the one over whom it is master. In this 'master/slave dialectic', there is a mutual dependence; and most relevantly for our discussion, *Self*-consciousness only emerges in relation to the Other.

> Self-consciousness exists in and for itself, when, and by the fact that, it so exists for another; that is, it exists only being acknowledged ...
> Action by one side only would be useless, because what is to happen can only be brought about by both ... they recognize themselves as mutually recognizing each other. (Hegel, 1807/1977, pp. 111–12)

The master/slave passage in Hegel had an important influence on key thinkers about subjectivity in the latter part of the twentieth century, especially writers within the tradition of French poststructuralism. This was partly because of a kind of historical accident. Alexander Kojève (1902–68), a Russian exile living in Paris, gave a series of lectures on Hegel in Paris between 1933 and 1939. The lectures were attended by the philosopher Jean-Paul Sartre, the philosopher, feminist and writer Simone de Beauvoir, the psychoanalyst Jacques Lacan, and the philosophers who were subsequently to become the teachers of two of the key figures in French poststructuralism (Michel Foucault and Jacques Derrida). They were also influential for the Marxist theorist Louis Althusser, who wrote his PhD on Hegel. French thought reinterpreted the passage to emphasize not so much the way in which the slave frees himself from the master through work, the standard Marxist interpretation, but the vulnerability of consciousness to processes of recognition by the Other, and the way in which social categories are involved in the process of recognition.

3.3   RECOGNITION AND RACISM IN COLONIAL SETTINGS: FANON

Colonialism provides a setting in which social categories, especially categories of race, are crucial to the way people are seen and come to see themselves. In his early text *Black Skin, White Masks* (1952/1967), Frantz Fanon (1925–61), the psychoanalyst, revolutionary and theorist of colonialism, explicitly draws on the Hegelian concept of recognition in his discussion of his own experience as a colonial subject. Born to a middle-class family in Martinique, a French colony in the West Indies (in French, *Les Antilles*), in 1943 he left Vichy-controlled Martinique to fight for the Free French resistance. A war hero, he was awarded the Croix de Guerre. He stayed on in France to study medicine and psychiatry in Lyon. *Black Skin, White Masks* was written in France and appeared in the year before he left to take up a senior post as a psychiatrist in Algeria, at the time of the outbreak of the Algerian War of Independence, where his treatment of victims of torture had a profound effect on his political attitudes, turning him into a revolutionary. The book describes the relationship of language and subjectivity in colonial Martinique, and the subsequent experience of colonial French-speaking subjects in France, his own experience.

The linguistic situation in colonial Martinique was that, as in other French colonies, French was the sole language of administration, and also of education, which was restricted to a lucky few (Fanon was one of only four per cent of Martinicans to receive an education). The vernacular language was Creole. In interaction with the colonial master, the colonial subject had a choice of French (if mutually known), Creole (if mutually known) or a simplified French pidgin; the choice of each had implications for subjectivity. This meant that one would be recognized as belonging to a certain category according to how one spoke; and consciousness of this being so recognized would have an influence on language choice in self-presentation to the Other. This meant that bilingual colonial subjects (those who knew both French and Creole) would be recognized as a different Self, depending on language choice and interlocutor. Language choice allows recognition, and recognition is the basis of subjectivity. Fanon writes: 'To speak is to exist absolutely for the other' (1952/1967, p. 17).

Perhaps one of the most damaging aspects of the experience of recognition in this way is an internalization of the categories, so that a process of self-stigmatization ensues, which is then expressed linguistically. Thus, the middle class in Martinique rejects Creole in favour of French:

> The middle class in the Antilles never speak Creole except to their servants. In school the children of Martinique are taught to scorn the dialect. One avoids Creolisms. Some families completely forbid the use of Creole, and mothers ridicule their children for speaking it. (Fanon, 1952/1967, p. 20)

This is not just an issue of sociolinguistic hierarchies; it goes to the core of the being of the colonial subject. In the eyes of the colonial master, and increasingly in his/her own eyes, the colonial subject only exists as a full human being when he/she speaks in a way which allows him/her to be recognized as in this respect 'like' the colonial master:

> The Negro of the Antilles will be proportionately whiter – that is, he will come closer to being a real human being – in direct ratio to his mastery of the French language ... A man who has a language ... possesses the world expressed and implied by that language ... Mastery of language affords remarkable power. (Fanon, 1952/1967, p. 18)

Fanon comments on the mystique of France for those living in Martinique. The following passage, like the previous one full of heavy irony, shows the transformation of subjectivity in the eyes of fellow Martinicans of those 'lucky' enough to be able to leave Martinique for France: 'He leaves for the pier, and the amputation of his being diminishes as the silhouette of the ship grows clearer. In the eyes of those who have come to see him off he can read the evidence of his own mutation, the power' (Fanon, 1952/1967, p. 23). The fact that language is a cue to recognition means that language encodes the relationship of power; and as language is not restricted to a particular location, as it is transposed, so is the encoding. Thus Fanon points out that in the French army, where colonial subjects often served, it was assumed by African soldiers who did not speak French that the Creole-speaking Martinicans were French speakers (a categorization rejected by French speakers themselves, who did not recognize Creole as French). The Africans tried to 'pass' as Martinicans by learning Creole, even though Creole was itself stigmatized within Martinique, and rejected by the French officers they were trying to impress. This ironic and painful example illustrates the possibility of 'misrecognition', where individuals are (mis)recognized as belonging to a social category to which in the eyes of powerful others they do not in fact belong. A parallel and equally painful example of misrecognition, in a very different colonial context, underlies the evolution of one of the two creoles spoken in Australia, the Torres Strait Creole. In the strait between the northern tip of Australia and New Guinea, the Torres Strait, lie islands populated by Melanesians which were colonized in the nineteenth century. From 1871, mixed-race missionaries from other parts of Melanesia were sent to do the proselytizing work in these islands and became desirable as marriage partners. These missionaries were seen by the Torres Strait Islanders to be speakers of English, although in fact they were speakers of Pidgin English, which was the language of communication in the marriages between the missionaries and their Torres Strait islander wives. Pidgin creolized in the children of these marriages, leading to the emergence of Torres Strait Creole. The speakers of this Creole initially had prestige as they were (mis)recognized as native speakers of English; but they were then subject to an opposite process of recognition when they encountered the reactions of speakers of Standard English, who did not recognize them as speakers of English, and for whom the speech of the Creole speakers was stigmatized (Shnukal, 1983; McNamara, 1987a).

Returning to Fanon: once the Martinican arrives in France, he monitors his French carefully for signs of non-metropolitan features. For example, the Martinican will try to avoid the influence of Creole on his French; Fanon gives a satirical picture of the Martinician practising the rolled 'r' and berates the tongue that has difficulty with it as 'wretchedly lazy': 'Yes, I must take great pains with my speech, because I shall be more or less judged by it. With great contempt they will say of me, "He doesn't even know how to speak French"' (Fanon, 1952/1967, p. 20). The situation is a perfect Catch-22, however. The Martinican who masters metropolitan French perfectly often encounters confusion and frustration, even anger, in his interlocutors in France, for whom the linguistic boundary used for categorization and recognition proves to be 'unreliable' in such cases. The metropolitan

French speaker may patronize the Martinican – Fanon (1952/1967, p. 38) gives a personal example:

> Rather more than a year ago in Lyon, I remember, in a lecture I had drawn a parallel between the Negro and European poetry, and a French acquaintance told me enthusiastically, 'At the bottom you are a white man.' The fact that I had been able to investigate so interesting a problem through the white man's language gave me honorary citizenship.

The impossibility of the racialized Other's situation is illustrated in this example. The French acquaintance's 'generous' endorsement of Fanon's French language and acculturation serves only to reinscribe the boundary. We will see further examples of this 'generosity' below, in our discussions of Said and Derrida. What can the racialized Other do in the face of this, both externally and internally?

3.4   THE OTHER IN COLONIAL DISCOURSE: SAID AND ORIENTALISM

In earlier chapters we saw, following Foucault, how subjectivity is constructed within discourse, and how such discourses typically focus on the 'abnormal', the Other, and in so doing define (often implicitly) a 'normal' Self as 'not Other'. In the previous section, we looked at the role of language in constructing the experience of the colonial Other. In this section we will examine the character of the discourse to which the colonial Other is subject. The best-known analysis of the construction of the Other in discourse in colonial settings is Edward Said's book *Orientalism* (1979). Said shows that language, or more specifically linguistic theory, played a crucial role in the emergence of this discourse.

In *Orientalism*, Said (1935–2003), a Palestinian from a Christian background who spent his adult life as an academic in the United States, traces the way in which the Orient, particularly the Islamic Middle East, is represented in Western thought, scholarship, art and literature. Orientalism is defined as how the West represents the East to itself as a scientific field of study, allowing the East to be 'recognized' in particular terms and thus to 'come into being' for the West.

The 'scientific', 'objective', systematic study of the Orient that constituted Orientalism was a form of surveillance, as in Foucault's discussion of the Panopticon (see Chapter 1 above). Said makes this link explicitly: 'Knowledge was essentially a *making visible* of material, and the aim ... was the construction of a sort of Benthamite Panopticon.

Scholarly discipline was therefore a specific technology of power' (1979, p. 127). The resulting representations of the Orient formed the basis for the political action of colonialism: 'The Orient that appears in Orientalism, then, is a system of representations framed by a whole set of forces that brought the Orient into Western learning, Western consciousness, and later, Western empire' (pp. 202–3). French Orientalism, combining scientific, intellectual study with colonial ambitions, became particularly clear in Napoleon's invasion of Egypt in 1798–9. Napoleon took several dozen scientific experts with him on his expedition and used the information gleaned as the basis for the establishment of an *Institut d'Egypte*, whose research led to a massive publication, the *Description de l'Egypte* in twenty-three volumes, published between 1809 and 1828:

> The other part [of Napoleon's project to dominate Egypt] was to render it completely open, to make it totally accessible to European scrutiny. Egypt was to become a department of French learning ... The *Institut*, with its teams of chemists, historians, biologists, archeologists, surgeons and antiquarians, was the learned division of the army. (Said, 1979, pp. 83–4)

There are two aspects of Said's account of Orientalism which particularly relate to the themes of this book. One is the key role of nineteenth-century philology, the forerunner of modern linguistics, in the development of Orientalism. Another is the way that, Said argues, Orientalism represented a continuation of earlier discourse associated with religious belief, under cover of secularism: Orientalist scholarship was academic and secular in character. Despite this, 'this is not to say that the old religious patterns of human history and destiny ... were simply removed. Far from it: they were reconstituted, redeployed, redistributed in the secular frameworks [of Orientalism]' (pp. 120–1). These two aspects are in fact one, for it was in the context of work in linguistics that the re-inscription of the old discourse in the new was accomplished.

Linguistics in this colonial period was known as philology and focused on what we would now call historical linguistics, the tracing of the evolution of particular languages over historical time, including the remote past. The pioneering investigation of Sanskrit by Sir William Jones (1746–94) following the British colonization of Bengal had identified surprising similarities between Sanskrit and three other languages, Latin, Greek and Persian, and this led to great interest in the historical relations between languages, and the study of language 'families'. The German scholar Friedrich Schlegel

(1772–1829) pioneered a study of the similarities and differences among these different 'Indo-European' languages, thus founding the field of comparative philology. Schlegel saw parallels between language and race, and used the term 'Aryans' ('the honorable people') to refer to the speakers of the original Indo-European language, the parent language of all the later languages in the family. The Indo-European family of languages was found to be unrelated to other language families, including (and in particular) the Semitic family of languages (which included Hebrew, Arabic and the languages of Ethiopia). The term 'Semitic' dates from this time: originally a linguistic term for the family of languages, it later came to refer to the cultures and ethnicities of the speakers of those languages. However, this comparison and contrast of language families was not only descriptive but evaluative:

> [For Schlegel] the Indo-European family was artistically simple and satisfactory in a way the Semitic ... was not ... [Such racism] was widely diffused in European culture. But nowhere else ... was it made the basis of a scientific subject matter as it was in comparative linguistics or philology. (Said, 1979, pp. 98–9)

It was those working in the field of comparative philology who played a key role in the development of the discourse of Orientalism:

> Almost without exception, every Orientalist [from the last decades of the 18th century] began his career as a philologist ... It is the extraordinarily rich and celebrated cultural position of [philology] that endowed Orientalism with its most important technical characteristics. (Said, 1979, p. 131)

One such figure was Ernest Renan (1823–92), Professor of Hebrew at the Collège de France. Renan was raised as a Catholic but lost his faith; he wrote a popular *Life of Jesus*, arguing that the life of Jesus should be studied historically like the life of any other man. Renan saw comparative philology in the tradition of Schlegel as the key discipline of modern (i.e. rational, critical, liberal) thought, 'a symbol of a modern (and European) superiority' (Said, 1979, p. 312), as it offered an account of the origins of humanity, civilization and language. But philology also had an additional significance for Renan as a replacement for his lost belief. According to Said (p. 135), 'The only way in which ... he could move out of religion into philosophical scholarship was to retain in the new lay science the historical worldview he had gained from religion.'

Renan worked on Semitic (Hebrew, Arabic, Aramaic) rather than on Indo-European languages and published his *Histoire générale et système comparé des langues sémitiques* in 1855. The goal of the study was to 'make language speak' by setting it in its context, and within a comparative frame (Semitic vs Indo-European). The Semitic languages and cultures were declared to be 'degraded', both biologically and morally, compared to Indo-European languages. The speakers of Semitic languages, the 'Semites', were in Renan's view 'rabid monotheists who produce no mythology, no art, no commerce, no civilization; their consciousness is narrow and rigid' (Said, 1979, p. 142).

As far as the languages themselves are concerned, Indo-European languages were seen as 'living', 'organic', 'generative', 'mature' languages. In contrast, Semitic languages were inorganic, unregenerative; thus representing the languages of cultures with 'arrested development'. In endorsing the view of Schlegel, cited above,[1] Renan is similarly ventriloquizing an older discourse, that of anti-Semitism. The organic/inorganic opposition is a familiar trope in Christian discourse in relation to Judaism, which over the course of the first century AD increasingly identified itself in opposition to Judaism, which it claimed to have superseded. Metaphorically, Christianity represents itself in its discourse as life-affirming, and signifying *new* life, while a 'literalistic', 'legalistic' Judaism is seen as a dead husk; empty and obsolete. Such metaphors have life in discourse and survive the loss of faith (as in Renan's case). The formulations characteristic of an older, anti-Jewish prejudice, reinterpreted in the 'scientific' discourse of early linguistics, thus formed a central trope within the discourse of Orientalism. It was now greatly extended to the Islamic cultures of the Middle East and became the context in which colonialism seemed natural and indeed creative and 'life-giving'. This ideology of colonialism as a liberal force for progressive change is echoed strongly in the next account of colonial subjectivity, that of the philosopher Jacques Derrida in colonial Algeria.

Oddly, Said does not explicitly comment on anti-Jewish prejudice – anti-Semitism – as the source of Renan's view of Semitic languages and peoples. In his Introduction to the book, he appears to recognize the link between anti-Semitism and Orientalist prejudice: he says of himself that he has 'found himself writing the history of a strange, secret sharer of Western anti-Semitism. That anti-Semitism and, as I have discussed it in its Islamic branch, Orientalism resemble each other very closely is a historical, cultural and political truth' (Said, 1979,

---

[1] Said (1979, p. 143, fn 50) points out that this view had also been expressed by Humboldt.

pp. 27–8). But nowhere else does he explore this or acknowledge explicitly the sources of Orientalist prejudice in the centuries-old cultural prejudices about Jews and Judaism circulating in the Christian cultural space. Perhaps this represents a blindness brought about by his own conditioning as a Christian; more likely it is politically inconvenient, as he uses the argument of the book to criticize Western positions on the Israeli-Palestinian conflict as a latter-day expression of Orientalism. Whatever the reason, the erasure is surely significant and can be seen as expressing the very anti-Semitism which he demonstrates as informing Orientalism. We will discuss the discourse of anti-Semitism further in Chapter 4.

3.5 DERRIDA AND RECOGNITION

Jacques Derrida (1930–2004) was born into an indigenous Algerian family and, like Frantz Fanon, was one of the relatively few among the colonized to have the benefit of education, which was conducted exclusively through the medium of French. Unlike the bilingual Fanon, however, Derrida grew up as a monolingual speaker of French, a fact whose significance he explores in a relatively late text, *Monolingualism of the Other* (Derrida, 1998). Derrida's family and community had experienced language shift to the language of the colonizer over the previous two generations, and in his upbringing and education there was little opportunity to learn the indigenous languages of Algeria (Arabic, which was treated as a foreign language at school, like English or German, and Berber, which was not taught at all). A key factor here was the colonial language policy, in which administration and education were conducted exclusively in French. The ideology of this policy held that the colonial project was actually a work of liberation, bringing with it the fruits of the French Revolution – the French term is *mission civilisatrice*. The French language, as the embodiment of these liberal values, was therefore a gift. In this sense, according to Derrida, the 'unilateral imposition of [a] "politics" of language' was 'disguised under alibis of "universal" humanism, and ... of the most generous hospitality' (Derrida 1998, p. 39).

Algeria forms part of the larger area of North Africa known as the Maghreb. Berber people were among the early settlers of the Maghreb (certainly by 3000 BC) and still make up approximately 20 per cent of the population of the country, speaking a range of Berber languages including Kabyle. The majority of Algerians (around 80 per cent) are

Arabs, who first settled the Maghreb in the AD 600s and developed their own Maghrebian variety of Arabic.

Derrida was a specific kind of colonial subject in Algeria, as a member of the indigenous Sephardi Jewish community in Algiers, growing up as (in his own words) 'a little black and very Arab Jew' (Bennington & Derrida, 1993, p. 58). The word Sephardi comes from the Hebrew word for Spain ('*Sfarad*') and represents one of the two broad cultural traditions of diaspora Jewish life (the other, Ashkenazi, deriving from central and eastern Europe). Jews and Muslims who refused to convert to Christianity were expelled from Spain in 1492 and sought refuge in the Ottoman Empire, including in North Africa. The term Sephardi was then extended to refer to Jews in general living in the Muslim world, even if they were not originally from Spain; that is, it was extended to members of the ancient Jewish communities in Arab countries who spoke Jewish ethnolects of Arabic known collectively as Judaeo-Arabic. The Arab settlement of Algeria had seen the development of a small Jewish community;[2] this community was supplemented after 1492 with Jews expelled from Spain, who brought with them a Jewish ethnolect of Spanish known as Ladino. Combined, the various Jewish ethnic communities constituted by the time that Derrida was born less than two per cent of the population of Algeria. The tiny indigenous Jewish community of Algeria thus had a tradition of speaking Ladino or Judaeo-Arabic, although this had been lost through linguistic assimilation in the generation preceding Derrida's birth.

The theme of recognition is prominent in the account Derrida gives of the process of the cultural and linguistic assimilation of the community into which he was born. This was marked by two contradictory moments of social 'recognition'. The first followed the colonial occupation of Algeria from 1830, which, as one of the liberal fruits of the French Revolution, brought with it, in 1870, the abolition of official state anti-Semitism (though a deep and pervasive anti-Semitism was revealed by the Dreyfus affair of the 1890s). Accordingly, the members of the long-standing indigenous Jewish communities of Algeria were 'recognized' as equal citizens and granted French citizenship; this led to a rapid assimilation to French culture and language and an abandonment of traditional mores and languages (Judaeo-Arabic and Ladino). This left the young secular Jews of Derrida's generation in

---

[2] There is some evidence of a Judaeo-Berber community predating the arrival of the Arabs.

a strange, absurd no man's land, speakers of no other language than that of the colonists.

The policy of favouring French over other languages in Algeria effectively erased the possibility of multilingualism for the newly assimilated generations, since it implied a kind of forbidding of other languages, an 'interdict', even though this was not spelled out in law:

> When access to a language is forbidden, nothing – no gesture, no act – is forbidden ... We had the choice, the formal right, to learn or not learn Arabic or Berber. Or Hebrew. It was not illegal, or a crime ... The interdict worked therefore through other ways. More subtle, peaceful, silent, and liberal ways. (Derrida, 1998, p. 32)

The monolingual French-speaking Algerian Jews were unlike the other colonized peoples of Algeria (the vast majority of Algerians), who maintained their languages (Arabic and Berber) even as they acquired French, to the extent that they did. Numerically vastly greater, and reluctant to surrender their traditions of Islamic education in favour of the secular French system, they were not given, nor did they seek, the same access to the French educational system as the assimilated Jewish minority (Heggoy, 1973).

Like the Martinicans of Fanon's generation, however, these young Jews spoke French with a non-metropolitan accent, which threatened them with social exclusion from the very language and cultural group they had embraced. But a more violent exclusion was about to be unleashed, and the deception of assimilation was to be revealed with shocking clarity.

The second moment of 'recognition' of the Jewish population of Algeria occurred in 1940, following the establishment of the Vichy Government, which administered Algeria (it was never occupied by German troops). The previous recognition of Algerian Jews as equal citizens was withdrawn; Jews were now 'recognized' in very different terms, this time not as equal citizens but as a race enemy, with the accompanying denial of all rights.

Derrida, who was in early adolescence during this period, was expelled from school as a result of these measures, and experienced the internalization of the new terms of recognition in a way similar to that described by Fanon:

> I was expelled from the Ben Aknoun high school in 1942, and beyond any anonymous 'administrative' measure, which I didn't understand at all and which no one explained to me, the wound was of another order, and it never healed: the daily insults from the children, my

classmates, the kids in the street, and sometimes threats or blows
aimed at the 'dirty Jew', which, I might say, I came to see in myself . . .
(Derrida & Roudinesco, 2004, p. 109)

A similar internalization was displayed by his father, when his
family's livelihood, security, and ultimate survival were threatened,
although this time Derrida was conscious of it:

> When state anti-Semitism was unleashed in Algeria, in 1940–42, my
> father was grateful to his employers for protecting us, for keeping him
> in their service, whereas they could simply have fired this Jewish
> employee, as some people were urging them to do, and as they had the
> legal right to do. I felt humiliated to see him overflowing with
> respectful gratitude to these people for whom he had worked for forty
> years and who generously 'consented' to 'keep him on'. (Derrida and
> Roudinesco, 2004, p. 108[3])

The result was the painful realization that Derrida's relation to his
'Self' and the society around him was constituted within the discourse
and language of the Other. He expresses this idea as a paradox:

> 'I only have one language; it is not mine.' I am monolingual.
> My monolingualism . . . feels like one to me, and I remain in it and
> inhabit it. It inhabits me . . . This monolingualism is me . . . I would not
> be myself outside it. It constitutes me . . . Yet it will never be mine, this
> language . . . (Derrida, 1998, pp. 1–2)

3.6 BEYOND SELF AND OTHER

So far, we have considered three examples of the role of language
either in constructing the terms of recognition of the Other (Said) or in
the experience of those so recognized (Fanon, Derrida). The account so
far can be read as a simple story of the denial of rights within this
construction of subjectivity. But particularly in the narratives of
Fanon and Derrida, the issues involved in their experience of subjectivity are more complex. In order to understand this, we need to return
to Hegel.

In Hegel's original discussion, recognition comes from outside,
from not-Self; it is recognition by the Other which leads to self-
recognition. He also situates this process of recognition politically:

---

[3] This is reminiscent of Freud's similar humiliation and anger as a child at the
reaction of his father when he was the victim of anti-Semitism; the father, an
observant Jew, had his hat knocked into the gutter; instead of protesting, he
meekly picked it up.

the formation of self-consciousness, often seen as a purely cognitive, individual phenomenon, is understood as operating in the domain of the social, and moreover within a social relation of struggle for dominance and power. The Self–Other dyad has been an important theme in discussions of subjectivity since Hegel's initial discussion, part of his larger argument about the emergence of the operation of spirit and the transcendent in human life.

Increasingly in these discussions, the binary character of Self and Other came to be emphasized. The Other came to be seen as what is not Self, what is excluded from Self, the defining point of difference from the Self. Often, the perspective of the dominant group was the point of reference, even in critical discussions, and the model of Self and Other came to be used to analyze many contexts of social domination. Racist Othering is fundamental in colonial settings, and in Orientalism, although as we have seen, this was obscured in the case of French colonialism in particular by 'alibis of "universal" humanism' (Derrida, 1998, p. 39) as well as by the 'dispassionate', 'scientific' character of Orientalist discourse. We have also seen how layers of racist Othering were at play in the development of Orientalism, and, in the case of Derrida, through the switch from one form of recognition, as not-Other (when civic rights were granted to Jewish subjects) to recognition as the racial Other under the laws of Vichy.

However, this viewpoint, while important and critically productive, potentially obscures the mutuality of the Other as envisioned by Hegel ('they recognize themselves as mutually recognizing each other'). From the point of view of the stigmatized minority, the powerful majority is Other, its Otherness demonstrated in the violence of the exclusion to which the minority is subject. The idea of the powerful excluding majority as Other is reflected in the title of Derrida's book, *Monolingualism of the Other*, because the monolingual's language is the language of the Other (in this case French culture). But even here this would suggest the persistence of a simple binary opposition, Self: Other.

However, while the form which domination takes is the definition of the Self in terms of the exclusion of (or by) the Other, the very fact that the Self is defined in terms of the Other involves in a paradoxical sense an incorporation of the excluded Other in the definition of the Self. It is impossible, in other words, to conceive of a Self wholly independently of the Other. Hegel's view that the Self is constituted in its relationship to the Other means that the Other remains a primary constitutive part of the Self: the Self is defined precisely in relation to the existence of the Other and requires the existence of the

Other for Self-definition to take place. In Butler's words (1999, p. 18): 'Hegel introduces the idea that self-identity is only rendered actual to the extent to which it is mediated through that which is different ... The grammatical subject is ... never self-identical.' Or in the words of Stuart Hall (1996, p. 4): 'Above all, identities are constructed through, not outside, difference ... It is only through the relation to the Other, the relation to what it is not ... that the "positive" meaning of any term – and thus its "identity" – can be constructed.' The philosopher Paul Ricœur, in explaining the title of his book *Oneself as Another* (1992), speaks of 'otherness of a kind that can be constitutive of selfhood itself'. He writes (p. 3): '*Oneself as Another* suggests from the outset that the selfhood of oneself implies otherness to such an intimate degree that one cannot be thought of without the other, that instead one passes into the other, as we might say in Hegelian terms.' So in fact we cannot construe Self and Other as a simple binary, despite the apparent meaning of the terms.

Let us now examine in detail the case of Derrida's account of his linguistic identity in pre-Independence Algeria. There is much more than a question of the benefits and costs of linguistic assimilation here, or simple frustration over the loss of multilingualism. Derrida does not regret being a speaker of French: he insists that 'there is nothing I respect and love as much' as the language (Derrida, 1998, p. 51); it is easier for him 'to bless than to curse [this destiny]' (p. 64) (that is, of having French as his primary language). Instead of retreating from French, or simply seeing himself as a victim of 'linguistic imperialism' (Phillipson, 1992), he explores the contradiction, the paradox, of his subjectivity being constituted in the language of the Other. What does this experience of subjection and subjectivity in language entail? And what is its broader relevance to an understanding of language and subjectivity in other, non-violent and non-colonial contexts? For that is what Derrida claims: although his relationship to French is contextualized within his autobiography, this does not mean that it is merely or primarily of biographical or historical interest. Instead, Derrida (1986/2005, p. 101) argues for its general applicability:

> I knew that what I was saying in *The Monolingualism of the Other* was valid to a certain extent for my individual case, to wit, a generation of Algerian Jews before the Independence. But it also had the value of a universal exemplarity, even for those who are not in such historically strange and dramatic situations as ... mine. I would venture to claim that the analysis is valid even for someone whose

experience of his own mother tongue is sedentary, peaceful, and without any historical drama.

First, given that speakers of languages are constituted in language, each speaker's whole being is involved in the relationship to the languages they speak. For Derrida, using French involves a range of complex, even contradictory feelings: on the one hand shame, pain, anger and the desire to hurt; but at the same time passionate attachment, expressed in images of physical desire. Thus, he scandalously claims that he both suffers *and takes pleasure in*[4] his paradoxical relationship to the language:

> But above all, and this is the double edge of a sharp sword that I wished to confide to you almost without saying a word: I suffer and take pleasure in [*jouis de*] what I am telling you in our aforementioned common language:
>   *'Yes, I only have one language; yet it is not mine.'* (Derrida, 1998, p. 2)

Second, the very possibility of communication of experience involves an external, shared, public medium. The experience of the individual can only be articulated in a language that does not belong exclusively to him or her, a position articulated in Bakhtin's notion of heteroglossia (1975/1981). Derrida (1998, pp. 19–20) asks: 'What happens when someone resorts to describing an uncommon 'situation', mine, for example, by testifying to it in terms that go beyond it, in a language whose generality takes on a value that is in some ways structural, universal, transcendental … ?' Third, however, the language available to us is 'a forbidding … speech' (p. 33). This is understood originally in Derrida's text as the way in which French, which permitted so much to its speakers in the colonial setting, also erased the possibility of multilingualism, by excluding local languages. But it illustrates a far more general potential of discourse. Languages make available to us a set of potentially inimical discourses within which our own subjectivity is inscribed; how can we think outside the terms which a language offers us? The use of language, any language, involves an ongoing wrestling with meaning and a struggle to escape the simple ventriloquizing of existing discourses which construct the subject in a constraining way, or worse. In Judith Butler's words (1997, p. 20): 'Bound to seek recognition of its own existence in categories, terms, and names that are not of its own making, the subject seeks the sign of its own existence outside itself, in a discourse that is at once dominant and indifferent.' Given this, how can individual experience

---

[4] The term Derrida uses, 'jouir de', suggests sexual pleasure.

be articulated in the language of the Other? Language can be used as a medium expressive of individual experience only by 'deforming, reforming and transforming it' (Derrida, 1998, p. 33). Thus, Derrida speaks of 'an impulse of love and aggression toward the body of [French]' (p. 66); in two extraordinary passages he imagines himself being sexually penetrated by French and (pp. 51–2) imagines the deconstructive rape of the French language. Derrida's notoriously difficult prose is an attempt to wrest meaning from French, to disrupt the normal readability – reminiscent perhaps of T. S. Eliot's iconoclastic, frustrating, disruptive poetry early in the twentieth century. Derrida's complex relationship with French and his struggle for meaning within French, the language of the Other, parallel those of the German Jewish writer Paul Celan in relation to German (McNamara, 2010).

Neither Fanon nor Derrida present the social, political and linguistic situation in which they grew up as involving a simple 'them and us' binary; in fact, they explicitly reject this position. Fanon, for his part, wants to step outside the terms of the black/white dichotomy, the colonizer/colonized. In this sense Fanon can be seen as anticipating Derrida's argument. For example, Fanon rejects the expectation from even such a sympathetic commentator as Jean-Paul Sartre that his reaction to his experience of colonialism will be simple anger. Fanon quotes Sartre's famous introduction, 'Orphée Noir', to an anthology of poetry written by black writers (Senghor, 1948), in which Sartre tells the (mainly white) readership of the volume that they should expect anger and defiance in the writing:

> What then did you expect when you unbound the gag that had muted those black mouths? That they would chant your praises? Did you think that when those heads that our fathers had forcibly bowed down to the ground were raised again, you would find adoration in their eyes?

Fanon answers Sartre's question as follows:

> I do not know; but I say that he who looks into my eyes for anything but a perpetual question will have to lose his sight; neither recognition nor hate. And if I cry out, it will not be a black cry. (Fanon, 1952/1967, p. 29)

In other words, he says he cannot be defined in terms of one of the terms in the binary: in place of the impulse to certainty that drives categorical recognition, there is a refusal of recognition, a questioning, uncertainty. This reflects closely Derrida's discussion of his paradoxical relationship to French and his attempt to transform the language by deforming it. What Fanon and Derrida are doing is subverting, questioning, as it were from inside, the very categories within which their subjectivity is inevitably constructed. We will explore further this theme of the potential instability of identity categories in subsequent chapters.

3.7 CONCLUSION

In this chapter we have used an exploration of the work of three authors writing about French colonialism to show how construction of the Other in colonial discourse has powerful implications for the subjectivity of those so constructed. We have also seen that this Othering is not a one-way street but is mutual. This has two implications: firstly, that the subjectivity of the Self even of the dominant group, because it is defined in relation to the stigmatized Other, is in a sense dependent on that Other for its own sense of Self. The Other is thus internal to the Self, not successfully and completely excluded from it, as its discourse of the Other would have it. It also means that the Self constructed in the experience of *being* the stigmatized Other cannot simply escape the stigmatizing power; Self and Other are in a mutual relationship which cannot simply be abnegated or rejected. This complicates greatly accounts of language in postcolonialism, an issue which needs urgently to be addressed in research. Derrida and Fanon indicate what an exploration of this complex experience of subjectivity in language might be like.

3.8 SUGGESTIONS FOR FURTHER READING

While postcolonial theory shares a heritage with poststructuralism (for example, Said draws heavily on Foucault in his presentation of Orientalism as a discourse), their assumptions are very different, as is evident in the presentations and discussions at the conference on racism called 'tRACEs: Race, Deconstruction and Critical Theory' held at UC Irvine in April 2003 (several of the key presentations are available at https://vimeo.com/album/1631670). The binary oppositions set out in Foucault are questioned in the work of Derrida in particular, for example in his classic *Monolingualism of the Other* (Derrida, 1998). Derrida's work is not easy; my advice to the reader is, 'Never read Derrida alone' – I have found that close textual reading in a group is the key to understanding it. Accessible guides to Derrida's thought are Reynolds and Roffe (2004) and Lucy (2004). Fanon's early work, discussed here, emphasizes the complexity of colonial relations, the internalization of racism in those subject to racist discourse, and contrasts with his later work where revolutionary violence is its focus, for example in his book *Wretched of the Earth* (1963).

4 Racist Discourse and Everyday Language

4.1 INTRODUCTION: THE POWER OF EVERYDAY LANGUAGE

On a seaside walk recently near Point King, on Port Phillip Bay near Melbourne, Australia, where I live, I came across a small stone monument commemorating the site of the arrival of the first European colonizers in that area in 1802. On one side there was a bronze plaque with an inscription dating from the erection of the monument in 1952, the 150th anniversary of the arrival, which reads:

> ON THIS SPOT ON 9TH MARCH 1802,
> ACTING LIEUTENANT JOHN MURRAY COMMANDING
> HMS LADY NELSON TOOK POSSESSION OF PORT KING
> LATER NAMED PORT PHILLIP, IN THE NAME OF HIS
> SACRED MAJESTY GEORGE III OF GREAT BRITAIN AND IRELAND,
> AND HOISTED THE UNION JACK.
> THIS WAS THE FIRST TIME THE UNION JACK
> WAS USED FOR THIS PURPOSE IN AUSTRALIA.

(The Union Jack, the flag of the new United Kingdom of Great Britain and Ireland, had only recently been commissioned in its present form following the Act of Union with Ireland in 1801 – and note the reference to Ireland in the King's title in the inscription.)

On the other side of the same monument there is another bronze plaque, placed there fifty years later, in 2002, on the 200th anniversary of the arrival, which reads:

> The people of the Kulin lived in the Port Phillip area
> for thousands of years.

> Acting Lieutenant John Murray from HMS *Lady Nelson* raised the
> Union flag here on 8 March 1802.

> This plaque was unveiled on 8 March 2002 by
> the Lieutenant Governor of Victoria, Lady Southey, AM.
> to commemorate the bicentenary of the event.

The two plaques were placed on the monument exactly fifty years apart. Their texts reflect the discourses of their times and form a revealing counterpoint. The earlier text is marked by a triumphalist tone of imperial expansion, emphasizing the hierarchies, symbols and rituals of empire. The latter is more subdued and careful in tone (notice that the text is in lower case), although the moment of colonization is still commemorated, and the imperial ranks, symbols and rituals remain, albeit in a more muted form. What is most striking, however, is the acknowledgement of the presence of Aboriginal people in the second text, which serves to highlight the fact that their presence is not recognized at all in the first.

John Murray's own account in his log of the events in the days after the first landing, a little prior to the flag-raising ceremony, deals with the first contact between the colonizers and the Kulin people, and makes poignant reading:

> 16 February
> I sent the launch with Mr Bowen and four hands armed to see if any natives were here, and before the boat was halfway on shore we had the satisfaction of seeing eighteen or twenty men and boys come out of the wood and seat themselves down on a green bank waiting the approach of our boat with which I had sent some shirts and other trifles to give them; the boat accordingly landed in the midst of them and a friendly intercourse took place with dancing on both sides – in an hour the boat returned ... They wished much to know what our arms were and their use and did not seem to believe Mr Bowen that they were only walking sticks ... (Flannery, 2002, p. 29)

By the following day the dancing had been replaced by distrust, with tragic consequences:

> 17 February
> The boat proceeded to the shore and was as before received in a friendly manner by the natives, all of whom were seated in a circle on a beautiful spot of grass near a high point of land. Mr Bowen and all the crew consisting of five men and the boy, Mr Brabyn, went up with their dinners in their hands and sat down in the midst of them (eighteen in number) and began to eat showing the natives how to eat bread, etc., and gave them anything they chose to ask for ...
> By this time our people had nearly finished their dinners and Isaac Moss having the boat in charge got up and was walking slowly down to her.
> At this time the boy Brabyn happened to turn his head towards the wood and saw a man in the very act of throwing a spear at Moss as well as a large body (not before seen) behind a large fallen tree with their spears all in readiness for throwing. The boy immediately cried out to

Mr Bowen ... But before the words were out of his mouth, a spear of
the most dangerous kind was thrown at and did not escape Moss by
a yard ... and in an instant ... the party in ambush ... began to throw
spears ... Our party was obliged to teach them by fatal experience the
effect of our walking sticks.

Thus did this treachery and unprovoked attack meet with its just
punishment ... (Flannery, 2002, pp. 29–31)

In neither of the texts on the monument is there any reference to or
reflection on the violence of the encounter. The complete erasure of
the Aborigines in the earlier inscription corresponds to the legal doc-
trine of *Terra Nullius* – that the land occupied by the colonists was
uninhabited, and belonged to nobody – which it has taken years of
legal argumentation in recent decades to successfully overthrow, and
which is now seen by contemporary opinion in Australia as racist and
indefensible. This explains the reference to the long tradition of occupation of the area by Aborigines in the later inscription, which functions as a form of intertextual response to the first (it is odd to have
a monument with two competing inscriptions such as this); it is
notable that this response is in the first sentence of the inscription,
thereby enhancing its salience. While the challenge in the second text
to the chilling absence of any reference to Aboriginal people in the
first text is clearly deliberate, its failure to acknowledge the actual
historical facts of conflict, violence and resistance constitutes another
kind of erasure – a silence about an issue with which Australian
society still finds it too hard to deal.

We see in this example how ordinary language use – here the
wording of public inscriptions – realizes instantiations of prevailing
discourses. But it does more than this: it reiterates and re-instantiates
such discourses. Each reader of the first inscription experiences afresh
the deletion or erasure of the existence of Aboriginal cultures in the
place where the colonization took place. The second perhaps implicitly raises the question of the relationship of the old and new cultures
on contact, but goes no further, creating in each reader, iteratively,
a somewhat painful, though ultimately comforting sense of the
acknowledgement of complexity which makes it easier for the reader
not to think things through to their conclusion.

In this example, we have focused on the impact of the wording of
the inscriptions on the reader. If the reader is an Australian non-
Aboriginal, the text contributes to the construction of the reader's
subjectivity as, in the first text, a member of a settler society with
a proud history of membership of a larger, victorious empire; in
the second, as member of a society conscious of its history, but also

conscious of its responsibilities. But what if the reader is of Aboriginal descent? The impact on subjectivity will be different: the first text represents an attempt to deny or erase the historical memory of the reader's people; the second similarly glides over or erases the issue of the violent conflict that accompanied the European colonization of Australia. What will be the response of such a reader to these texts? What role do texts situated in the context of violent intergroup relations play in the construction of the identity of the minority – and the majority?

In this chapter we consider the issue of subjectivity in the context of exposure to everyday discourse and will use the example of racist ideologies and racist discourse as the context for the discussion. The first part of the chapter deals with an account of the power of everyday language in the construction of the subjectivity of majority German citizens under Nazism. The second part explores how racist discourse in everyday conversation may be studied empirically, given its fleeting nature. It illustrates an attempt to do this by the documentation of the exposure to everyday anti-Semitism of Jewish immigrants to Australia from Israel. It then deals with how this exposure is 'read' by its targets, how they incorporate this awareness into their existing subjectivity, which has been constructed within other, competing, paradigms. In general, I hope to show the inescapability but also the complexity of the impact of the experience of everyday racist discourse on those who are constructed as Other within it; as well as the enduring role of racist discourse in acting as a reservoir or a site for the reproduction and renewal of racist violence among those whose subjectivity is constructed as 'not Other' within this discourse.

4.2 VICTOR KLEMPERER: EVERYDAY LANGUAGE UNDER NAZISM

The power of everyday language use in enforcing ideologies is the subject of Victor Klemperer's extraordinary account of language under Nazism in his book *LTI* (1947/2000), an acronym for *Lingua Tertii Imperii*, Latin for 'The Language of the Third Reich'. The book, drawing on his notebooks written in Germany during the period 1933–45, is an account of ordinary language use in Germany under the Nazis. Klemperer (1881–1960) was a veteran of the First World War, and a Professor of French Literature in Dresden when the Nazis came to power in 1933. He was a Protestant, born to assimilated Jewish parents, and was married to a German woman who was not Jewish. Despite this, his parentage meant that he was defined as Jewish under the Nazis' Nuremberg Laws and as a result lost his university post in 1935, and was then subject to the extreme sanctions directed at Jews in Germany at that time. His marriage to a German Gentile meant that he initially avoided deportation and death and continued to live in Dresden until late in the war. When the order for his deportation finally did come, in February 1945, he ironically managed to escape during the bombing of Dresden. He lived to be a leading cultural figure in East Germany and died in 1960.

From the time in which he was subject to the sanctions against those identified as Jews, Klemperer kept a kind of linguistic diary and notebook, although this was a very dangerous occupation, as had he been caught with it he would almost certainly have been sent to a concentration camp and killed. The notebook is a record of the way in which language use changed under the regime as a reflection of and a deliberate reinforcement of Nazi ideology. Klemperer's data came from written texts such as posters, obituary notices and advertising; he had to rely on publicly visible texts such as these as, like others subject to the Nuremberg Laws, he was denied access to books or newspapers. But Klemperer also used oral data: he noted popular sayings and made mental notes during conversations. Klemperer's book was published in 1947 in East Germany (it only became known in the West after 1968).

The acronym *LTI*, which forms the title of the book, is itself a reference to language use under the Nazis, a time during which acronyms proliferated as a way of getting people to think differently about the realities they referred to. Klemperer argues that the Nazis deliberately subverted the language in order to change the way in which the German people thought about politics and life in the society of the time. Each of the thirty-six mostly short chapters of the book is a comment on a different aspect of the linguistic manipulation of ordinary people's thought by *LTI*. Writing at the time, he comments: 'It isn't only Nazi actions that have to vanish, but also the Nazi cast of mind, the typical Nazi way of thinking, and its breeding ground: the language of Nazism' (p. 2). The role of oratory in Nazi Germany has often been commented upon – Hitler and other senior Nazis were famously powerful orators, and the effect of the oratory at Nazi political rallies was evident to all. But Klemperer says that this was in fact not the most powerful use of language under the regime:

> No, the most powerful influence was exerted neither by individual speeches nor by articles or flyers, posters or flags; it was not achieved by things which one had to absorb by conscious thought or conscious

emotions. Instead Nazism permeated the flesh and blood of the people through single words, idioms and sentence structures which were imposed on them in a million repetitions and taken on board mechanically and unconsciously ... language does not simply write and think for me, it also increasingly dictates my feelings and governs my entire spiritual being the more unquestioningly and unconsciously I abandon myself to it.

And what happens if the cultivated language is made up of poisonous elements or has been made the bearer of poisons? Words can be like tiny doses of arsenic: they are swallowed unnoticed, appear to have no effect, and then after a little time the toxic reaction sets in after all. The Third Reich coined only a very small number of the words in its language, perhaps – indeed probably – none at all ... But it changes the value of words and the frequency of their occurrence, it makes common property out of what was previously the preserve of an individual or a tiny group, it commandeers for the party that which was previously common property and in the process steeps words and groups of words and sentence structures with its poison. (Klemperer, 2000, pp. 15–16)

Klemperer's text can be seen as an early example of what is now known as Critical Discourse Analysis (CDA), an attempt to examine ordinary language use to reveal its ideological function (Fairclough, 1989; 2001; 2013; Fairclough and Wodak, 1997). While most CDA focuses on public written and spoken text – newspaper and other media texts, for example – there is less attention paid to analysis of informal discourse, particularly casual conversation. The problem is that references to prevailing discourses such as racism are likely to be fleeting in casual conversation. Klemperer took mental notes of conversations which he recorded subsequently; this is not a method which is sanctioned by contemporary social science conventions, unfortunately. An example is the following: Klemperer comments on a remark made in conversation with a young academic colleague, a close family friend:

There were a few shameless communists in Okrilla, so we organized a punitive expedition [*Strafexpedition*].
What did you do?
You know, we made them run the gauntlet of rubber truncheons, a mild dose of castor oil, no bloodshed, but effective all the same.
A proper punitive expedition in fact.

Klemperer traces the word *Strafexpedition* to the violent German colonialism in South-West Africa. He comments: 'you could hear the encircled Negro village ... the cracking of the hippopotamus whip'. The expression then made its way into more general use in German and was one of the first examples of the ideological use of language noted in Klemperer's diary.

4.3   RACIST DISCOURSE IN CASUAL CONVERSATION

Racist discourses are shared discourses, which are not authored but 'ventriloquized' by individuals who cite them. They circulate at the everyday level and are experienced in everyday interaction; they are endlessly repeated, or *iterated*, a term whose importance we introduced earlier in this book. (Note that Klemperer in the quote above is conscious of the iterability of racist discourse: 'Nazism permeated the flesh and blood of the people through single words, idioms and sentence structures which were imposed on them in a million repetitions.') Everyday racism in casual conversation, because of its occasional and ephemeral nature, is somewhat difficult to study systematically, other than by noting down examples that one encounters, as Klemperer does, and as the British novelist and essayist George Orwell did as evidence of everyday anti-Semitism in Britain towards the end of the Second World War, at the same time that Klemperer was writing. In his essay on anti-Semitism published in February 1945, Orwell (1945/1968, p. 332) writes:

> Here are some samples of anti-Semitic remarks that have been made to me during the past year or two:
> Middle-aged office employee: 'I generally come to work by bus. It takes longer, but I don't care about using the Underground from Golders Green [an area of north London with a significant Jewish population] nowadays. There's too many of the Chosen Race travelling on that line.'
> Tobacconist (woman): 'No, I've got no matches for you. I should try the lady down the street. She's always got matches. One of the Chosen Race, you see.'
> Young intellectual, Communist or near-Communist: 'No, I do not like Jews. I've never made any secret of that. I can't stick them. Mind you, I'm not anti-Semitic, of course.'
> Middle-class woman: 'Well, no one could call me anti-Semitic, but I do think the way these Jews behave is too absolutely stinking. The way they push their way to the head of queues, and so on. They're so abominably selfish. I think they're responsible for a lot of what happens to them.'
> Milk roundsman: 'A Jew don't do no work, not the same as what an Englishman does. 'E's too clever. We work with this 'ere' (flexes his biceps). 'They work with that there' (taps his forehead).

> Chartered accountant, intelligent, left-wing in an undirected way: 'These bloody Yids are all pro-German. They'd change sides tomorrow if the Nazis got here. I see a lot of them in my business. They admire Hitler at the bottom of their hearts. They'll always suck up to anyone who kicks them.'
>
> Intelligent woman, on being offered a book dealing with anti-Semitism and German atrocities: 'Don't show it me, please don't show it to me. It'll only make me hate the Jews more than ever.'
>
> I could fill pages with similar remarks.

Casual anti-Semitism remains a pervasive and little-remarked feature of culturally (post-)Christian societies at all levels of society to this day. I also keep an occasional diary of my experience of incidents such as these. An example is the following:

> March 2011
> It's just before the Oscars, and I'm having dinner with three friends from my book group. X reports that there is a campaign in Hollywood against the idea of the film *The King's Speech* getting an Oscar, on the grounds that it is anti-Semitic, led by Jews, who (quote) 'have infiltrated Hollywood', he says, without irony. 'Infiltrated?' I say ...

The choice of wording ('infiltrated') is the essential constitutive element of the racist nature of this remark, as Klemperer would have understood. But these anecdotal methods are often attacked for being subjective, selective and decontextualized, although the evidence from an accumulation of such remarks, such as those cited by Orwell, and the evidence emerging from Klemperer's diary, makes this criticism less persuasive.

How then can casual racism be studied? Because of the ephemeral nature of racist discourse in spoken interaction, some researchers on racist discourse have tended to focus on the analysis of publicly available material such as newspapers, television and radio, and the Internet (for example Van Dijk, 1991; Reisigl & Wodak, 2001; Hill, 2008; Campbell, 2010). Other researchers have developed strategies for collecting evidence of racism in spoken interaction. One method allows the accumulation of instances through the collective action of a group of researcher/informants. Such was the method used by Myers (2005; Myers & Williamson, 2001) in her study of everyday racist discourse in the United States. The researcher asked volunteers from her classes of undergraduate sociology students to keep observation notes of racist remarks or incidents that they noticed over the course of a month. When the evidence of the notes was collated and analyzed, substantial evidence of the prevalence of everyday racism emerged. Picca and Feagin (2007) used a similar method with their students in the United States, getting them to keep journals to record incidents of everyday racism, for example remarks from family, friends, roommates and colleagues. This was supplemented with data from individuals who agreed to be interviewed on the subject of racism. While the interview data offered relatively little support for the prevalence of racist discourse, reflecting the widespread unacceptability of overt racism, analysis of incidents of talk in private settings ('backstage': Goffman, 1959, p. 112) yielded extensive evidence of racist language and attitudes, not confined to whites. The finding that interviews appear to lead people to say what they think should be said has led to a reluctance on the part of some researchers to rely on data from interviews. Yet interviews yielded relevant data in an early study by Van Dijk (1987), who conducted discourse analysis of interview data from white Dutch informants, supplemented with data from white Americans in California. The structure of the Dutch informants' narratives of incidents illustrating their (negative) attitudes to immigrants from Surinam was analyzed, and occasional conversational interactions among informants interviewed in groups of three also provided useful data.

A related but somewhat different interview method is to conduct interviews with people who are themselves the potential target of racist discourse, rather than the perpetrators of it. This was the method used by Essed (1990; 1991) in a comparative study of the experience of racist discourse by black women in the Netherlands and the United States. This was also the method used in an interview study I conducted some years ago of the experience of anti-Semitism of Jewish Israelis who had chosen to live permanently in the Diaspora, in this case in Melbourne, Australia (McNamara, 1987b). Before introducing this study and its follow-up, we need to consider the nature of anti-Semitism, the racist discourse which is the focus of the study.

4.4   WHAT IS ANTI-SEMITISM?

Anti-Semitism, racist prejudice against Jewish people, is a particularly clear example of what Foucault meant by a discourse, which, as we saw earlier, is defined by Stuart Hall (1997, p. 44) as: 'A group of statements which provide a language for talking about – a way of representing the knowledge about – a particular topic at a particular historical moment.' Anti-Semitism, in other words, involves a particular kind of representation of 'the Jew' and 'Jewishness' which may bear little relationship to the actual character and way of life of Jewish people. At any 'particular historical moment', the detail of the representation may change, that is, it will reflect relevant contemporary contexts and mores, although there is a remarkable persistence of tropes over time.

Evidence of the prevalence and routine character of anti-Semitism in contemporary society is not hard to find. For example, consider the following exchange about the role of Jews in the media involving the former US President Richard Nixon and the evangelist, the Reverend Billy Graham, revealed in tapes of a conversation from 1972 which were released in 2002:

GRAHAM: This stranglehold has got to be broken or the country's going down the drain.
NIXON: You believe that?
GRAHAM: Yes, sir.
NIXON: Oh, boy. So do I. I can't ever say that, but I believe it.
GRAHAM: If you get elected a second time, then we might be able to do something.[1]

A phone call from February 1973 between Nixon and Graham provides another example. During the call, Mr Graham complained that Jewish-American leaders were opposing efforts to promote evangelical Christianity, such as the Campus Crusade. The two men agreed that the Jewish leaders risked setting off anti-Semitic sentiment. 'What I really think is deep down in this country, there is a lot of anti-Semitism, and all this is going to do is stir it up,' Nixon said. This might suggest the opposite of anti-Semitism, in that Nixon was aware of the prevalence of the phenomenon and its potential as a source of hostility to Jews. However, he goes on to say: 'It may be they have a death wish. You know that's been the problem with our Jewish friends for centuries.'[2]

The American singer Michael Jackson was involved in a controversy over the lyrics of his song 'They Don't Care about Us' (1995), which included the lines

'Jew me, sue me, everybody do me
Kick me, kike me, don't you black or white me ...'

In response to criticism that these lines expressed anti-Semitic attitudes, Jackson indignantly defended himself in the following words:

[1] 'Graham regrets Jewish slur', *BBC News*, 2 March 2002, http://news.bbc.co.uk/2/hi/americas/1850077.stm, retrieved 8.2.2018.
[2] Charlie Savage, 'On Nixon tapes, ambivalence over abortion, not Watergate', *The New York Times*, 23 June 2009, www.nytimes.com/2009/06/24/us/politics/24nixon.html, retrieved 8.2.2018.

The idea that these lyrics could be deemed objectionable is extremely hurtful to me, and misleading. The song in fact is about the pain of prejudice and hate and is a way to draw attention to social and political problems. I am the voice of the accused and the attacked. I am the voice of everyone. I am the skinhead, I am the Jew, I am the black man, I am the white man. I am not the one who was attacking. It is about the injustices to young people and how the system can wrongfully accuse them. I am angry and outraged that I could be so misinterpreted.[3]

However, in 2005 a different side emerged, as indicated in the following press report:

Pop star Michael Jackson was caught on tape making anti-Semitic remarks, calling Jews 'leeches'. In a series of audio tapes broadcasted Wednesday on ABC's 'Good Morning America', Jackson is heard using anti-Semitic language in a voice message to one of his former advisers. 'They suck … they're like leeches', Jackson is heard saying. 'It's a conspiracy. The Jews do it on purpose.' The tapes are part of a lawsuit filed against Jackson by two of his former advisers. According to the ABC report, Jackson, who was restricted by his business managers in the amounts of cash he was allowed to spend, used to ask his advisers for cash loans that sometimes reached millions of dollars. When he did not receive the money, Jackson became abusive and would leave harsh messages.[4]

Given the prevalence of anti-Semitism even among public figures such as these, where does it come from? The term 'anti-Semitism' itself originated in the context of nineteenth-century philology. As we saw in the previous chapter, the identification of the existence of families of languages in the late eighteenth and early nineteenth centuries distinguished the Indo-European family, with its original speakers known as Aryans, and the Semitic family (Hebrew, Arabic, etc), with its speakers known as Semites. In the view of philologists such as Renan, as we saw, the Semitic languages and cultures, and by extension their speakers, were found to be degraded, both biologically and morally, compared to Indo-European languages (and their speakers).

Anti-Semitism is a very ancient discourse (Wistrich, 2010; Nirenberg, 2013). Its origins lie in the pre-Christian rivalry between Greeks and Jews in trade in the eastern Mediterranean; a Hellenized

---

[3] Bernard Weinraub, 'In new lyrics, Jackson uses slurs', *The New York Times*, 15 June 1995, http://query.nytimes.com/gst/fullpage.html?res=990CE4DF113DF936 A25755C0A963958260&scp=11&sq=Michael%20Jackson%20-%20HIStory&st=cse, retrieved 8.2.2018.

[4] Nathan Guttman, 'Michael Jackson calls Jews leeches', *The Jerusalem Post*, 24 November 2005, www.jpost.com/Jewish-World/Jewish-News/Michael-Jackson-calls-Jews-leeches, retrieved 8.2.2018.

Egyptian priest in 270 BC is the first person to articulate representations of Jews which are notably anti-Semitic. This Greek tradition was picked up by Hellenized Jews who promulgated early Christianity, notably Paul, so that by the time of the writing of the books of the New Testament the responsibility of the Jews for the death of Jesus is enshrined in the sacred text, for example in this famous passage (Matthew 27: 24–25):

> When Pilate saw that he was not succeeding at all, but that a riot was breaking out instead, he took water and washed his hands in the sight of the crowd, saying, 'I am innocent of this man's blood. Look to it yourselves.' And the whole people said in reply, 'His blood be upon us and upon our children.'

The metaphors of anti-Semitic discourse have a life which is independent of their origins in Christian ideology and belief. Anti-Semitism has survived the decline of Christianity and is no longer an exclusively or even primarily a religious prejudice. Indeed, it is often the subject of scrutiny and critique by contemporary Christian thinkers, aware of the tragic heritage of anti-Semitism. A plaque installed by the Archdiocese of Vienna in Judenplatz in Vienna for example reads:

> 'Kiddusch HaShem' means 'Sanctification of God'. With this awareness Jews of Vienna in the synagogue here on Judenplatz – the center of a significant Jewish community – chose a voluntary death at the time of the persecution of 1420/21, in order to escape the forced baptism they feared. Others, about 200, were burned alive at a stake in Erdberg.
>
> Christian preachers of that time spread superstitious anti-Jewish ideas and agitated against Jews and their faith. Under this influence Christians in Vienna accepted the crime without resistance, they approved it and became perpetrators. In this way, the destruction of the Viennese 'Jewish City' in 1412 was already a threatening omen for the events that took place in all of Europe at the time of the National Socialist tyranny.
>
> Medieval popes turned without success against this anti-Jewish superstition, and individual believers fought in vain against the racial hatred of the National Socialists. They were too few.
>
> Today, Christianity regrets its share in responsibility for the persecution of Jews and realizes its failure. For Christians today, 'Sanctification of God' can only mean asking for forgiveness and hoping in God's saving action.

But such awareness among progressive Christians has not spelled the end of anti-Semitism. It is common among secular people, including those who are otherwise progressive. Note also that its target is not only religiously observant Jews. Being seen as 'Jewish' in the lens of anti-Semitism has nothing to do with the affiliation with Judaism of the individual concerned; the possibility of a secular Jewish identity has been normal in many societies since the beginning of the twentieth century at least, and it is no protection against anti-Semitism. Nor indeed is conversion to Christianity, as the example of Klemperer and so many others shows. And anti-Semitism has spread to non-Christian cultures as a corollary of Western colonialism, so that it now represents a postcolonial, globalized phenomenon. Consider the following, part of Article 22 of the Covenant of the Palestinian Islamist organization Hamas, adopted in 1988 and as yet unchanged:

> ... With their money, they took control of the world media, news agencies, the press, publishing houses, broadcasting stations, and others. With their money they stirred revolutions in various parts of the world with the purpose of achieving their interests and reaping the fruit therein. They were behind the French Revolution, the Communist revolution and most of the revolutions we heard and hear about, here and there. With their money they formed secret societies, such as Freemasons, Rotary Clubs, the Lions and others in different parts of the world for the purpose of sabotaging societies and achieving Zionist interests. With their money they were able to control imperialistic countries and instigate them to colonize many countries in order to enable them to exploit their resources and spread corruption there ... They were behind World War I, ... making financial gains and controlling resources. They obtained the Balfour Declaration, formed the League of Nations through which they could rule the world. They were behind World War II, through which they made huge financial gains by trading in armaments, and paved the way for the establishment of their state.[5]

In other words, despite the role of Christianity in promoting anti-Semitism, the function of the 'Jewish Other' in (anti-Semitic) discourse circulating within (post-) Christian and postcolonial societies cannot be understood primarily in ethnic or religious terms. It is best understood as an ideology of the Christian, post-Christian and now globalized world. The British psychoanalytic theorist and cultural historian Stephen Frosh (2005, p. 215) writes:

> The other is ... an absolutely central element in social life ... Historically and culturally, otherness and the sense of the alien is deeply embedded in Western society. Whilst there are several forms that this takes, including vicious modes of anti-Black and other colour

---

[5] *Hamas Covenant 1988: The Covenant of the Islamic Resistance Movement,* 18 August 1988. Available at: http://avalon.law.yale.edu/20th_century/hamas.asp, retrieved 8.2.2018.

racism, anti-Semitism has been and remains a potent signifier of the underside of Western culture. The Jew is a *principle* of otherness for the West, articulating (through contrast) what is safe and unitary by embodying difference. The two-thousand year history of Christian anti-Semitism has created a figure that is more than a symbol of the splits in Western society; the Jew is rather the kernel of otherness, that which is always found everywhere, but which is never allowed in ... The Jew is the materialisation of that otherness which is most feared and least understood ... *All* otherness in the West is Jewish, including that inner otherness which is unconscious desire.

If this is an extreme formulation, then this is because what has to be thought about is an extreme phenomenon: the recurrent, never-ending, barely even cyclical reiteration of anti-Semitic ideology and practices.

4.5 REPORTS OF EXPOSURE TO RACIST DISCOURSE BY ITS TARGETS

Let us turn now to the study of the experience of anti-Semitism by its targets: an interview study I conducted of Israeli-born long-term residents of Melbourne, Australia. Melbourne is a city of some 4.8 million people, with a Jewish community of some 60,000, forming some 1.25 per cent of the population. Of this community, approximately 12 per cent are Jews who were born or grew up in Israel, native speakers of Hebrew, who emigrated to Australia as adults (Porat, 2015; 2018).

One distinctive feature of the experience of this group was that, while as Israelis they had obviously known *about* anti-Semitism before they left Israel – it is a fundamental rationale for the existence of the Israeli state – and may even have come from families who in previous generations had direct experience of the violence of the Holocaust, they had had no direct experience of anti-Semitism themselves in their own lives while living in Israel. This changed when they came to live in the Diaspora. Most of my informants were secular, perceived themselves as culturally Jewish and Israeli, but were usually not religiously observant and therefore not easily identifiable as Jewish by wearing religious clothing or styles.

Following an earlier in-depth interview study of Israelis in Melbourne involving about fifty individuals (McNamara 1987b), some fifteen years later I returned to re-interview nine of the same subjects with whom I was able to re-establish contact. The semi-structured interviews lasted up to an hour and were tape recorded. Sections related to awareness of and experience of anti-Semitism, and

Table 4.1 *Analytic categories of data from Israeli informants*

PRIVATE DOMAIN				
EVIDENCE OF ATTITUDES			EVIDENCE OF VIOLENCE	
IMPLICIT	EXPLICIT	VERBAL ABUSE	EVIDENCE OF THREATS OF VIOLENCE	EVIDENCE OF ACTUAL VIOLENCE
PUBLIC DOMAIN				
EVIDENCE OF ATTITUDES			EVIDENCE OF VIOLENCE	
IMPLICIT	EXPLICIT	VERBAL ABUSE	EVIDENCE OF THREATS OF VIOLENCE	EVIDENCE OF ACTUAL VIOLENCE

reactions to it, were transcribed and their content coded. Evidence from the domain of direct private experience (in the course of inter-actions with individuals in daily life) was coded separately from aware-ness of anti-Semitism in the public domain (via media including radio and print media, graffiti and so on). Within each domain, a distinction was made between evidence of anti-Semitic attitudes, either implicit or explicit (with outright verbal abuse further distinguished from other explicit statements), and evidence of anti-Semitic violence, either threats of violence or incidents of actual violence. There is a continuum therefore from anti-Semitic attitudes which are implicit in remarks through to actual incidents of violence. Table 4.1 shows the analytic categories that were used in the study.

The evidence of anti-Semitism reported by the nine informants in the second set of interviews was extensive. Table 4.2 summarizes the findings under each heading. Where the evidence is within the direct experience of the informant or his/her family (as opposed to hearing about it from others), this has been placed in **bold** in the table.

Examples of the informants' direct experiences of explicitly stated anti-Semitic attitudes in the private domain include the following.

> That has happened to me. For example, I went to change the wheel on my previous car, on the Mazda. The guy who put it on, got the spare wheel out of the back of the car. All the other wheels had Mazda on them, the spare wheel didn't. I said to him, the spare wheel hasn't got Mazda written on it. He said, yes, they're very Jewish about it. That made me sort of prick up my ears, you know, what do you mean? I suppose that is a sort of incident. (S8)

Table 4.2 *Awareness of anti-Semitism in Melbourne among Israeli Jewish residents*

| | PRIVATE DOMAIN | | | | |
| | EVIDENCE OF ATTITUDES | | | EVIDENCE OF VIOLENCE | |
S#	IMPLICIT	EXPLICIT	VERBAL ABUSE	EVIDENCE OF THREATS OF VIOLENCE	EVIDENCE OF ACTUAL VIOLENCE
1	• Social segregation in schoolyard • Lack of reciprocation to social invitations • 'You're so different [from other Jews]'	• Job discrimination • 'Jew' = miser • From patient at work • Child at school – from teacher, other kids			
5	• Queuing – 'you people' • 'You're so different [from other Jews]' • Sense that others are monitoring their speech	Resentment by fellow lawyers at appointment of Jews to Victorian Supreme Court	2 or 3 incidents		
8		• Inferior spare tyre – 'so Jewish' (mechanic) • New Testament interpretation at private school (friend) • 'Jewish boss – no time off' (husband)	• Hate mail (friends) • Phone calls (friends)	• Hate mail (friends) • Phone calls (friends) • Swastikas in letter box (friends)	
12	• Accused of theft by neighbour		Skinheads at work (stallholder in market)		Pushed into public urinal

Table 4.2 (cont.)

	PRIVATE DOMAIN			EVIDENCE OF VIOLENCE	
	EVIDENCE OF ATTITUDES				
S#	IMPLICIT	EXPLICIT	VERBAL ABUSE	EVIDENCE OF THREATS OF VIOLENCE	EVIDENCE OF ACTUAL VIOLENCE
18	• Message of nativity play - Christian colleague	• Explicit job discrimination – comments of boss when drunk • Christian workmates	Direct experience in street		• Father-in-law and friend bashed • Own children bullied in park • Children from Orthodox Jewish school bullied
19		• 'You difficult Jews' (at home, carpenter) • Polish friend, drunk • Comments at Polish cultural events			
20		• Priest after sermon • About colleague from Head of Department • Priests, private school			
26		'Jews killed Christ'			

Table 4.2 (cont.)

	PUBLIC DOMAIN				
	EVIDENCE OF ATTITUDES			EVIDENCE OF VIOLENCE	
S#	IMPLICIT	EXPLICIT	VERBAL ABUSE	EVIDENCE OF THREATS OF VIOLENCE	EVIDENCE OF ACTUAL VIOLENCE
5	References to Jewish identity of accused in newspaper reports of crime (embezzlement)	Ukrainian community response to literary hoax involving Holocaust	Official reports on incidence of abuse	Official reports on incidence of threats	Official reports on incidence of violence
8	• References to Jewish identity of accused in newspaper reports of crime (embezzlement). • Public discussion of literary hoax involving Holocaust	• Ukrainian community response to literary hoax involving Holocaust • Caller, talk-back radio			
12			Graffiti	• Guards at synagogue	• Annual arson attempts on local synagogue • Witness to arson attack at local synagogue • Reports of arson attack in Sydney
13				• Guards at synagogue • Swastikas on synagogue • Guards at Jewish high school	Arson attack at local synagogue

Table 4.2 (cont.)

		PUBLIC DOMAIN			
		EVIDENCE OF ATTITUDES		EVIDENCE OF VIOLENCE	
S#	IMPLICIT	EXPLICIT	VERBAL ABUSE	EVIDENCE OF THREATS OF VIOLENCE	EVIDENCE OF ACTUAL VIOLENCE
18		• Comments of Victorian Premier on 'unforgiving' Jews • Discrimination at exclusive men's club		**Fences around synagogues**	• Arson attack at local synagogue • Reports of arson attack in Sydney
19		**Church sermon on Jewish Pharisees**			

So, and then, the only other time, I came [across] something in regard to the son of [names an extremely prominent Jewish Australian]. His son became a very pious Hasidic Jew. He was doing his PhD at [University X] and at the time he was becoming very orthodox. The family I think are originally reformed Jews. Very Anglo. Well he and I, we applied actually for the same job at [that university]. The head of the department called me in started asking me questions about [him], and at that time I didn't even know [him], I'd just sort of saw him once or twice. And I said to him, 'Why are you asking me all this?' And he said, 'Ah, I'm not sure. He applied for the job.' Why not? it was a job in political sociology, and [he] was doing his PhD on Max Weber. How more suitable can you be? So he starts saying things like, 'You know the way he dresses and ... ' I said to him, 'Listen, I don't believe this conversation is actually taking place. It's not going to ... ' He said, 'Oh he's got all these things hanging up, his shirt'. I said 'It's not like he's going to work in a factory near the machines and these little things can be caught, you know. I don't think the students worry about the way he dresses'. (S20)

Non-Jews are sensitive particularly those who are not successful ... uh last year there were ... during the last years 3 judges were appointed to the Federal Court ... Merkel, Goldberg and what's the third? I can't get the third one ... so you know there were people you know who said the Jews are taking over I heard it you can take it you can call it anti-Semitism maybe it is so what ... ah Finkelstein sorry the third judge .... so you know maybe those who wanted to be appointed to the bench came with this remark you know ... (S5)

In the public domain, S8 gives the following example of explicitly stated attitudes, involving the media (talkback radio):

I was just driving and listening on talkback. Someone from Ringwood rang back. It had to do with the David Irving [the revisionist historian]. And she was saying how she thought he should be allowed in. Then she said, 'Did you know that really the Jews have always worked together with the Nazis any way. And the word Nazi comes from Ashkenazi.' And she was speaking with this great authority. It was sort of like the old brainwashed Soviet days, you know? And she was saying it on the radio. And I thought, I wonder how many people think like that? And when somebody talks like that to you, they know nothing, you're obviously going to be brainwashed by that.

Sometimes, there is direct experience of episodes of explicit violence, though this is rarer, reported by three of the nine informants:

My ex-father-in-law was bashed ... one Saturday afternoon his friends and he came out synagogue ... my kids when they went to the park with a skull cap er some kids came and threw the skull cap down er so the thing that are are there [mm] er anti-Semitism . er . that's a hard word. (S18)

The same subject had described these same incidents in greater detail in an earlier interview:

Er my father-in-law and his neighbour ... went one day home Saturday af- evening and they were bashed by a couple of people saying 'Jews give us the money' so as they are very religious on Saturday they don't go and 'We have not got money' 'No you have money give us some money' they started to run away screaming 'Help help help' so they took up and disappeared. My kids and their friends were bashed around the corner once because they were going after this Bnei Akiva party and I was in the park came to me they were with their skull cap so a few older boys that sort of bullied them say 'you fucking Jew' or something of that kind ... I would have said that there is.. there is anti-Semitism.

This example is from a man who sells goods at a stall in a popular market:

Yeah um first of all you see those the how you call them the bodgies [old-fashioned Australian slang for skinheads] I don't know whatever so they they speak openly about the Jews and bad language so of course we are we quiet ... once I have been in the toilets and those people the bodgies were there and the bicycle bike I don't know how you call that so they've been next to the toilet and once I was wearing the kippah [skullcap worn by Orthodox Jews] it was very very hot day so someone pushed me on the back you know it was passing so when I would try to hnh it was very uncomfortable so I I saw him I didn't see who was the man but I saw there and um on the toilet it says 'Jews go out' and so on there is you know. (S12)

Evidence of explicit verbal abuse in the public domain involved graffiti ('there were drawing with a swastika on the benches in the park here I'm not talking about the City too' (S18)), while evidence of violence involved reports of arson attacks:

Croatim and the Yugoslav each citizen more or less safe but em for the Jews we felt different ... you see it mostly in the synagogues which many places ... when you go in Sydney you go and burned everything ... it was a trust of Australia and it was shame for Australian. (S12)

It is clear that there is extensive experience and awareness among the Israeli informants of anti-Semitism in the community; often this experience is direct. The evidence is more often of attitudes rather than of the directly violent outcomes of those attitudes; but the attitudes represent a culturally reproduced potential for violence which, when the occasion presents itself, can result in actual violence. The relationship between attitudes and actual violence is voiced by one of the informants as follows:

> At [names well known exclusive private school in Melbourne, where the informant was a teacher], the only thing I found offensive . . . was the New Testament, or my interpretation of it. It sounded horrible to me. The Jews did this, and the Jews did that. The Jews did . . . And I remember I went to the priest, he was a very nice fellow, and I said to him, I'm a bit concerned about all these terms, you know these young kids, they hear that the Jews did this and that and the other, one day they are going to march down to Balaclava [an area of Melbourne in which observant Jews live] and beat on the Jews who didn't listen to Jesus. He said, 'Oh you are completely misunderstanding'. (S20)

The following media reports of an incident which took place in Balaclava itself in 2006 seems to bear out this informant's fears:

> Police will interview an entire busload of footballers after some players allegedly bashed a Jewish man after a day at the races in Melbourne on the weekend.
>
> About 20 players from the Ocean Grove Football Club had spent Saturday at the Caulfield Guineas [a horse race meeting] when their bus pulled up alongside 33-year-old Menachem Vorchheimer, who was wearing traditional Jewish dress as he walked with his two children along Balaclava Road, Caulfield, about 6.30 pm.
>
> He was allegedly bashed when he approached the bus, which was carrying about 20 football players, after passengers began yelling racist comments at him . . .
>
> Passers-by are believed to have surrounded the bus to prevent it leaving the scene until police arrived.
>
> Mr Vorchheimer alleged the footballers motioned to him and his children as if they were shooting a gun.
>
> The men yelled 'F . . . off Jews' and 'Go the Nazis,' Mr Vorchheimer [said].
>
> He said he approached the minibus when it stopped at a red light. 'I wanted to find out where they were from so that . . . I could make approaches to that organisation.'
>
> When the lights changed to green the bus moved off and two of the players grabbed his hat.
>
> The bus stopped a short distance away and when Mr Vorchheimer went to retrieve his hat he was pulled towards a window and punched.
>
> 'I was pulled toward the open window and then punched by a right hand into my left eye by a passenger in the bus,' he said. 'Meanwhile my kids are on the sidewalk crying and screaming.'

Mr Vorchheimer said he had suffered headaches and nausea since the attack, while his children had received counselling.[6]

Vorchheimer promptly sat in front of the bus. Meanwhile, passers-by gathered around. Despite the driver's demands not to call the police, someone did.

The officers soon learnt an inconvenient truth: the driver was an off-duty [policeman, Senior Constable Terry Moore] ... When Vorchheimer said that whoever punched him was wearing a pink tie, Moore got on to the bus and spoke to his passengers and within seconds all of them removed their ties. It was then impossible for Vorchheimer to clearly identify his attacker.[7]

(Terry Moore was subsequently promoted to Leading Senior Constable. Eventually, the footballers were charged and found guilty, and fined.)

Outside court, Mr Vorchheimer said he was pleased.

'The message I would like to get to the wider community is that prejudice is often found in misconceptions of people and who they are,' he said.

'They assume that I'm not Australian, which I am; they assume I'm not part of the Australian society, which I believe I am in every regard.

'People should really take the time to get to know people before pre-judging them.'[8]

4.6   THE REACTION OF THE TARGETS OF RACISM: SUBJECTIVITY AS A SITE OF STRUGGLE

The data from the study of the Israelis in Melbourne also provide us with an opportunity to observe the process of construction of subjectivity in discourse. Often, the discourses to which we are subject have been there since birth, for example discourses of gender and sexuality, and although these may and will change over time, the process is unlikely to be abrupt, except in the case of someone coming out as gay, for example. This makes the way in which discourses construct our subjectivity somewhat harder to observe, as our subjectivity in

---

[6] Jane Holroyd, '"Nazi" hate attack probe', *The Age*, 17 October 2006, www.theage .com.au/news/national/footy-trip-race-attack-probe/2006/10/17/1160850895893 .html, retrieved 8.2.2018.

[7] 'Victory, Australia – the Jewish hero who fought the law, and the law won', *Vos Iz Neias*, 27 November 2010, www.vosizneias.com/69756/2010/11/27/victory-austra lia-the-jewish-hero-who-fought-the-law-and-the-law-won/, retrieved 20.2.2018.

[8] Kate Uebergang, 'Racism anger in court', *Herald Sun*, 18 April 2007, www.herald sun.com.au/news/victoria/racism-anger-in-court/story-e6frf7kx-1111113368487, retrieved 8.2.2018.

terms of these discourses is likely to be stable and undisturbed, leading to a feeling of 'naturalness' and inevitability in our identity, as Butler observed. In the case of immigrants, however, they are subject to, and the subject of, new discourses, not least as immigrant Other in many cases. The result is a feeling of conflict or struggle among competing discourses, reflected, for example, in Norton's study of immigrant women in Canada (Norton Peirce, 1995; Norton, 2000), discussed in Chapter 1.

Subjectivity as a site of struggle is particularly evident in the case of the Israelis in the Melbourne study, and in this part of the chapter we will examine in detail the nature of this struggle. On the one hand, the exposure, direct and indirect, to the discourse of anti-Semitism has clear implications for their subjectivity: they have to deal with being seen by non-Jewish others in the terms that the discourse of anti-Semitism constructs. But this presents particular difficulty in the case of Israelis choosing to live in the Diaspora, as their subjectivity as Israelis in Israel was a function of a very different discourse. The establishment of the State of Israel meant the creation of a new way of being Jewish, building on the historical experience of Jewish life in the Diaspora but claiming to supersede it. In this discourse, not only does the existence of Israel make the Jewish experience of anti-Semitism something to be conscious of but no longer inevitable, but the new Israeli post-Diaspora identity renders the old Diaspora identity obsolete. The condition of freedom from anti-Semitism in the Jewish state was there for all Jews who chose to avail themselves of it. This meant a contrast between Israeli Jewish identity and the traditional way of being Jewish in the Diaspora, where coping with living a minority existence in an anti-Semitic environment was central. Israeli Jews by contrast have a very different, national Jewish identity. Israel is a secular state, not a theocracy (unlike, say, Iran), with significant Muslim and Christian minorities enjoying many of the rights that Jewish Israeli citizens do. The majority of Israeli Jews are secular, and religious affiliation and practice is a contentious social and political issue there. The subjectivity as Israelis of the informants within this study was formed within that discourse: they saw themselves as fundamentally different from Diaspora Jews, whom they continued to see as unliberated. One informant discussed what she saw as the typical oversensitivity of the Jew in the Diaspora as distinguishing Diaspora Jews from Israelis:

> Jews here have this shield around them have this barrier now people who are under threat need a barrier and that's how you survive you know and if you've been exposed to abuse and hostility and so on and

> most things you will do that I mean you'd be silly not to do that
> anyway it's a subconscious thing anyway and people do that in order
> to feel more secure but as soon as you put your barrier up to protect
> yourself you also keep yourself in and everyone else out right . . .
> whereas I think that Israelis are very different in that way they are far
> more open they're far more alive indeed don't need so many barriers
> to keep them they don't need the barrier like you know there are
> some animal they have external skeletons and the moment you
> touch the external skeleton it's a life-threatening experience for
> them because without it they cannot survive and that's the
> difference I don't think Israeli need that or have that . . . (S1)

However, if, like Diaspora Jews, the Israeli immigrants are subject to
the same negative discourses, their awareness of the reality of these
discourses, targeting directly or implicitly they themselves, produces
a potential crisis of subjectivity. The Israelis are caught in competing
discourses through which to understand and interpret their consciousness of the issue of anti-Semitism within the immigrant setting.
They are aware of this:

> There used to be a time where I sort of, all the problems of a Jew and all
> their fears of anti-Semitism and this and that. I didn't consider that
> they were relevant to me. You know I was Israeli, and Jewish to a lesser
> degree in that sense. Now it is the other way round. (S19)

In what follows, a number of strategies are adopted by the informants
in order to make sense of their awareness of anti-Semitism in the
immigrant setting as a way of resolving the conflict they are experiencing. These strategies involve calling on various discourses to interpret their experiences. One could simply situate one's experience
within a discourse which stresses the universality in time and space
of anti-Semitism outside Israel:

> You ask me about anti-Semitism. There is no shortage of it . . . They get
> their anti-Semitism with their mother's milk . . . so ok so what so what
> are you going to do about it? That children will stop to get to have their
> mother's milk? It is part it's been part of the culture for 2000 years. (S5)

But situating one's experience within such a discourse is problematic
for some informants for whom it is associated with the conditioning
of their youth in Israel, which they reject as naive:

INTERVIEWER: What does it do to Israelis to live among Gentiles?
S20:   Well the first experience you see I never knew any Gentiles.
                        So the first experience was like nearly unimaginable, like
                        relating to people from another planet. And I expected
                        them to be anti-Semitic.

INTERVIEWER: Can you explain a bit more about your set of expectations when you arrived, you said that Gentiles were very unfamiliar, and you expected them to be anti-Semitic ...
S20: Either overtly, or covertly.
INTERVIEWER: Why? Is this because of your education in Israel?
S20: Because of the education. Because what I now consider a big brainwash at school, you know, that all Gentiles hate Jews, because of history and persecution.

Given the kinds of difficulties in identifying with a subject position which on other grounds they have learned to reject, what alternative readings of the significance of the anti-Semitism they have indicated their awareness of are open to the Israelis? It is possible to identify three major strategies, as follows.

Ambiguation ▬▬▬▬▬▬▬▬▬▬▬▬▬▬▬▬▬▬▬▬▬▬▬▬

The first strategy is to dispute whether the incident constituted conclusive evidence of anti-Semitism. By utilizing the potential ambiguity of the reported phenomena, the issues arising if they were indeed examples of anti-Semitism are deferred or avoided. Some examples of this strategy include the following.

S12 has just described his efforts to thwart an arson attack on a synagogue early one morning, which saved the building. His wife (S13) disputes whether it's absolutely clear that it was a deliberate arson attack motivated by anti-Semitism. She says:

> They know who burnt it? They know who burnt it? They don't know. Isn't that funny, maybe it's drunks ... who knows? They never caught them ... it's an arsonist ... who knows? They didn't find them.

S1 has just described an incident in her workplace which revealed a colleague's hostility to her. However, she questions the interpretation that it was motivated by anti-Semitism:

> What happened in the hospital was maybe not because I was Jewish maybe it was because I was just a foreigner I do not know whatever the case was this was blunt experience for me to feel unwanted and you know I never heard things like 'go back to where you came from'.

S18 narrates what at first sight appears to be a clear example of discrimination at work: his boss explained that his (obviously Jewish) name was the reason why he had been passed over in favour of an Anglo-Australian, considerably junior in experience, to go on an overseas trip. However, the informant then goes on to consider a range of other explanations for the decision. These include his own competence, his general attitude at work, the possibility that it represents a general prejudice on the part of his boss against immigrants in general, not Jews specifically, and his limited language proficiency compared to that of a native speaker.

Universalizing

When this strategy of ambiguating the phenomenon is not relevant, or unsuccessful, further strategies come into play. One is an appeal to the universality of forms of ethnic intergroup conflict and discrimination. One subject gives the example of the prejudices experienced by Asians in Australia; another talks about the prejudices between Arabs and Jews within Israel; a third refers to the prejudices within the Jewish community about different Jewish groups, both in Israel and in the Diaspora. One informant says that remarks can be discounted as jokes, and compares it to jokes about gendered relations:

> I tend to ignore it because it does not appear to be as ..er a danger at present it's not open you never know if it is a joke because yes there are some differences between Jews and non-Jews the same as there are differences between men and male and females so you can't say how males are anti-females or vice versa so I take it as a joke for that minute whether there is something beyond that I don't er look at it . . . (S18)

Individualizing

A third and rather common strategy is to locate the significance of the experience within a discourse of the individual rather than the group. It can take a number of forms. The first involves the psychology of the individual Israeli himself or herself, which is seen as contributing to the dynamics of interactions, and the resulting attributions:

> But er from comments that I heard I was looked at as a different . . . kettle of fish to use the Australian expression . . . because of this I was a queer . . . person . . . maybe I'm queer because I find myself that I'm as I told you I mean I don't listen to the news I'm more individualist or I can't really say that I was queer because I was Jew or because I'm queer by nature so . . . (S18)

> I think mostly it's because I get on ok with people I don't they you know so much of every interaction is about the spirit so even if you want to generalize and say how many Jews are subjected to anti-Semitism in the end you have to go down to the nitty gritty of what the interaction contains. (S1)

Second, the significance of incidents reported can also be interpreted in terms of the personality structure of prejudiced individuals:

> Yes once once I think I heard someone saying something about Jew
> being a miser but maybe I think many years ago I would take it very
> badly and angry and but now I just know how people are just looking
> for another structure to be and if they hate someone it's like it gives
> them that strength they've got a purpose shocking purpose terrible or
> whatever but its it just puts their life in some sort of perspective which
> they might not have otherwise. (S1)

Finally, a third individualizing strategy is to dispute the existence or
relevance of group categorizations at all:

> To me everyone's a human being and that's it. I mean, when I went up
> to somebody, I don't consider the person say as a Gentile or a Jew. It's
> a human being. It makes no difference. (S26)

In the following quote, the strategy of individuality involves disman-
tling the whole possibility of a meaningful group identity. The role of
ideology in the early years of the establishment of Israel as stressing
a shared Israeli identity is seen as obsolete; the false insistence on
similarity within the group categorized as 'Israeli' disguises the enormous diversity of individuals so categorized. The conclusion of this
informant is that 'there is no such group' (Israelis) at all, only
individuals:

> Maybe when thirty years ago we had established or forty years ago we
> were still establishing a State we fought wars we brought into
> a situation ideals now the ideals disappeared it's the it's a purely
> commercial materialistic society like anywhere else so what do you
> expect ... you know even to go to the concert as if there is an Israeli
> group in Melbourne er there's nothing to substantiate it there are
> people who came from Israel and they and they come in the whole
> range of ... intelligence money beliefs and there are there are people
> who came are of Indian origin and they look much more like Indians
> they even live among the Indians not among [other Israelis or Jews] ...
> you know there is no such a group in fact. (S5)

The result then is to focus on one's individual fate, independently of
that suggested by one's membership of a group:

> So what one does about it I mean maybe the action the reaction is let's
> take the suitcases and go to Israel but it's so many thing I mean take
> my own case that's anti-Semitism case but I'm not here to solve anti-
> Semitism cases I'm here to solve my own personal life ... trying to do it
> the best that I can. (S18)

Underlying all such strategies is a conflict over the meaning of the
experiences that are their subject, as constructed within the competing discourses of what it is to be a Diaspora Jew, and what it is to be

a post-Diaspora Israeli Jew. The experience of anti-Semitism triggers a struggle over subjectivity. While such experiences might seem to reinforce the suggestion of the perennial and ubiquitous character of anti-Semitism in the Diaspora, it conflicts with the decision of the Israelis to choose to live permanently in the Diaspora but *qua* Israelis, with their rejection of the obsolete identity of Diaspora Jews, not as Diaspora Jews – hence the temptation to 'explain away' the phenomena as a way of avoiding the feelings of conflict in the first place. Racism of all kinds no doubt triggers similar struggles in the individuals subject to it; while racist discourses construct us as a particular kind of Other, other discourses construct us in very different, sometimes competing ways. One form of a kind of agency, then, is to interpret one's experience within terms offered by alternative discourses – though the range of alternative discourses on offer may represent a limited choice. And notice that the 'agency' is constructed within discourse, not outside it.

Another way of thinking about the kinds of experiences reported in the study discussed here, and the sense that is made of them by their targets, is in the light of Erving Goffman's discussion in his book *Stigma* (1963). Goffman draws our attention to the Greek origins of the term, referring to visible bodily marks used to identify the inferior moral status of a slave, a criminal or a traitor. Today, of course, the bodily evidence of what he refers to as 'disgrace' is no longer the focus – instead, he defines stigma as follows: 'a stigma is an undesired differentness from what we had anticipated' (p. 15). An incident with a friend I was working with as a teacher many years ago is a perfect instance of what Goffman means. The friend, who was Jewish, had not been identified as such by her immediate supervisor, a colleague with whom she had worked for two years; she had 'passed', in Goffman's terms. At lunch with the three of us one day, my friend's Jewish identity emerged explicitly in the course of the conversation. Her colleague reacted with a bodily expression of surprise, and then said, 'Oh X, I hadn't realized you were ... [pause] anything in particular' ... The euphemistic wording, as Klemperer would have said, is everything.

Face-to-face interactions such as these involving an encounter between the stigmatized and what Goffman (1963, p. 24) refers to as normals often have an awkwardness:

> When normals and stigmatized do in fact enter one another's
> immediate presence, especially when they there attempt to sustain
> a joint conversational encounter, there occurs one of the primal

scenes of sociology; for in many cases, these moments will be the ones when the causes and effects of stigma must be directly confronted by both sides.

But 'normals' and 'stigmatized' are not discrete categories. Rather, as Goffman insists, they are perspectives:

> Stigma involves not so much a set of concrete individuals who can be separated into two piles, the stigmatized and the normal, but a pervasive two-role social process in which every individual participates in both roles, at least in some connection and in some phases in life. The normal and the stigmatized are not persons but perspectives.

We can see this in a literal sense in the dilemma of subjectivity of the Israeli informants. One of the goals of the establishment of the Jewish state was to 'normalize' Jewish life, to render obsolete the unfree condition of the Diaspora. The Israeli Jew was a new kind of Jew, freed from the impact on subjectivity of the experience of anti-Semitism. The Israelis in Melbourne potentially find themselves stigmatized in their encounters with the discourse of anti-Semitism, but this conflicts with their sense of themselves, constructed within Israeli discourse, of being free of the impact of such stigmatization. In this particular case the instability of the construction of subjectivity through exposure to discourse, and the resulting struggles of subjectivity, is plain to see. We have here an instance of Derrida's remarks about the instability and conflicted nature of subjectivity:

> Our question is still identity. What is identity, this concept of which the transparent identity to itself is always dogmatically presupposed by so many debates on monoculturalism or multiculturalism, nationality, citizenship, and in general, belonging? ...
>   To be a Franco-Maghrebian, one 'like myself', is not ... a surfeit or richness of identities, attributes, or names. In the first place, it would rather betray a disorder of identity [trouble d'identité] (Derrida, 1998, p. 14)

4.7   EVERYDAY RACISM AS A RESERVOIR OF VIOLENCE

Where does the casual reproduction of racist discourse lead? As we have seen in the incident of the footballers, it can act as the seed ground for the reproduction of violence. More terribly, in the eyes of many, including contemporary Christian scholars, the discourse of anti-Semitism circulating in culturally Christian societies in the period before the Second World War constituted a kind of tinder, dry material waiting to catch fire, providing material for the extreme anti-Semitic violence of the Holocaust. The eminent Christian Holocaust scholar John Roth writes that 'While Christianity was not a sufficient condition for the Holocaust, nevertheless it was a necessary condition' (2000, p. 6).

In Claude Lanzmann's nine-hour documentary film *Shoah* (1985), based on a series of interviews with all those involved in the project of the Holocaust – victims, perpetrators, witnesses – we see the realization in acts of horrific violence of the potential for violence embodied and repeatedly reproduced in racist discourse. In one of the many extraordinarily painful interviews in the film, Lanzmann interviews two Jewish men, Motke Zaïdel and Itzhak Dugin, who late in the war were forced to dig up and burn the bodies of victims killed previously near Vilna in order to cover up evidence of the crimes of the Nazis. Vilna was the centre of the largest Jewish population in Lithuania. Most of the victims were shot in Ponari, a forest outside Vilna, and then buried in graves. Later, the Nazis forced Jews like these men to dig up these graves and burn the bodies. Lanzmann interviews these men in Israel, where they are living. The two men are surrounded by other members of Motke Zaïdel's family, including his 20-year-old daughter Hanna, visible behind Itzhak Dugin as he speaks. The following is a translation into English of the interview (the interviewer, Lanzmann, speaks in French, which is then translated into Hebrew for the men, who reply in Hebrew, subsequently translated into French for Lanzmann. Lanzmann's questions are given in bold). The interview not only shows the extraordinary level of violence and cruelty that marked the crimes of the Holocaust, an indication of the extremity of anti-Semitic hatred that underlay it, it also shows the way in which language itself could be a tool for further violence, a literal playing out of the reality of language use observed and noted by Klemperer.

So it was they who dug up and burned all the Jews of Vilna?

Zaïdel (voiceover): Yes. In early January 1944 we began digging up the bodies.

Dugin (voiceover): When the last grave was opened, I recognized my whole family.

[The audio and video tracks become synchronized as the camera cuts to a shot of Motke Zaïdel and Itzhak Dugin in the Zaïdels' apartment in Israel, Zaïdel on the left, Dugin on the right with Hanna Zaïdel just behind him. The camera moves in on Dugin:]

Which members of his family did he recognize?

Mom and my sisters. Three sisters with their kids. They were all in there.

How could he recognize them?

They'd been in the earth four months, and it was winter. They were very well preserved. So I recognized their faces, their clothes too.

They'd been killed relatively recently?

Yes. [Camera cuts to shot of Motke Zaïdel seated on Dugin's right.]

And it was the last grave?

Yes.

The Nazi plan was for them to open the graves, starting with the oldest? [Camera cuts back to Dugin.]

Yes. The last graves were the newest, and we started with oldest, those of the first ghetto. In the first grave there were twenty-four thousand bodies. [Camera inclines slightly to focus on the face of Hanna Zaïdel just behind Dugin.]

[Camera then cuts to what appear to be a rocky area of the Ben Shemen forest in Israel. Motke Zaïdel speaks:]

The deeper you dug, the flatter the bodies were. Each was almost a flat slab. When you tried to grasp a body, it crumbled, it was impossible to pick up. [Camera cuts to Motke Zaïdel and Itzhak Dugin seated with the forest in the background.] We had to open the graves, but without tools. They said: 'Get used to working with your hands.'

With just their hands!

Yes. When we first opened the graves, we couldn't help it, we all burst out sobbing. But the Germans almost beat us to death. We had to work at a killing pace for two days, beaten all the time, and with no tools.

They all burst out sobbing? [Dugin clears his throat; the camera moves in on him as Zaïdel continues.]

The Germans even forbade us to use the words 'corpse' or 'victim'. The dead were blocks of wood, shit, with absolutely no importance. Anyone who uttered the words 'corpse' or 'victim' was beaten. The Germans made us refer to the bodies as Figuren, that is as puppets, as dolls, or as Schmattes, which means rags.

(Lanzmann, 1985, pp. 12–13)

4.8 CONCLUSION

The crimes of the Holocaust were triggered and implemented by deliberate policy of the Nazis, but attracted support, often enthusiastic, among people not only in Germany but in each of the countries where German forces spread during World War II. What was the nature of this fertile ground on which the Nazi seed fell? Racist discourse circulating in the barely noticed material of everyday conversation acts as a kind of reservoir in which the potential for racist violence lurks. The fact that it is barely noticed, despite its endless circulation and repetition, is what gives it its power, as Klemperer realized. One particularly becomes aware of these discourses if one is the subject of them. We may stumble on the evidence of racist and other discourses in casual conversation all the time, if we pay attention. The study of language has a role in documenting and making explicit the phenomenon of the widespread, mundane circulation of racist discourses, often below the level of consciousness.

The highly mechanized crime of the Holocaust would not have been possible but for the myriad acts by ordinary people who absorbed, circulated and reproduced the anti-Semitic narrative. Its success depended on endlessly iterated actions by individuals. What makes poststructuralism particularly appropriate for the study of racist and other discourses is its attention not only to the macro dimension of discourse, its content, the representation of reality that it invites, but also to the micro dimension, how it circulates in the minute-by-minute experience of everyday interaction. The power of discourse does not operate by fiat; its effect is not automatic, not one-off, top down, but is endlessly dispersed and iterated in the interactions of individuals. Foucault speaks of the need for an analysis of power not in the traditional terms of sovereignty and obedience but in terms of 'power at its extremities, in its ultimate destinations, with those points where it becomes capillary' (1980, p. 96). In the second half of this book, we will explore the relation between the macro and the micro in order to witness and understand the capillary action of discourse in everyday interactions.

4.9   SUGGESTIONS FOR FURTHER READING

There are a number of key studies of the presence of racist and other discourses in everyday conversation, including Essed (1990; 1991), Myers (2005) and Picca and Feagin (2007). There is an extensive more general literature on language and racism within the tradition of Critical Discourse Analysis (CDA); key figures are Van Dijk (e.g. 1987; 1991) and Reisigl and Wodak (2001). The classic introduction to the techniques of CDA is Fairclough (1989, revised 2001), and there are important critiques by Blommaert (2005) and Pennycook (1994; 2001), the latter from a poststructuralist perspective.

The most powerful representation of the Holocaust is Claude Lanzmann's extraordinary nine-hour documentary *Shoah*, which avoids historical footage and relies solely on interviews with victims, perpetrators and witnesses conducted by Lanzmann himself in the early 1980s. The antecedents of the Holocaust in the history of anti-Semitism are documented in Nirenberg (2013) and Wistrich (2010).

5 Language Learning and Subjectivity

5.1 INTRODUCTION

Like many people, I have learned or acquired a number of languages in my life – Latin at school and university, Italian when I was an adolescent, French as a young man and since, Hebrew on and off throughout my adult life, and most recently German. I am not communicatively fluent in any of them, alas. But the learning of each language has had an important meaning for me as a person, and has been both an expression of, and a force for change of my sense of self. There is an extensive literature on language learning in relation to identity, including classic studies such as Kramsch (2009), Norton (2000; 2013) and Block (2007). Nunan and Choi (2010) and Ros i Solé and Fenoulhet (2013b) present personal accounts of the impact of language learning on the identity of learners. Burck (2005) and Pavlenko and Blackledge (2004) look at the lived experience of multilinguals, and what each of the languages a multilingual speaks means in the lives of the subjects. Pavlenko (2006) and Dewaele (2010) explore the links between multilingualism and emotion. This chapter will not attempt to do justice to the literature on this subject. Instead, it has a more specific focus, in line with the themes of this book. It asks, where do the meanings associated with the object of language study, and the process of language learning, come from? It will argue that choices in language learning involve subjectivity framed within specific social discourses. This might seem surprising on the face of it, as the choice to learn any particular language seems like a private, individual choice, and the meaning of the choice, and the experience of learning, can feel very personal (Ros i Solé and Fenoulhet, 2013a). But given that languages, and the speakers of languages, are the subject of a variety of discourses, such choices can be understood in another way, as involving positioning the self in relation to how the choice of languages to be learned, and the process of language learning, are situated within discourses to which we are subject.

For much of the history of applied linguistics, thinking about the social meaning of language learning in terms of the subjectivity of the learner has not been favoured, owing largely to the principal disciplines drawn on to act as a theoretical framework for studies of language learning. The relatively asocial character of much linguistic theory has meant that linguistics as a source discipline does not encourage consideration of the social context of language learning. Saussure, the founder of modern linguistics, saw language as structure (*langue*), abstracted from actual use in context (*parole*) (Saussure, 1916/2013). Accordingly, structuralist linguistics, which has had an enduring impact on approaches to language learning, emphasizes the conscious learning of linguistic form (grammar, vocabulary, phonology). Chomsky's great contribution to linguistic theory also indirectly had a profound influence on theories of language learning, but again at the cost of forcing the social context into the background. Chomsky's focus on *competence* (the intuitive grasp of language structure, biologically ordained and thus independent of cultural specificity), and his disregard for *performance* (the actual use of language) (Chomsky, 1965) underlay his famous claim that linguistics was a branch of cognitive psychology (Chomsky, 1972). Chomsky was not himself interested in second language learning and made this clear when he addressed a conference of language teachers and argued that they had little to learn from him (Chomsky, 1966). Indeed, relatively few second language acquisition researchers have chosen to work within the strict biological paradigm of Chomsky. Yet despite this, his focus on unconscious knowledge and the subsequent debate about the learning mechanisms by which children acquire language prompted revolutionary changes in conceptualizing second language acquisition. The British applied linguist Pit Corder argued that second language acquisition can be shown to involve processes which are not conscious, in addition to conscious learning (Corder, 1967/1981); Larry Selinker, who came to Edinburgh to work with Pit Corder after completing his thoroughly structuralist PhD on language learning in the United States, understood the significance of Corder's insight and, while also rejecting Chomsky's nativist theory, began to theorize the learning mechanisms underlying this unconscious acquisition in his discussion of the development of what he called the second language learner's *interlanguage* (Selinker, 1972). Here again, the focus was on the cognitive and the psychological.

There existed, in fact, a thoroughly social approach to linguistic theory in these early decades, the British-Australian linguist Michael Halliday's Systemic Functional grammar (Halliday, 1985); he was one of the founding teachers on the Edinburgh course in Applied Linguistics established in 1957. But it was less often taken up in other courses in applied linguistics in Britain and elsewhere, and for a long time lacked a theory of learning, so that its potential to inform understanding of language learning was limited. (It is worth noting in passing that its modernist, totally systematizing character is at odds with poststructuralism's focus on discourses and its emphasis on iterability and instability.)

In other areas of linguistics such as sociolinguistics and pragmatics, there has of course been extensive attention to the social dimension of language and language use. Its influence on language learning has been strongly felt as an underpinning of the communicative movement, to be discussed in detail below. The sociolinguistics of Labov, which identified a parallelism between (usually) unconscious features of language use and a set of macro-social categories (gender, ethnicity, age, social class) drawn from mainstream sociology, has been less influential. Another important contribution to language learning theory from a social perspective has come from studies of interaction, the topic of the second half of this book, and these have had an enduring influence on understanding how second languages are acquired through conversation and in other face-to-face interactions (see, for example, Seedhouse, 2005 and Wong & Waring, 2010). But they again do not focus in the first instance on the social identities of the participants. Even the well-known theory of integrative vs instrumental motivation developed in the 1950s in such a potent and divided sociopolitical context as Québec (Gardner & Lambert, 1959) seriously under-theorized the significance of the social context in which these motivations were generated.

In short, then, for a long time many of the main sources of input into studies of second language acquisition have not focused on the broader social context of language learning, particularly framed in terms of its impact on the subjectivity of the learner. While this has certainly changed in recent years, since the work of Kramsch, Norton, Block, Pavlenko and the many others cited above, poststructuralist perspectives on the subjectivity of the language learner continue to be under-investigated. In this chapter we will consider the social meaning of language learning in poststructuralist terms. How do discourses shape the position of both the language being learned and the subject who learns it? The chapter will begin by considering why students choose to study a particular language, and the process of learning that language, in the light of discourses of nationalism, gender and ethnicity. This will be followed by a personal account of the discourses involved in my own language learning, which will then be used as a point of departure to critique the dominant paradigm of language learning over the last fifty years – communicative language teaching and learning – and in particular its expression in the Common European Framework of Languages (CEFR) (Council of Europe 2001).

5.2 LANGUAGE LEARNING AND DISCOURSES OF NATIONAL IDENTITY

One of the salient discourses within which languages and language learning may be located is within discourses of national identity. Why does language learning seem to be such a struggle in the English-speaking world? A functional explanation that does not involve issues of subjectivity would be that as English increasingly becomes the language of international communication, English speakers feel less and less need to learn other languages. There is no doubt that simple economic and political forces shape the options of individuals in relation to language learning, as in so much else. Yet what role do discourses play within this? I will argue that discourses of national identity play a major role in determining attitudes to language learning in the anglophone world, as elsewhere.

Within Britain, for example, plurilingualism is not expected of public figures, with the possible exception of Scotland and Wales, particularly the leaders of the nationalist parties in those countries. Even such an ardent Europhile as the prime minister who led Britain into the European Union, Edward Heath, had a ludicrously strong English accent in his occasional speeches in French. Queen Elizabeth's even more occasional speeches in French are also marked by an assertion of her English identity with the strongly English features in her delivery of French. In my own country, Australia, public figures who are fluently bilingual are considered marvels. The election of Kevin Rudd as Australian prime minister in 2007 provoked endless discussion of the wonderful fact that he was able to deliver a speech in Mandarin. Things are somewhat different in the United States, where the ability to address political rallies in Spanish as well as in English is a distinct political advantage for presidential candidates wishing to win the votes of Spanish speakers, the largest linguistic minority in the United States. In Canada things are of course different, as it is an officially bilingual country; the current prime minister, Justin Trudeau, is fluently bilingual in French and English. Within Australia at least, monolingualism in English is the default within discourses of Australian subjectivity.

Nevertheless, discourses of national identity are subject to change, and changes in these discourses may have implications for the languages which are the targets of language learning in national language policy and in public discourse. This is clearly the case in Australia. Until the early 1970s, Australia was a strongly Anglo-oriented society, with an explicitly racist immigration policy known unapologetically as the White Australia Policy. In this period, discourses involving language learning favoured those foreign languages which were being learned in England – specifically French, and to a certain extent German. A cultivated Australian, just as a cultivated Englishman, might be expected to know some French. The election of the first socialist government in nearly twenty-five years in 1972 led to the final abolition of the White Australia Policy, an upsurge of nationalism, an embrace of the benefits of immigration, and the adoption of a policy of multiculturalism. In the context of these renewed discourses on what it meant to be an Australian, preferred choices of languages to be studied changed. The immigrants who had most obviously and successfully integrated and contributed to the diversity of Australian culture were the Italians (there had been large-scale immigration from Italy in the 1950s and 1960s), and it helped that the language was associated with a rich European cultural heritage (even if most of the immigrants were poorly educated, came from impoverished areas of the south and did not speak Standard Italian). Language learning was encouraged in schools, including in primary schools and in the early years of secondary education, and in a system which allows choice at the local level many school councils chose Italian as the language children would learn, as an expression of the new possibilities of Australian subjectivity – freed from British cultural influence, expressive of an immigrant society, tolerant and multicultural.

The rapid advances made in the economies of East and South-East Asia and the emergence of Japan, the enemy nation of the Second World War, as Australia's principal trading partner in the 1980s and 1990s led to a major reassessment of Australia's place in the region. The 1990s saw the emergence of new discourses of Australia as 'part of Asia', and young people, when they left Australia to travel and broaden their horizons, now often chose Asia rather than Europe as their destination. Official language policy followed, which stressed the learning of languages of the nation's trading partners in Asia:

generous funding was provided for the learning of Japanese, Indonesian, Chinese and Korean. Indonesian was selected because it was an Asian language that was relatively easy to learn and is written using the Roman alphabet. Indonesia is also Australia's nearest neighbour. There was a huge upsurge in the learning of Japanese in particular, both in schools and in universities. However, with the election of the conservative government of the Anglophile John Howard in 1997, older cultural values in Australian identity were reasserted, with a turning away from Asian languages and a turning back to Britain, the United States and Europe. This period saw reductions in the funding of the study of Asian languages and a decline in the number of students studying Japanese and Indonesian in particular. More recently still, there has been increased demand for Mandarin, again expressive of Australia's realignment as an Asian country and the growing power and influence of China in the region.

In recent years we have seen an upsurge of enrolments in Spanish. How can this be accounted for? What does Spanish represent? My own speculation is that it is a way of aligning discourses of Australian national identity more in the direction of the United States without appearing too obviously to do so. The choice of Spanish is reflective of the rapidly growing interest of young Australians in travelling in Latin America, a hemisphere still dominated in many ways by the United States. An anti-American spirit of exploration of Latin America gives Spanish a kind of covert prestige in the new configurations of what it means to be a young Australian. It is a way of asserting an Australian identity of being anti-American, while expressing covertly a preoccupation with, and indeed envy of, the United States.

In other words, learners of languages locate themselves in relation to prevailing discourses in which languages and their speakers are subjects of the discourse. They can identify either with the subject positions on offer, either those favoured by the discourse, or stigmatized by it. For example, security discourse, 'the war on terror', has led governments to promote learning of languages which are useful for military purposes – the languages of the current theatres of war, 'the languages of the enemy' (Kramsch, 2005). The fact that these languages and their speakers represent a new kind of Other has led some individuals to study them through identification with this Other, a kind of act of resistance on the part of the learner. (This is a further example of Foucault's 'reverse discourse': see the discussion of this point in Chapter 2.) And in general it must be said that all languages and their speakers represent a kind of Other in discourses of nation and ethnicity; an exoticized other in which the exotic might be attractive, representing scope for fantasy of the self as a learner of the language making contact with this exoticized world.

5.3 LANGUAGE LEARNING AND DISCOURSES OF ETHNICITY

Language learning in the context of immigration is also configured within discourses of national and ethnic identity. There are many pressures on individuals to prioritize learning the majority language of the new environment over the maintenance of the language of the immigrant family, and studies of language maintenance and shift in immigrant societies demonstrate that the typical pattern is for the children of immigrants, and particularly the grandchildren of immigrants, to neglect learning the language of their parents or grandparents. Immigrant languages are often not held in the same esteem as the main foreign languages taught at school, given how the latter feature in discourses of national identity, as shown above.

What about the immigrants themselves? The new social context means that the pattern of ingroup and outgroup which was the basis for identity in the previous society may no longer be relevant. In my study of Israeli Jews who had settled permanently in Australia (McNamara, 1987b) (see Chapter 4 above), many of the discourses that had framed their subjectivity in Israel were no longer salient; a new set of discourses had replaced them. In Israel, the secular–religious divide was paramount, as was the division between Ashkenazi and Sephardi communities – communities whose forebears had lived in Europe on the one hand, or in the Ottoman or Arab world on the other. So acute was the secular–religious issue that many Israelis I interviewed said they were 'not Jewish', by which they meant they were not religious; they made a sharp distinction between 'Israeli' (secular) and 'Jewish' (religious) identity. And while discourses of anti-Semitism were familiar to Israelis, and in many cases had caused profound suffering in earlier generations in their immediate families, or even in their own lives, they had mostly not experienced anti-Semitism directly before coming to Australia, certainly not in Israel, whose very existence is to relieve Jews of the direct experience of anti-Semitism. Another discourse to which they were subject in Israel involved Jews living in the Diaspora, who were seen as living subject to anti-Semitism and were configured as weak and vulnerable, compared with Israel which had put an end to such positioning for its Jewish citizens. All of this changed when the

Israelis came to Australia, as none of these were prevailing discourses in the new context of Australia. Instead, the Israelis had to negotiate the general prejudice against immigrant groups (collectively known by the racist terms 'wogs') and their languages, and their first direct encounter with anti-Semitism (see Chapter 4 for details of this). The net result of this was a reluctant realignment with the Diaspora Jewish community and an acceptance that their children would grow up as monolingual speakers of English, with some limited, symbolic knowledge of Hebrew, exactly like children growing up in other Australian Jewish families (the Australian Jewish community is largely monolingual in English). What was found for this group was similar to what has been found for many other immigrant groups in Australia, Canada, the USA and the UK, although the dynamics in each case are different. For the individuals subject to such transformation, the immigrants themselves, the experience of transformation of their subjectivity is complex and often painful, as documented, for example, in Eva Hoffman's (1989) *Lost in Translation*. Pavlenko (2007) draws attention to this and other accounts in memoirs of writers of their experience of language learning in the context of migration.

5.4 LANGUAGE LEARNING AND DISCOURSES OF GENDER

The choice to learn a language and the process of language learning are also the subject of discourses of gender. In Chapter 1 we looked in some detail at Bonny Norton's study of immigrant women in anglophone Canada negotiating the learning of English, and how salient their gendered identity was in some aspects of their investment in learning English (Norton Peirce, 1995; Norton, 2000). Again, there is a considerable literature on different aspects of the relationship of gender to language learning (Pavlenko et al., 2001), too much to do justice to in a short chapter. In many parts of the world, language learning is an overwhelmingly female activity and is associated with discourses of gendered identity (Carr & Pauwels, 2005). Discourses of masculinity are particularly relevant, with their othering of the female (and the associated fear of homosexuality). In a study of the motivation of Grade 9 school students in Ontario, Canada, to learn French, the impact of gendered identity on motivation to learn among boys was found to be overwhelming:

> As the study progressed, it became apparent that traditional views of what is appropriate for a boy and what is appropriate for a girl were

weighing significantly on the results. Boys were reporting that they felt less capable than girls in French because society has told them in no uncertain terms that they are not supposed to be as capable. Boys reported being less interested in learning about French culture because society has made it clear that that is more of a female concern. (Kissau, 2006, p. 415)

I will give here just two glimpses of the way gendered discourses may structure attitudes to language learning and the experience of language learning in very specific ways, often not overtly. Akiyama (2004) explored the reasons for the low valuation of speaking skills in the Japanese education system in the 1990s, despite the efforts of the Japanese Ministry of Education to emphasize spoken language skills in the curriculum for junior and senior high schools. The reason was associated with the highly influential and consequential role of tests in the Japanese education system, particularly the tests at the end of the years of schooling which govern access to the most prestigious universities. Such tests include tests of English language proficiency, but (at the time of Akiyama's study) not of speaking skills in English. Akiyama interviewed policy-makers responsible for this situation. Part of the reason for the disparagement of oral skills was that speaking was seen as a 'woman's thing', that is, of lesser value; the scores in English were taken as indicators not of English proficiency, which was in itself not particularly valued, but of the hard work and intelligence of the students. Oral proficiency was not seen as a marker of hard work and intelligence in the way that, say, mastery of the grammatical system was.

Gendered identity may structure learning opportunities for young children acquiring a second language in classroom settings. Turner (2002) studied two Mandarin-speaking immigrant children, a girl and a boy, in a mixed first-year primary school class as they began literacy in English. Turner conducted a year-long ethnographic study focusing on interactions among the children at the tables at which they were working together on literacy tasks. She found that relationships with peers were crucial for understanding the children's literacy development, as the children struggled to establish their identity as belonging to the group at the table at which they were working. The tables were segregated on gender lines, so that the female Mandarin-speaking learner was at the girls' table, and the boy was at the boys' table. The socialization processes in each case were heavily gender-marked. In the case of the girls working at the girls' table, the overriding social task was friendship and who was entitled to be best friends with the most popular girl in the group. Writing tasks accordingly involved learning to write names, and sentences such as 'I love X'. At the boys' table the Mandarin-speaking boy learner whom Turner was studying was not the only Mandarin speaker at the table, and there was interaction in Mandarin between the boy and the other Mandarin speakers. At one point the boy was completely ostracized from the table and in fact spent many lessons lying by himself on the floor. When the recordings of the interaction in Mandarin between the boy and the other boys at the table were inspected, it turned out that the conversation was very competitive, with the other boys attempting to insult and humiliate Turner's subject, with derogatory references to his father, swearing and so on. Turner argued that the gendered identity of her subjects was crucial to their experience of engaging with English literacy. The social processes that were involved were relatively invisible to the busy teacher – particularly the exchanges in Mandarin, which she did not speak, but also in general, as the teacher was not able to monitor all the conversations at the tables in the classroom.

5.5 LANGUAGE LEARNING: A PERSONAL HISTORY

In this part of the chapter, I will use an account of my own language learning history and its association with aspects of my subjectivity as the context for a critique of the managerialist and globalizing discourses which form the basis for current approaches to language learning and teaching, and particularly as expressed in the Common European Framework of Reference for Languages (CEFR) (Council of Europe, 2001). I will argue that the goals of language learning cannot be properly described nor achievement adequately measured within such a framework. I am not communicatively fluent in any of the languages I have learned over the years. Yet each of the languages I have learned has powerful associations with my changing sense of myself. In this section, I will try to identify the discourses within which my language learning has had meaning for me, and the subjectivity involved for me as a language learner.

The first language I learned was Latin. Two discourses were involved here. I grew up in an Australian Irish Catholic family and was educated in Catholic schools. When I began learning languages at secondary school in the 1960s, where I was taught by the Christian Brothers, an Irish teaching order, Latin was the only language the school offered. This was expressive of the ideology of the school: since the Mass in those days was still said in Latin, one of the functions of the school was to prepare anyone who might be considering the priesthood with the necessary background in the language. We sang hymns in Latin, at Mass, and on special occasions, for example to mark the diamond jubilee (sixty years) of the establishment of the school: '*Haec dies quam fecit Dominus: Exultemus et laetemur in ea*' ('This is the day that the Lord has made, let us rejoice and be glad in it'), a setting by William Byrd (1540–1623) of verses from Psalm 118. Although I have long since moved away from the tenets of my faith, I appreciate the access that learning Latin has given me to better understanding the liturgy and the rich tradition of liturgical music of the Church, and to the centuries of Christian tradition which still inform the post-Christian world of today (for example, Derrida and his fellow philosopher Jean-Luc Nancy see globalization as involving the Christianization of the world: see Banki, 2018). I studied Latin for a total of ten years, including four at university, and have a degree in the language. As I started reading Latin literature in the last years of school and through my university degree, a secular discourse now structured my experience of learning the language: I was introduced to the rich aesthetic, historical, literary and intellectual world of ancient Rome, a powerful imaginative resource for a colonial subject far from the Metropole such as myself (see the discussion of Fanon and Derrida in Chapter 3). I somehow did not take seriously the possibility that this civilization actually existed in the way that my own life existed until I visited the Roman Forum some years after graduation, when I realized that this was a real world, not just the private world of the imagination. This kind of 'language study' sees language 'as an object of linguistic and cultural reflection for general education purposes', its aim being to develop 'the capacity of the educated elite to read and interpret literary texts' (Kramsch, 2005, p. 547), although I do not think this does justice to the meaning of this experience for me, which was profound in shaping my aesthetic, literary and historical consciousness.

The next language I began learning was Italian. Although my all-boys school did not offer any modern languages, partly for the reasons discussed earlier about the negative association of language learning with masculinity, I was stimulated to study Italian by the presence of children of recent immigrants from Italy who were my classmates. I did these studies for two years at another, government school in special Saturday morning classes. My insistence on this commitment, which involved financial expense on the part of my hard-up parents, and the need to travel to the Saturday school on my own part, was mildly transgressive. This is perhaps partly because I was failing to live up to the expectations of masculinity (I had an older brother who conformed unambiguously to those expectations), but more perhaps because Italian was the language of many of the recent immigrants to Australia. These immigrants were generally families from largely poor rural areas of Italy, whose presence the Australian Irish-Catholic hierarchy barely welcomed in our parishes. Nevertheless, my parents supported my decision. They need not have worried: in fact, we learned standard Italian and were introduced to some of the history and culture of Italy, and its literature. I was favoured over fellow-students from Italian families, one from my own school, who infuriated the teacher by their use of dialect words – no such risk with me, who knew nothing. Again my communicative attempts were an abysmal failure. At the end of the second year of study, I took a formal examination in Italian, including an oral component conducted at the university. Preparation for the oral included the memorization of a poem: I chose Giuseppe Giusti's *Sant'Ambrogio*, a poem of the Risorgimento, detailing an incident involving Austrian soldiers – who were occupying northern Italy at the time – in the Basilica of Sant'Ambrogio in Milan. The poem offers an ironic and poignant insight into how oppression damages the oppressors as well as the oppressed. I managed my recitation without problems, and the examination was over. As I left, the examiner said something to me in Italian which I could not at all understand. She repeated it more slowly and again I understood nothing. Finally, she said in English 'Leave the door open' – she must have said 'Lascia aperta la porta' or something similar. Again, in terms of the CEFR, my two years of study had apparently not taken me very far. But I value the experience of learning Italian in those years very highly. Again, as with Latin, it was an introduction to the history, literature and culture of Europe, an imaginative world for someone who was starved of imaginative possibilities. A few years ago, I happened to spend a few hours in Milan, my first time in the city. I was unaware that it was the city of the Basilica in the poem; but when I started investigating what I might see in Milan in the few hours I had there, I was delighted to discover that Sant'Ambrigio was in Milan and spent a couple of hours visiting it, affirming the trust that I had clung to in my unhappy adolescence that the world could be different. The meaning of my experience of learning Italian could not be measured using the instruments of the communicative movement, which emphasizes functional proficiency, especially in the spoken language – it was in entirely other terms, a boundary crossing, and a sign for the future.

Perhaps the clearest examples of discourse framing the subjectivity of the language learner involved my learning of Hebrew and German. I have written about this in detail elsewhere (McNamara, 2013).

Language learning involved for me crossing the boundary policed by anti-Semitism: the boundary between the Catholic world in which I grew up, marked by explicit anti-Semitism, and the experience of the violence of the Holocaust in the lives of two particular Jewish people whom I grew to love. In the case of Hebrew, my learning was the result of a brief relationship and a subsequent lifetime's friendship with Lillian, a Polish Jewish fellow student who was the only child of two sole survivors of the Holocaust. We began our friendship at a time of crisis in my own life, a growing alienation from the values of my family and culture, and a dawning, terrifying awareness of my possible homosexuality. Lillian was born in Poland but had spent seven years of her childhood in Israel before the family's emigration to Australia, and her stories of her childhood and the Hebrew expressions she used in her narratives were full of wonder and promise for me. After graduation, we travelled to Israel together for a holiday. I was unable to communicate my growing feelings for the significance of the languages within Lillian's world, both Yiddish and Hebrew, to my parents, siblings, friends, and the feelings themselves were a source of great confusion. On the one hand, my growing understanding of the potential for violence associated with anti-Semitism within culturally Christian societies and its ultimate expression in the Holocaust, vividly present in the lives of Lillian and her parents, forced me to become conscious of the violence of the discourses that were central to the cultural world of my family from which I was growing increasingly, and anxiously, detached. On the other hand, understanding the nature and depth of this violence was frightening. I unconsciously used an imaginative engagement with the victims of anti-Semitism as a sort of proxy for the psychological and possible physical violence I feared that my dawning awareness of my homosexuality provoked. I have visited Israel several times since, and on two occasions, one recently, I attended *ulpanim* (intensive Hebrew courses designed for immigrants) to begin learning the language seriously and to explore all that it continues to mean for me. In CEFR terms, I am still a low-level learner after forty-five years of exposure; however, that precisely is not the point.

My learning of German has a different trajectory, beginning only ten years ago, but it involved a similar boundary. Near the end of my degree, a time of great personal crisis for me, as I've said, I met the elderly uncle of a fellow student. We called him 'Uncle Paul', and he became an important father figure to me – my relationship with my own father, and all that that symbolized, was in deep trouble. Uncle Paul was a Jewish refugee from Vienna who had made it to Britain just before the outbreak of the war but was arrested as an 'enemy alien' in the panic of 1940. Like many others he was deported to Australia on a ship called the *Dunera*. The story of the 'Dunera Boys' is relatively well known in my generation (Bartrop & Eisen, 1990; Inglis et al., 2018). They were interned in remote rural locations, some until the end of the war. They had nothing to return to in Europe, having lost their families in most cases, and their contribution to post-war Australia was enormous. Uncle Paul died six or seven years after I met him, but the memory of what he meant to me remained intensely strong, and many years later I felt the need to explore the meaning of that memory on a series of extended visits to Vienna, his city. When I arrived there, it felt that Vienna was his gift to me – he had wanted to show it to me, but I had never taken up the opportunity. I have copies of the many letters he wrote (in German) to relatives who had made it to the United States at the time of his escape to Britain, and subsequently. The letters are very poignant as he becomes aware of the unfolding tragedy involving his wife, his mother and his mother-in-law, who were still in Vienna:

18. September 1939
Meine Mutter ist noch in Wien und es ist mir doch eine gewisse Beruhigung wenn ich weiss, dass sie nicht ganz allein mit Wilden zu tun hat, sondern, dass auch Paula manchmal bei ihr ist ... traurig? ich weiss nicht mehr was traurig ist da ich ganz sicher nicht mehr weiss was lustig oder sagen wir was nicht traurig ist.

(18 September 1939
My mother is still in Vienna and it is a certain comfort to me to know that she is not dealing with these savages all by herself, but that Paula is sometimes with her ... sad? ... I no longer know what sad is – I certainly don't know what happy is or rather what is not sad.)

My learning of German, which I undertook to be able to read the letters in the original (they had already been translated for me), similarly evokes an intense sense of his emotional presence – the language resonates for me, it is a 'Vatersprache', a 'father tongue'. Engaging with German in this intensely personal way also involves struggle: I resist the bland cultural materials in the coursebooks we use at the Goethe Institut, where I am learning German. All of them are appropriately tied to the CEFR levels, which make no acknowledgement of the emotional and historical and cultural context in which the language has meaning for me. What is the nature of the barrier that these materials and the courses in which they are used create for me?

5.6 LANGUAGE LEARNING AND DISCOURSES OF GLOBALIZATION: THE COMMUNICATIVE MOVEMENT

The answer I think lies in the fact that the prevailing discourse on language learning and teaching – the communicative movement – has itself tended to obscure the variety of personal meanings language learning has for individuals. Contemporary language learning and teaching is located firmly within discourses of globalization and managerialism (Block and Cameron 2002; Brutt-Griffler 2002). These discourses shape the subjectivity of the learner as a mobile individual, a worker or a traveller, who will need to communicate, particularly in the spoken language, in functional domains relevant to work or travel. The emergence of discourses of managerialism and globalization is clear if we look at the history of the communicative language movement in Europe since its introduction in the early 1970s (Kramsch, 2005). A major player from the beginning has been the Council of Europe, a cultural and policy organization (not related to the EU: its membership is far broader, with currently forty-seven states as members), whose announced goals (according to an earlier version of its website[1]) were these:

> The Council of Europe is the continent's oldest political organisation, founded in 1949 ... [It] was set up to ... develop continent-wide agreements to standardise member countries' social and legal practices [and] promote awareness of a European identity based on shared values and cutting across different cultures.
> Within the area of education, its mission involves carrying out major projects on education policy, content and methods in and out of school ... Special importance is attached to ... the mutual recognition of competences to improve mobility and employment prospects, and lifelong learning for participation in an international society.

These goals represent a Europe-wide version of what we would today call globalization, emphasizing managerial concerns such as labour mobility and the training of a workforce for the globalized marketplace. A comparison with the goals of the Organisation of Economic Cooperation and Development (OECD) is instructive. The mission of OECD (2008, p. 10) is as follows: 'The Organisation's mission is essentially to help governments and society reap the full benefits of globalisation, while tackling the economic, social and governance challenges that can accompany it.' It may be worth comparing the

---

[1] http://www.coe.int/T/e/Com/about_coe/, date accessed: 10.01.2006, subsequently revised; this revealing text is no longer available.

Table 5.1 *A comparison of the goals of the OECD and the Council of Europe*

OECD	COUNCIL OF EUROPE
The Organisation's mission is essentially to help governments and society reap the full benefits of *globalisation*,	... the mutual recognition of competences to improve *mobility and employment prospects,* and lifelong learning for *participation in an international society*
while tackling the economic, *social and governance challenges* that can accompany it.	[It] was set up to ... develop continent-wide agreements to standardise member countries' *social and legal practices* ...

actual wording of the goals of the two organizations, as in Table 5.1 (goals that seem shared have been italicized).

While the OECD specifically focuses on economic development, and the Council of Europe focuses on education, in a deeper sense they share the same mission. They share another feature, which is that assessment regimes of educational achievement, including in languages, are central to the fulfilment of the goals of each organization: for OECD, these are the PISA assessments (McNamara, 2011b); for the Council of Europe, it is the assessments tied to the Common European Framework of Reference (CEFR) (Council of Europe, 2001). We will say more on the question of assessment in the penultimate chapter of this book.

The initial motivation of the work of the Council of Europe in this area was to permit transfer of credentialing for language proficiency across national and linguistic boundaries, to allow recognition to be given outside particular national settings for standards of language proficiency among immigrant workers and professionals. A key moment in this early development was the commissioning of the development of what were known as functional language syllabuses (e.g. Wilkins's Notional/Functional syllabus (1973)) and the definitions of successive levels of achievement in language (Waystage (Van Ek & Trim, 1998a), Threshold (Van Ek & Trim, 1998b) and Vantage (Van Ek & Trim, 2001)) as part of a single unit/credit scheme for credentialing of language proficiency in different languages, to allow portability of language credentials. The culmination of this work was the development of the Common European Framework of Reference for Languages (CEFR) (Council of Europe, 2001). The CEFR defines six broad levels of proficiency, from A1 (the lowest) to C2 (the highest). The actual formulation of the wording of the levels of the CEFR was the result of a project to develop level descriptors: short, detailed statements of aspects of functional communicative competence, often in the form of 'can-do' statements, the wording of which was drawn from a large number of existing scales (North, 2000). The basic building blocks of the scale development were functional descriptors faithfully reflecting the fundamental underlying construct of the assessment, a 1970s notional/functionalism (Wilkins, 1973) whose goal was to facilitate the recognition of language competencies across national boundaries in the context of labour migration.

The setting of language learning within discourses of globalization and labour mobility has far-reaching implications. In constructing the language learner as a member of the globalized workforce, it sees all languages as functionally equivalent. In the frameworks and scales that describe the terms in which this functional equivalence is established, it both defines the construct of language learning and sets up an accounting system for languages so that achievement in language learning and language proficiency can be compared across languages. The CEFR is a kind of Euro for languages, so that all are seen as freely convertible (they are all defined in exactly the same functional terms). Defining the goals and meaning of language learning in purely functional, communicative terms ignores the role of language learning in the subjective experience of the learner as an individual with a history, both personal and cultural. What the functionalist globalizing discourse of the communicative movement and its expression in the CEFR does is to erase all historical and cultural differences among languages and learners in their specific socio-cultural and historical contexts as determining influences on the motivation to learn languages and the meaning of language learning; it is a hegemonic discourse. What is needed instead is to give an account of how language learning in different societies and cultures will have specific social meanings, and hence potential meanings for individuals, within the history of contact, culturally and politically, with the societies and communities in which the target language is spoken, and the resulting discourses involved. These historical conditions will mediate the encounters of individuals from different societies with the same language, so that the learning of the same language may have very different meanings according to the specific social and cultural background of the learner.

There are historical parallels for the cost of unification in the interests of economy on linguistic diversity. The French sociologist Pierre Bourdieu, writing about the linguistic unification of France in the eighteenth century, states (1991 p. 49):

But it was doubtless the dialectical relation between the school system and the labour market – or, more precisely, between the unification of the educational (and linguistic) market, linked to the introduction of educational qualifications nation-wide, independent (at least officially) of the social or regional characteristics of their bearers, and the unification of the labour market (including the development of the state administration and the civil service) – which played the most decisive role in devaluing dialects and establishing the new hierarchy of linguistic practices.

The quote from Bourdieu thus reminds us that the cost of unification is the devaluing of the local interpretation of the goals of education. In particular, the imposition of a single set of cultural meanings and social and political values for language education, for each language and in each country of the vast and historically complex continent of Europe, and now far beyond Europe, eviscerates the traditions of language teaching which are incompatible with the CEFR. It is simply not the same for a French person, a Dutch person, a Russian, a Croatian, an English person to learn German, speaking culturally and historically. Each learner from those backgrounds is potentially awake to the cultural and political significance of the act of language learning, unless, in an act of collective amnesia, they are invited to wipe the slate clean and re-identify themselves as citizens of the new globalized Europe.

The CEFR, in other words, is not like the Euro, because the currency of language is not convertible. Managers, lawmakers and administrators love the CEFR and other standards-based frameworks all over the world because they provide a certain kind of quantitative accountability in a way that was not possible before. But this all-too-ready surface translatability denies the untranslatable, the part of language and language learning which gives the enterprise value beyond labour force mobility: personal, emotional, *subjective* value. And being capable of 'participation in an international society' is not best achieved through historical amnesia, tempting though that may be given the unfathomable horrors of the past.

5.7 CONCLUSION

For some time now, researchers in applied linguistics have been exploring the complex relationship of multilingualism and the experience of language learning in particular to the subjectivity of the learner and language user. This has sometimes been used as a fulcrum for a critique of the tenets of the communicative movement and for the central preoccupations of applied linguistics more generally (e.g. Kramsch, 2005; Pennycook, 2001). There is a universalizing character of the communicative movement, in which all languages are interchangeable and the complex subjectivities of learners are bleached out. I have tried to show from my own personal experiences of language learning what a complex relationship to the subjectivity of the learner such experiences can have. If we wish to rescue language education as fulfilling the goals of the education of the person, not just the goal of the creation of a mobile and flexible workforce, we will need to insist on the complex personal meanings of the experience of language learning. The problem is that the managerialist ethos of the CEFR, the clearest articulation of the spirit of the communicative movement, has been so thoroughly enshrined in curriculum and in educational and other policy (immigration, citizenship and so on) that it has become a juggernaut whose momentum it becomes increasingly difficult to resist (McNamara, 2014).

5.8 SUGGESTIONS FOR FURTHER READING

Accounts of the personal experience and subjective meaning of language learning began with the diary studies tradition, with its largely cognitive focus, but in recent years there have been a number of collections focusing on the broader social context of learning, such as Kramsch (2009), Nunan and Choi (2010), and the special issue of *Language and Intercultural Communication* edited by Ros i Solé and Fenoulhet (2013b). The classic study of gender and language learning is Norton (Norton Peirce, 1995; Norton, 2000), updated in Norton (2013). Sociopolitical critiques of the role of English in the world and its implications for language learning can be found in Phillipson (1992), Pennycook (2001), Block and Cameron (2002), Brutt-Griffler (2002) and Canagarajah (1999), with a particularly powerful contribution by Kramsch (2005). The development of the Common European Framework of Reference (CEFR) is described in North (2000), building on the logic of the communicative movement in Europe, a key early text of which is Wilkins (1973). There have been relatively few published critiques of the CEFR, exceptions being Hulstijn (2007), largely from a cognitive perspective, and Fulcher (2004), from a more social and political perspective.

6 Discourse and Subjectivity in Face-to-Face Interaction (1): The Interaction Order

6.1 INTRODUCTION

When I go to my local pharmacy to have a prescription filled, as I have been doing for the last twenty years, I often speak to the pharmacist, whom I have known throughout that time. We both happen to be male, of roughly similar ages, and are both gay; both Australian, both professionally educated. Are these facets of our subjectivity evident in this interaction? Would what we say, or the nature of the interaction, be different if one of us were a woman, or younger, or straight, or of a different nationality or educational level? Or are our institutional roles, as pharmacist and customer, more relevant here?

This example raises the more general issue of the extent to which 'big D Discourses' (in the Foucauldian sense, as discussed in Chapter 1) are evident in 'small d discourse' which is the focus of linguistic study, and how the skills of the discourse analyst may best address the issue of their operation. What is the impact of prevailing discourses in the day-to-day interactions of individuals, particularly where the character of the discourse indicates the potential for systematic disadvantage or actual harm? For example, in a health context, in the case of an immigrant female patient being seen by a male doctor from the majority culture, is the patient in a kind of triple jeopardy by virtue of the fact that she is a woman, an immigrant and a patient? The resolution of such a question turns out to be unusually difficult and complex, not only methodologically, but also theoretically. The issue to be explored here is that interaction is the potential site for not one but two quite independent orders of social action: the macro-context of social relations as a function of big D Discourse, and the micro-context of face-to-face interaction which, in the view of an important group of sociologists, is in principle independent of the first. The proposed existence of two independent social orders has triggered considerable controversy, a controversy that can potentially, as we shall see in this and the next chapter, be reinterpreted in the light of poststructuralist theories of determinism, iterability and agency.

6.2   FACE-TO-FACE INTERACTION: THE INTERACTION ORDER

The idea that face-to-face interaction represents its own social order, in principle independent of but potentially articulated with the larger social forces within the context in which interaction takes place, was formulated by the American sociologists Harold Garfinkel and Erving Goffman in the 1960s. Garfinkel developed a tradition in sociology known as ethnomethodology (Garfinkel, 1967; Heritage, 1984), the study of practical everyday reasoning in social settings, as a complement to the more usual focus of sociology, that is, the role in behaviour of macro-social categories such as class, race, gender, ethnicity, age and so on.

The difference between the two social orders can be understood by thinking about freeway driving. The macro-social order is like the explicitly formulated and externally imposed and policed constraints of road rules: for example, which side of the road to drive on, speed limits, how overtaking is to be done, rules for giving way at intersections, and so on. The micro-social order resembles the immediate situation of driving which involves ongoing mutual monitoring of and adaptation to other drivers, what ethnomethodologists refer to as 'local practices'. The local practices which respond to the immediate contingencies of freeway driving are too particular and variable to be summed up in rules; the flow of traffic, the occasional traffic jams are the result of the sum of these local practices. In the same way, according to Garfinkel, the behaviour of practitioners in their negotiation of social interaction can be best understood as being guided by general principles or maxims which are interpreted locally and minute by minute. It is not simply an automatic top-down application of rules. The study of this locally situated and motivated interaction is the subject of ethnomethodology and its subsequent discipline, Conversation Analysis.

In an important paper entitled 'The Neglected Situation', Goffman (1964) rejected the idea that the larger social context could simply be read off the detail of social interaction, that social situations are merely the site of intersection of macro-social variables and 'do not have properties and a structure of their own' (p. 134). (Note that Goffman's critique is also relevant to variationist sociolinguistics, where the impact of factors such as gender, class, race, age and so on is examined quantitatively, across instances, and the context of particular interactions is ignored.) Goffman defined the social situation as 'an environment of mutual monitoring possibilities ... Cultural rules ... socially organize the behavior of those in the situation' (p. 135).

In a later paper, Goffman develops this idea as follows: 'Social interaction ... [is] that which uniquely transpires in social situations, that is, environments in which two or more individuals are physically in one another's response presence' (1983, p. 2). Goffman argues that 'Face to face interaction has its own regulations; it has its own processes and its own structure' (1964, pp. 135–6). The 'processes' involved include how turn taking, requesting the floor, giving up the floor and leaving the interaction are socially coordinated. Goffman compares these processes with the rules and procedures which characterize a variety of rule-governed social interactions including card games, ballroom dancing, fist fights, and the work of surgical teams. The systematic nature of face-to-face social interaction, in this sense, he calls the *interaction order*, a micro-social order of social life which is in principle, and crucially, independent of other, macro-social orders: 'This face-to-face domain ... [is] an analytically viable one ... which might be titled the *interaction order* ... [and] whose preferred method of study is microanalysis' (Goffman, 1983, p. 2). By 'order' Goffman means a domain of social activity, whose goal is the 'sustained, intimate coordination of action' (1983, p. 3).

Harvey Sacks and his contemporary and colleague Emanuel Schegloff, both of whom were students of Goffman at Berkeley in the 1960s, and who had frequent contact with Garfinkel at UCLA during the same period, developed a method for the 'microanalysis' to which Goffman refers. Sacks (1935–75) taught at UCLA and UC Irvine from 1964 to 1975 until his death in a car accident. Schegloff (b. 1937) continued the tradition of Sacks's work in his teaching at UCLA. Their method of microanalysis came to be called Conversation Analysis (CA), or the study of language in social interaction.

The term Conversation Analysis is in a sense misleading, as it involves an analysis of conversation not because of an interest in the characteristics of the language of conversation for its own sake but because language is typically the medium, though not the only one, through which interaction is conducted. As Goffman put it, the regulations, processes and structure of interaction 'don't seem to be intrinsically linguistic in character, however often expressed through a linguistic medium' (1964, p. 136). Key to the notion of interaction is the visibility of the actions of interactants to each other. That is, in an 'environment of mutual monitoring possibilities' (Goffman, 1964,

p. 135), any move by one of the participants, for example any turn at talk, is visible and thus interpretable as an action by the other participant(s). As Schegloff puts it, 'Each participant's talk is inspectable, and is inspected, by co-participants to see how it stands to the one that preceded, what sort of response it has accorded the preceding turn' (2007b, p. 1).

Turns, in other words, constitute social actions and are of interest to Conversation Analysts as actions: 'Turns are inspected for what action they perform, rather than what they are about' (Schegloff, 2007b, p. 1). Parties monitor the talk-in-a-turn to see where they might enter the interaction, whether someone is being nominated as next speaker, and what action(s) the speaker might be doing. These interpretations are guided by the maxim: 'Why that now?' (meaning, 'What action is being performed by that turn?'). The motivation for this inspection is not idle curiosity, but the action's possible implications for the hearer in terms of what the next action should or might be in response. (The emphasis on reception and recognition of social actions provides an intriguing echo of the discussion of recognition in subjectivity, following Hegel, in Chapter 3.)

Conversation Analysis has developed a complex set of procedures for the analysis of interaction. There is no time to go into this in detail here; introductions are available in Schegloff (2007b), but also in Sidnell (2010), Liddicoat (2007), Ten Have (2007), Wooffitt (2005) and others. To give one example: a key term in the analysis of language in interaction within CA is the turn constructional unit, or TCU. TCUs are the building blocks out of which turns are fashioned. Resources for building and recognizing TCUs include the grammar of sentences, clauses, phrases, lexical items, as well as intonation. The criterial feature of a TCU is that it constitutes a recognizable action in context. Turns can have multiple TCUs. Each TCU as it nears its end is a *transition relevance place*, that is, a place where transition from one speaker to another becomes routinely possible. Speakers signal that they are nearing the end of a turn in subtle ways, including by the use of grammatical cues (the completion of a syntactic clause), intonational or prosodic cues (the use of a rising or falling terminating pitch contour), lexical cues such as the use of several stereotyped expressions (*but uh, or something, you know* ...), vocal paralinguistic cues including the lengthening of the final (stressed) syllable, or a possible drop in pitch and loudness; and through body movements such as hand gestures, a left and down movement of the head, or a steady gaze towards the selected next speaker. Coordination between speakers in interaction is a surprisingly complex achievement, and an analysis will try to capture the delicately orchestrated deployment of resources involved. CA is accordingly extremely detailed, with recognized conventions about the degree of fidelity of transcription required, and time-consuming; this is inevitable given what it is trying to achieve. Its achievements are already considerable, in describing the frequent patterning of interactional moves and sequences in specific social actions such as offers, invitations, assessments, requests and so on; it as if there is a set of typical or preferred 'dance steps' for each type of social action. Importantly, though, the performance of the steps is not somehow automatic, cannot simply be assumed – each has to be iteratively enacted and may not be so enacted in any particular case; a fact which itself is likely to have interactional consequences and implications for the participants' interpretation of the social actions thereby performed.

6.3 CONVERSATION ANALYSIS AND INTERACTION IN INSTITUTIONAL SETTINGS

Given that the focus of Conversation Analysis is on the interaction order, and not directly on macro-social categories of gender, ethnicity, age and so on, can it say anything about the operation of macro-social categories in interaction? Critics of CA, of whom there are many, answer in the negative, mistaking its focus on the interaction order as a blindness to the relevance of macro-level discourses. But this is a misunderstanding, and I will try to argue in this chapter in what way CA can and does address the operation of discursive categories in its analysis of interactional data. I will also argue that accounts of the operation of macro-level categories must be able to account for their impact at the level of micro-interaction, given that it is an *independent* order of sociality. In other words, for such discourses to have any impact on interaction, they must be inscribed in the interaction order; and this has to be mutually achieved by the participants – it is not a 'given' or an automatic, top-down projection from the very existence of discourses, as it were.

One place in which it is possible to see how macro-level social roles are inscribed in the pattern of interaction is in institutional talk, that is, talk between individuals acting in prescribed social roles that are oriented to by the participants in the interaction. While the primary data of Conversation Analysis is often casual conversation, in which the identities of the participants as members of social categories are often or even typically not foregrounded, and the participants are not oriented to the completion of an institutionally relevant task, from its very beginning CA has also explored whether and, if so, in what ways, the patterns of interaction discovered in casual conversation in non-institutional settings are carried over into those occurring in institutional settings. In what follows, we will give three examples of the character of interaction in institutional settings and see that the 'dance steps' that characterize them differ systematically from those of everyday conversation. The first is from the medical setting and involves the interactional practices of nurses ('health visitors') visiting new mothers in the United Kingdom. The second is from the domain of media, the news interview. The third is from the educational domain of language testing, specifically interaction in the conversation between examiner and candidate in assessments of spoken language proficiency.

Note that in each of these cases, the issue is the extent to which the institutional role is detectable in the patterns of interaction, that is, it is distinguished from the patterns that are observed in casual conversation where no institutional role is involved. Most of the social roles or 'identities' in the examples that follow do not involve the specific aspects of subjectivity (gendered, national, sexual, ethnic and so on) that have been the focus of earlier chapters (the issue of gender does arise in the third example). The institutional roles of health visitor/new mother, interviewer/interviewee and examiner/candidate are all reflective, however, of the institutionality and bureaucratic character of modernity (Foucault, 1977). Although the Conversation Analysis tradition developed independently of poststructuralism and was not informed by it, these examples demonstrate that, in principle, externally imposed social categories such as those central to a discourse may be visibly oriented to in the interaction order by the participants. In the following chapter, we will show via a detailed example how CA can reveal the operation of discursive regimes of gender in the interaction order.

Health Visitors

In a classic study, Heritage and Sorjonen (1994) report on the conversational interaction between health visitors and new mothers. In the UK, health visitors are professionally trained nurses, one of whose jobs it is to assist the new mother in accommodating to the demands of the infant; topics covered might include feeding (especially breast feeding), nutrition and care. In general the aim is to provide support for the new family. The study focused on the first visit of the health visitor to the new mother, usually about ten days after the birth of the mother's first child. The health visitor is required to fill in a form as part of the visit and has to elicit the information relevant to the form through the interaction with the mother, who is often busy with the infant. The interaction is typically informal and conversational rather than formal and bureaucratic. Despite its informal, conversational character, however, Heritage and Sorjonen were able to show how it systematically differed from informal conversations that lacked such an institutional agenda. In particular, they noticed what they call '*and*-prefacing' in the speech of the health visitor as he/she goes through the questions, as in the following example (HV = health visitor, M = mother; arrows indicate the interactional phenomenon of interest, in this case *and*-prefacing):

```
 1   HV:        Has he got plenty of wo:rk on,
 2   M:         He works for a university college.
 3   HV:        O:::h.
 4   M:         So: (.) he's in full-time work all the ti:me.
 5   HV:        °Yeh.°
 6              (0.4)
 7   HV:    →   And this is y'r first ba:by:.
 8   M:         Ye(p).
 9              (0.3)
10   HV:    →   .tch An' you had a no:rmal pre:gnancy.=
11   M:         =Ye:h.
12              (1.1)
13   HV:    →   And a normal delivery,
14   M:         Ye:p.
15              (1.4)
16   HV:        °Ri:ght.°
17              (0.7)
18   HV:    →   And sh' didn't go into special ca:re.
19   M:         No:.
20              (1.8)
21   HV:    →   °An:d she's bottle feeding?
22              (1.2)
23   HV:    →   °Um:° (0.4) and uh you're going to Doctor White for
                your (0.6) p[ost-na:tal?
24   M:                    [Yeah.
```
                                        (Heritage & Sorjonen, 1994, pp. 3–4)

Note here that the 'institutional setting' is not constituted by location – these conversations take place in the homes of the mothers, not at the clinic – but by the professional character of the task at hand. This is unlike casual conversation in which there is no such task – imagine a casual conversation with your partner, in which you introduce *and*-prefacing – you would soon get a negative reaction! In general, according to Heritage and Sorjonen (1994, p. 7), '*and*-prefacing ... is used to underscore the user's orientation to a question as a routine or agenda question within an activity'. They point out (p. 1) that:

While *and* as a question preface is rarely found in ordinary
conversation between peers or acquaintances, it is a commonplace
feature of interaction in 'institutional' settings such as law courts and
certain types of medical encounter, where the parties are occupied
with a restricted set of tasks, or address one another as incumbents of
particular social roles.

In other words, at the level of micro-interaction in the interaction order,
the presence of relevant social categories and roles is evident because the
normal interactional patterns are replaced with those indicative of these
roles. The rules of interaction in the interaction order, in other words,
may reflect the kind of institutional work that is being done.

The News Interview

Our second example of the way in which institutional roles, which are
examples of macro-level orders of social organization, are visible in
distinctive patterns of interaction at the micro-interactional level is in
the news interview. News interviews may superficially resemble
casual conversation but differ from them interactionally in important
respects. In casual conversation, as the speaker turns proceed, at each
transition relevance place there is a negotiation of next speaker turn.
Typically, in casual conversation, speakers use 'continuers' in the
form of acknowledgements, news markers and so on to pass up their
turn at talk, thus allowing the current speaker to continue with
a subsequent turn in a narrative sequence, as in the following example
(continuers are marked with arrows).

```
1      S:              =.hhh Uh:m::, .tch.hhhh Who w'you ta:lking to.
2                      ...
3                      ...
4      G:              I: wasn't talking to a:nybody. Bo-oth Martin'n
5                      I slept until about noo:n,=
6      S:      1→      =O[h.
7      G:               [.hhhh An' when I woke up, I wanted to call
8                      my mother
9      S:      2→      Mm[hm
10     G:               [.hhhh An' I picked up the pho:ne, a:n I
11                     couldn't dial out.'n [I thought our phone was
12     S:      3→                           [Oh: ( ),
13     G:              out'v order. ['n I-
14     S:      4→                   [Yeh,
```

(Clayman & Heritage, 2002, pp. 108–9)

In news interviews, however, interviewees rarely produce such acknowledgements. Because the turn structure is in the control of the interviewer, there is no similar available turn for the interviewee to pass up; instead, the interviewee simply waits for the next question to be asked, as in the following example, from a BBC radio interview. A librarian is being interviewed and is asked whether the library might be in a position to afford to purchase some historic letters which are coming up for auction and which it would, funds allowing, normally be interested in purchasing. Note that at the arrowed transition relevance place at the end of line 2, instead of there being an acknowledgement or other kind of continuer, which we would expect in casual conversation, there is silence as the interviewee waits for the formulation of the question from the interviewer.

```
1  IR:  1→  .hhh The (.) price being asked for these letters
2           is (.) three thousand pou::nds.
3  IR:  2→  Are you going to be able to raise it,
4           (0.5)
5  IE:      At the moment it ... (continues)
```
(Clayman & Heritage, 2002, p. 105)

The existence of this interactional convention in news interviews allows us then to notice the significance of occasions in news interviews when this is *not* observed. In the following example,[1] the then Leader of the Opposition in the Australian Federal Parliament, Mr Tony Abbott (later elected prime minister), is being interviewed on a popular television current affairs programme, Q&A, in front of a studio audience, members of which are allowed to pose questions. Questions can also be emailed or texted in to the host, Tony Jones, who reads the question out, as in the example below; there may also be follow-up questions from the host himself, again as here. Abbott, who studied for the Catholic priesthood as a young man though was never ordained and was well known for his avowed Catholic faith, had recently, after an internal party struggle, been elected the head of a rather divided and fractious Liberal Party. Despite its name the party is conservative politically, and has supported hard-line policies on the reception and treatment of migrants and asylum seekers arriving by boat at Christmas Island, an island which is territorially part of Australia but is relatively close to Indonesia. (The boat arrivals are currently subjected to internment in remote areas and may experience lengthy delays in the processing of their asylum applications; the harshness of the treatment of these individuals arriving by boat is the

---

[1] www.youtube.com/watch?v=f0N4SQ4R5K4.

subject of great controversy.) The question read out by the host, Tony Jones, is: 'When it comes to asylum seekers, what would Jesus do?' This triggers audience laughter, which Abbott participates in; he initially tries to dismiss the question by making a joke about his folly at allowing himself to become leader of a divided political party; however, the host of the programme returns to the question and insists he answer it.

```
1   TJ       A web question has come in, it's from [name] in Canberra: 'When it
2            comes to asylum seekers (.) what would Jesus do?'
3   Aud      ((laughter, applause))
4   TA       Well uh Je- Jesus
5   Aud      ((applause))
6   TA       ((turns to TJ)) um (.) er Jesus wouldn't have put his hand up to lead
7            the Liberal Party I suspect hhh
8   Aud      ((audience laughter))
9   TA       or or (.) or the Labor party for that matter (.) ha ha ha
10  Aud      ((applause))
11  TA       ha ha ha
12  TJ       ok
13  TA       ha
14  TJ       but but someone who be[lieves
15  TA    →                       [yeah ye[ah
16  TJ                                    [in the principles that he [espoused
17  TA    →                                                          [yeah    mm
18  TJ       did do that so it is a legitimate question
19  TA    →  yeah (.) uh (.) uh don't forget Jesus drove the traders from the temple
20           as well now I I mean (.) [you
```

Note that as the host formulates his request (ll. 14, 16, 18), Tony Abbott does not wait for its formulation as might be expected of an interviewee, as in the previous example. (Admittedly the interviewer's turn is not formulated grammatically as a question, but it is motivated by Abbott's failure to answer the question in l. 2 and elaborates the grounds for the legitimacy of the question.) Instead, Abbott overlaps with the host with three continuers ('yeah', ll. 15, 17); moreover, these do not occur at transition relevance places but instead are either in mid-word or in mid-clause, and he adds a further continuer ('mm') at the end of a dependent clause, but still in mid-sentence. When Abbott does finally get his turn to answer, he in a way accepts the grounds of the question by responding to it with a possible scripture-based precedent for his policy of excluding boat arrivals: he quotes an incident in the New Testament: 'Don't forget Jesus drove the traders from the temple as well.' The biblical text in question reads as follows:

13 It was nearly time for the Jewish Passover celebration, so Jesus went to Jerusalem.

14 In the Temple area he saw merchants selling cattle, sheep, and doves for sacrifices; he also saw dealers at tables exchanging foreign money.

15 Jesus made a whip from some ropes and chased them all out of the Temple. He drove out the sheep and cattle, scattered the money changers' coins over the floor, and turned over their tables.

16 Then, going over to the people who sold doves, he told them, 'Get these things out of here. Stop turning my Father's house into a marketplace!'

(John 2:13–16 (New Living Translation))

Following this remark of Abbott's, the host, Tony Jones, pursues the analogy by pointing out that in the New Testament account Jesus used violence, implying that the biblical text might also be seen as a precedent for the government taking violent measures (the actions of Australian navy vessels in relation to the boat arrivals had long been controversial).

```
1   TJ      It's (.) it's er it's quite quite an interesting analo[gy be[cause [as you
2   TA  →                                                        [mm    [mm    [mm
3   TJ      know um an a whip was used  on that occasion
4   TA  →                        mm                   mm [mm
5   TJ                                                   [to drive people [out of
6           the temple um you know if that's the analogy
7   TA  →                                                  [mm
8   TJ      you're u[sing should we take it at face value?
9   TA  →          [mm
10  TA      no no I I I'm I'm just saying that (.) um look (.) Jesus was the best man
11          who ever lived (.) uh (.) but that doesn't mean that he said (.) yes to
12          everyone that he was permissive to everything and and this idea yeah that
13          Jesus would say (.) uh to every (.) to every person who who wanted to come
14          to Australia 'Fine' uh 'the door's open' I just don't think is necessarily
15          right now let's not verbal Jesus
```

As the interviewer pushes the issue and insists on formulating the next question to Abbott, Abbott again 'interrupts' several times with continuers, usually not at transition relevance places, often in mid-word, sometimes at a clause or noun phrase boundary in mid-sentence.

We have then a clear breach of the normal convention of interviews, that interviewee continuers are typically absent at transition relevance places in the interviewer's turn. The initial question to Abbott by the audience member is both political and very personal, as it tries to embarrass him by suggesting a lack of alignment between his private (although publicly declared) Christian convictions and his hard-line policies on boat arrivals. In both of the extracts cited above, Abbott's use of continuers is in breach of the norms of news interviews. On the one hand, as Clayman and Heritage (2002) have shown, the use of continuers at all by interviewees is dispreferred and therefore marked; it can be seen as disrupting the institutional character of the action *as interview*, and thus implicitly the right of the interviewer to ask the question. Moreover, the placing of the continuers in non-transition relevance places intensifies their disruptive effect. This is despite the fact that Abbott's turns are formulated as continuers ('yeah', 'mm'), which preserves the surface form at least of cooperation with the intention of the interviewer, even though their placing suggests an urgent insistence on his right to reply. The disruptive effect of Abbott's use of continuers can be understood only in relation to the unmarked institutional practice of news interviewing. His disruptive moves suggest resistance, urgency, perhaps the urgent need to defend his identity as a political leader and as a devout Christian; and perhaps his resentment at the line of questioning which his disruptive use of continuers challenges as somehow unfair. Whatever the interpretation, his actions are meaningful only within the frame of the interactional conventions both of casual conversation on the one hand and the departures from them that constitute the institutional character of the news interview.

Language Testing: The Oral Proficiency Interview

The final example of evidence of distinctive patterns of interaction in institutional talk emerges in studies of the institutional character of oral proficiency interviews initiated by Van Lier (1989) and continued within the collection of studies in Young and He (1998). Annie Brown (Brown 2003, 2005; Brown & McNamara, 2004) studied face-to-face interaction in the course of the oral proficiency interview given as part of the International English Language Testing System (IELTS) test, a British-Australian test of English for academic purposes. Although the interview is conducted in a generally friendly and relaxed manner, intended to put the candidate at ease so that, according to the British Council IELTS website, the interview 'is interactive and as close to a real-life situation as a test can get',[2] the overt structuring of the

---

[2] British Council, IELTS, 'Understand the Speaking test', https://takeielts.britishcouncil .org/prepare-test/understand-test-format/speaking-test, retrieved 5.3.18.

interaction reflects its institutional character. In the words of Young and He (1998, pp. 10–11):

> Interviews reflect the institutional context in which they are embedded through their speech exchange system and its goal-orientedness. In ordinary conversation, topics and turns are not prescribed by specific speech activity; none of the participants has a predefined role in managing the interaction. In L[anguage] P[roficiency] I[nterview]s, however, there are specific constraints on participants' contributions in terms of turn-taking and reduction or re-specification of conversational options ... Another way in which the LPI, as a genre of institutional discourse, differs from ordinary conversation is in its goal-orientation ... Interviewers have as their goal to extract language samples from the interviewee and often have a predefined agenda for the encounter.

The agenda is evident in the structure of the interview (University of Cambridge Local Examinations Syndicate, 2000, p. 3):

Introduction
The candidate is encouraged to talk briefly about their life, home, work and interests.

Extended Discourse
The candidate is encouraged to speak at length about some very familiar topic either of general interest or of relevance to their culture, place of living, or country of origin. This will involve explanation, description or narration.

Elicitation
The candidate is given a task card with some information on it and is encouraged to take the initiative and ask questions either to elicit information or to solve a problem.

Speculation and attitudes
The candidate is encouraged to talk about their future plans and proposed course of study. Alternatively, the examiner may choose to return to a topic raised earlier.

Conclusion
The interview is concluded.

Brown's study of interaction in the IELTS interview found extensive evidence for an orientation to this institutional role in the actions of the interviewer. This involved a number of features:

(a) an overt orientation to the interviewer role (Brown, 2005, p. 154):

```
(I = Interviewer; C = Candidate)
1  I  →  °right° .hh e:rm °let's see let's think I'm expected to talk to you about a few
2        things° but erm (1.6) in Hong Kong, (.3) erm (1.8) d'y- (.8) >what are the
3        wor king< hours in Hong Kong. so your father goes to work.
4
5  C     ye:s [e:r
6  I          [what- what is a typical working day. [(.) in terms of hours.
7
8  C                                                 [mm
```

(b) topic priming (gradual introduction of the topic with preparatory material, rather than a bald question) (Brown, 2005, p. 97):

```
1  I  →  .hh so- (.) do you have a room, on your own?
2  C     no I'm sharing with my friend=
3  I     =mhm can you describe your room to me?
```

(c) *and-* and *so*-prefacing (Brown, 2005, p. 98):

```
1  I  →  [°yeah° and: erm: (0.5) do you have any special duties that you have to do in the
2         hostel?
3  C     yeah: (.) we have to wash the: dishes. [(.) (n- n-) (.) a one month (1.4) =
4  I                                            [mm:?
5  C     = once in a month.
6  I     do you? [(.) ye]ah? mhm .hh is that washing dishes for everybody?
7  C             [yeah
8  C     yeah for everybody. (0.3) but three person in one (0.6) one duty.
9  I  →  mhm,° ri:ght.° (.) .hhh and: anything else you have to do?
```

(Brown, 2005, p. 97)

```
1  I  →  did they? [(.) ye:s (.) yeah.. hh so (.) do you have a room on your own?
2  C               [yeah
3  C     no I'm sharing with my friend.
4  I     mhm can you describe your room to me?
```

(d) formulations and assessments (Brown, 2005, p. 106):

```
1  I  →  ...°right.° yeah so you also have family there. ye:s; yeah. .hh UM .hh now;
         (0.7) when you ....
```

The interaction overall is clearly then institutional in character and thus unlike casual conversation, in which these moves to control the interaction would be likely resisted (and possibly resented). Specifically, the institutional role of the interviewer is achieved interactionally in the way Brown describes. But what about other potential aspects of the subjectivity of those conducting the interview, for example gender? The literature on gendered speech that we have considered in Chapter 2 tends to suggest that women's speech is more supportive and collaborative (e.g. Coates, 1997b, 2013; Cheshire & Trudgill, 1998; Davies, 2003) – is this also evident at the level of the interaction order in this institutional context, where it could then potentially affect the candidate's contribution, and thus their score? Brown arranged for a number of candidates to take the test twice with different interviewers each time, including interviewers of different genders. Audio-taped recordings of the interactions were made and these were then rated by trained judges. The scores on the two performances were then compared, and where there was a large discrepancy between the scores on the two occasions, the interviews were transcribed and carefully analyzed. Was the gender of the interviewers the cause of the difference in scores given by the independent judges? With one of these interview pairs with the same candidate, Brown identified differences in the approach of the male interviewer (Ian) and a female interviewer (Pam) with the female candidate (Esther), who achieved significantly higher scores with Pam than with Ian. Brown found that the interaction of the female interviewer (Pam) had a number of notable features. Consider the following extract (Brown, 2003, p. 8):

```
1    P    →    ... do you live in a fla:t?
2    E         er no hostel
3    P    →    in a hostel.
4    E         Carlton College.
5    P    →    is it? [(.) tell me about the hostel, (.) I
6    E              [°mm°
7              (1.6)
8    E         oh um: it's aum: international college, =
9    P         = mm,
10             (0.8)
11   E         er >I mean a hostel,< er: (1.0) and I knew- (.) I- (1.0) knew: that
12             (.) hostel: by: (0.9) a counselling centre, (1.2) and: (1.9) and
13             it's: (0.5) er: quite good for: (0.8) u:m: (.) >suitable for me;<
14   P    →    [Is it¿
15             what do you like about it Esther?
16   E         um: (3.0) er >the food< (0.8) yeah is: >quite good< er: but it's (.)
17             everyday f- western food.
18   P    →    is it¿ [(.) what do they give you: to eat.
19   E                [yeah
20   E         er (.) potatoes,
21   P    →    oh yes.
22   E         yeah (.) everyday potatoes, er: a:nd (0.6) sometimes got er:(.) beef
23             (0.8) lamb chops (.) and: (.) others (.) like noodles ...
```

First, topical sequences were structured: the topic was introduced with one or two closed questions (one to introduce the topic (e.g in l. 1 above), another to elicit background information relevant to it), and this was followed by explicit requests for elaborated responses (e.g., 'Tell me about ...' in l. 5 above). Pam gave regular feedback on the candidate's turns, via news markers (e.g. l. 5, l. 14, l. 18, l. 21), echoes (e.g. l. 3), assessments and formulations.

The interaction with the male interviewer, Ian, showed a number of features which contrasted strongly with these (Brown, 2003, p. 11):

```
1    I    →    ... >in Kelang is it- is it many Malay or there a lot of Chinese or (.) or
2         →    what is it (.) in Kelang (.) [the population.<
3    E                                      [yeah more Malay.
4    I    →    >more Malay is it.<
5    E         °°mm°°
6    I    →    °right.° (1.2) erm (.) >what about the< foods there.
7              (1.2)
8    E         er: they are Indian food (.) Chinese food (.) a:nd Malay food
9              [(.) th]ey are a:ll (0.8) mix.
10   I         [ mhm]
11             (1.0)
12   I    →    they're mixed are they.
13   E         yea:h (0.4) all mix (0.6) e:verything (xxxxx) hhnhhn
14   I    →    yeah? (.) >is it good that way is it.<
15   E         yeah hhh.
16             (1.2)
17   I    →    ah- which is the spiciest food.
```

Ian's questioning techniques were less explicit and used closed questions (l. 1, l. 2, l. 6, l. 17), statements, echoes (l. 4, l. 12) and tokens such as 'Yeah?' (l. 14); he was also much less likely to acknowledge or otherwise respond to Esther's talk.

Was it the case then that Pam's and Ian's gendered subjectivity was evident in the interaction, with consequential arguably unfair consequences for the candidate? Before reaching this conclusion, Brown analyzed another pair of interviews in which again the candidate, this time male, scored significantly lower with one interviewer than with the other. But this time both interviewers were female (Cath and Jean). The interviewers were again found to have distinct interviewing styles, with the candidate scoring more highly with Cath, who again appeared to be more supportive. With Jean, with whom the candidate got a lower score, there was more interruption and talking over the candidate (ll. 10, 13, 15, 17), which appeared to inhibit him. Jean also produced rapid-fire closed questions (ll. 1-3) to which the candidate had little option to respond reactively (Brown, 2005, p. 191):

```
1   J   →   wha- what's the distribution of income what I mean by that is that .hh
2           are there some very poor people and some very rich or a lot of middle
3           class people (.) how- how is it based.
4   L       e:r middle class (.) I think middle class er
5   J       a lot of [middle class?
6   L                [a lot of middle class.
7   J       okay are there some very poor? (.) or [m-
8   L                                             [poor erm I (.) I don't think so it
9           [just (.) a small [amount (.) of them very poor
10  J   →   [no              [oh right .hh and what about very rich (.) are there
11          some very rich people?
12  L       yah [>quite a lot of very<
13  J   →       [yeah so: SO: quite a big middle class (.) [mainly. (.) probably a =
14  L                                                      [yeah middle (.) °middle =
15  J   →   = [bit like Australia?
16  L       = [class°
17  J   →   [you know a large middle [class? .hhh okay =
18  L       [yeah                    [middle class
19  J       = .hh (.) ^what about if somebody erm (1.0) somebody <is poor and =
```

On the other hand, describing Jean's behaviour in terms of 'interruptions'
begs the question interactionally; they could perhaps be read as supportive. For example, O'Loughlin (2002) counted Coates's 'typical' features of
male/female conversation in IELTS interviewer data and found the counts
to be unrevealing. He showed that many overlaps were facilitative of talk,
and needed to be seen in context. If then Jean is to be read as 'supportive',
then all three female interviewers are supportive. Is this the elusive
gender effect? Or is the gender effect simply a function of competence
in the institutional role of interviewer? Is it possible, in fact, to distinguish
'institutional' and 'gendered' identities in this interactional data?

In summary, then, Brown found abundant evidence of the institutional role of the interviewer in the micro-interactional data but
ambiguous evidence of gendered subjectivity. Are the differences in
interviewing style an issue of competence as interviewers, rather than
gender? Or is competence a function of gender here? This is an example of the difficulty of disentangling the evidence of the subjectivity
associated with a particular discourse given that we are subject to
multiple discourses. We will return to the issue of the performativity
of gendered subjectivity in interaction in the next chapter.

6.4 RECONCILING THE TWO SOCIAL ORDERS

Given the existence of the interaction order, in any interaction there
are potentially two kinds of social action happening: the social action

in the interaction order (the micro-level of the detail of interaction), and the social action of big D Discourse (the macro-level of social categories such as gender, sexuality, institutional identities, and so on). What does the existence of two independent orders imply for their relationship? A parallel with the study of physiological processes may be drawn. One of the great achievements in the history of medicine occurred in the seventeenth century with the publication by William Harvey of an account of the circulation of the blood in the human body. In the same century Robert Hooke initiated the conceptualization and study of cell biology using a microscope; subsequent work identified the mechanisms for transmission of ions across the cell wall. We can think of the circulation of the blood as an example of a macro-structure of the human body; the cell is an example of a micro-structure. Clearly, the two accounts need to be compatible, if both are correct. In other words, any account of the circulation of the blood in the human body, given that at some level it involves cellular processes, must be compatible with what is known about the biology of the cell. In the same way, Conversation Analysis advocates would argue, any account of the operation of macro-sociological forces must be compatible with what is known of the interaction order. In other words, once the existence of the interaction order is accepted (and the evidence for it, after over fifty years of work, is massive), then the social action of discursive forces at the macro-level must also be visible within the social action of the interaction order. For Goffman, as for CA practitioners, 'the institution of interaction underlies the operation of other social institutions, mediating the business they transact' (Heritage, 2009, p. 301).

Given the complexity of the interaction order, and the effort required to analyze it, there is a tendency simply to ignore it and to attempt a more immediate and direct analysis of the effect of the macro-social order of discourse in interaction. In fact, practitioners of discourse analysis in other schools such as Critical Discourse Analysis and Discursive Psychology, and other sociolinguists of a socially critical bent, often express impatience with the project of Conversation Analysis, and its exacting demands. In particular, they claim that what they see as the procedures and assumptions of CA, with its focus on identifying features of the interaction order, make it blind to the operation of macro-social discursive regimes in discourse (Pennycook, 2001). This has led to fierce debates between advocates of CA, particularly Schegloff, and its critics (see, for example, the exchanges in Cicourel, 1992; Schegloff, 1992a, 1997, 1998a, 1998b, 1999; Wetherell, 1998; Billig, 1999a, 1999b). In a debate with proponents of Critical Discourse Analysis, an approach which attempts to reveal the ideological basis of textual organization, including in spoken texts, Schegloff (1997, p. 180) articulates clearly what is at stake:

> There is nothing in the preceding analysis which necessarily either undercuts or underwrites critical discourse analysis. The upshot is only that critical discourse analysis be applied to a world refracted through the prism of disciplined and molecular observation, observation at the level of the lived reality of the events which compose it, and not to the world as refracted through the prism of 'casual' vernacular observation, constrained neither by the discipline of interactional participation nor by that of systematic empirical inquiry.
>
> Though it prompts impatience in those who aspire to more global claims and assertions, over and over again close examination of brief exchanges which may initially appear to casual inspection to be utterly unremarkable, or even transparently characterizable in vernacular or commonsense terms, turn out to yield rather more complex, and differently complexioned, understandings. More sweeping accounts appear then to depend on *not* examining single moments or episodes closely, and this may help understand the common impatience, and often intolerance, of close analysis . . . this, and the fact that such analyses often yield results uncomfortably at variance with commonsense understanding or ideological predilections.

We will look at this debate further in the next chapter.

6.5 CONCLUSION

In this chapter we have seen how macro-level institutional roles such as health visitor, language test examiner and news interviewer and interviewee are visible in the micro-level detail of interaction. But are other subjectivities constituted within discourse ('big D Discourse') also regularly visible at the micro-interactional level? If so, given the, in principle, independence of the two levels, how is this achieved? In other words, how is the operation of big D Discourse mediated at the micro-interactional level? Is the level of interaction simply a place in which discourses are inscribed, as it were automatically? This cannot be the case, given the independence of the interaction order, in which coordination is not just given but is achieved, turn by turn. In interaction, we may be able to see the operation of discourses in what we may think of as real time, turn by turn, so that if there is inscription, it is an inscription that is demonstrably oriented to by participants and built, step by step, not simply given.

The notion of turn-by-turn building of interaction corresponds in an important way to the notion of *iterability* in poststructuralism, that is, that nothing is given a priori, as it were, but has to be achieved in each iteration. This has two important consequences. Firstly, we might expect to be able to see in interaction the routine inscription and re-inscription of discourses in the orientation of participants. Further, it is possible that in interaction we may *fail* to see evidence of the operation of discourses; this will have important implications for our understanding of the impact of discourses on everyday life. And finally, as Butler and Derrida remind us, the process of iterability also leaves open the possibility of slips, of failures of inscription. The interaction order, then, is a site where resistance to discourses may be observed. We will consider each of these possibilities in relation to discourses of gender in the following chapter, in an analysis of a discussion in a university class of the notion of gender as 'performed' (see Chapter 2 above).

6.6   SUGGESTIONS FOR FURTHER READING

Fundamental texts in the ethnomethodological and Conversation Analytic tradition include Heritage (1984) on the beginnings of ethnomethodology in the work of Garfinkel, the collected lectures of Sacks (1992), with an illuminating introduction by Schegloff (1992b), and the first volume of Schegloff's own definitive account of CA (Schegloff 2007b). Useful introductions to CA can be found in Wooffitt (2005), Liddicoat (2007), Ten Have (2007) and Sidnell (2010). Benwell and Stokoe (2013) is a sympathetic treatment of CA in the context of a more general discussion of discourse and identity; Speer (2005) also situates CA within a broader discussion of a variety of approaches to discourse analysis. Blommaert (2005) is an example of a socially critical scholar who makes the conventional case against CA, unsuccessfully in my view. The debates between Schegloff and proponents of Critical Discourse Analysis and Discursive Psychology can be found in Cicourel, 1992; Schegloff, 1992a, 1997, 1998a, 1998b, 1999; Wetherell, 1998; and Billig, 1999a, 1999b.

7 Discourse and Subjectivity in Face-to-Face Interaction (2): Inscribing Gender

7.1 INTRODUCTION

Discourses of gender pervade social life. As we saw in Chapter 2, in poststructuralist accounts of subjectivity we iteratively perform our gendered identities in order to make ourselves recognizable as normally gendered subjects. Discourses of gender, like other discourses, typically define behaviours indicative of what is considered to be 'abnormal' as gendered behaviour so that there is pressure on individuals to avoid displaying any such signs; what is 'normal' is defined by default as 'non-abnormal'. Thus, individuals are permanently required to offer evidence to others of their 'normality' in gendered terms by the details of their behaviour, including what they say, their gestures and so on. In this way the discursive regime operates at the level of everyday social interaction. But this raises the question we began to explore in the previous chapter: is this view of the performativity of gender, so central to poststructuralist accounts of gendered subjectivity, compatible with what is known about the social order at the level of interaction, as revealed, for example, by the techniques of Conversation Analysis?

As we saw in the previous chapter, there have been a number of responses to this general problem of the relation of these macro- and micro-orders of sociality. One is to ignore the problem presented by the existence of the interaction order altogether, and to assume, in the case of gender, for example, that the macro-structure of patriarchal power is simply 'beamed down' to the fine details of interaction, in which it is automatically acted out. This assumption is criticized by Goffman in his famous paper 'The Neglected Situation' (1964). He writes (p. 134):

> At present the idea of the social situation is handled in the most happy-go-lucky way. For example, if one is dealing with the language of

respect, then social situations become occasions when persons of
relevant status relationships are present before each other, and
a typology of social situations is drawn directly and simply from chi-
squaredom: high-low, low-high and equals. And the same could be said
for other attributes of the social structure. An implication is that social
situations do not have properties and a structure of their own, but
merely mark, as it were, the geometric intersection of actors making
talk and actors bearing particular social attributes.

I do not think this opportunistic approach to social situations is
always valid ... It can be argued that social situations ... constitute
a reality *sui generis* ... and therefore need and warrant analysis in their
own right, much like that accorded to other basic forms of social
organization.

While the focus of Conversation Analysis is on revealing the structure
of the interaction order, it is not in principle blind to the existence of
other orders of sociality, as some of its critics have assumed. It insists
on the recognition of the interaction order, but it also recognizes the
role of gender, as of other macro-social categories, as potentially
(although not necessarily always) influencing interaction at the
micro level. It sees gender as 'omnirelevant', that is, it is potentially
relevant in interaction at any moment. But not necessarily so; gender
becomes relevant when gender is demonstrably oriented to by the
participants in interaction, and when it is, it is observable not so much
in the content of what people say, as in the micro-details of interaction – the interaction order.

In this chapter, then, we will consider issues arising from what we
will argue are these complementary perspectives, the macro and the
micro. We will begin by looking at ways in which close analysis of
interaction has contributed to debates on the operation of patriarchal
discourses in interaction. We will look briefly at two sites for this
debate: first, a famous text on the operation of gender in interaction
by Schegloff (1997), originally presented in a colloquium at an applied
linguistics conference on differing approaches to discourse analysis;
and second, a study by Kitzinger and Frith (1999) on refusals in date
rape. This will be a prelude to the main part of this chapter, an analysis
of a discussion of the performativity of gender among young adult
students in a university setting. Here we will argue that close analysis
of the interaction among the students demonstrates their routine
reproduction of gendered subjectivity in their actions, even as they
are debunking gender stereotypes in the overt content of their speech.
The extended example demonstrates the way in which the techniques
of Conversation Analysis lend themselves well to poststructuralist
discourse analysis, particularly in revealing the iterability in

performance which is so central to the poststructuralist perspective on social interaction.

7.2 THE DEBATE ABOUT THE RELEVANCE OF GENDER

The question of the appropriate way to analyze the interaction order, and the relation of the interaction order to macro-orders of discourse, is the subject of a series of debates between Emanuel Schegloff on the one hand, and adherents of Critical Discourse Analysis and Discursive Psychology on the other hand, who (among others) have criticized Conversation Analysis for what they see as its neglect of the broader social context. Schegloff and others have long argued, following Goffman, that the interaction order (the micro-level) is in principle an organization of social life independent of other kinds of organization of social life at the macro level (e.g., gender). In the words of Drew and Heritage (1992, p. 48): 'The rules of conversation operate in ways that are, in principle at least, independent of the extradiscursive identities of the participants ... the turn-taking rules themselves operate in terms of locally constructed discourse statuses rather than, for example, positions in a social hierarchy.' This means that, for example, the preference structure rules (the sequence of preferred moves) identified in CA operate in a single way independently of gender: they are the same for male and female speakers.

How, then, can gender be inscribed in interaction? Schegloff warns us against a simple top-down reading of the impact of gender in discourse as potentially resulting in misleading conclusions. In a paper presented at a symposium on the question of the relevance of extra-textual context in the analysis of discourse (Schegloff, 1997), he sets out his argument via an analysis of some data from a telephone conversation in which a divorced husband (Tony) learns from his ex-wife (Marsha), who lives hundreds of miles to the south, that their young adult son's car has been vandalized during a visit to her, leaving it undriveable. The son (Joey) is stranded and dependent on his friend Steve to take him to pick up the car later. Marsha, for whom the vandalism is no longer news, focuses on what now needs to happen, not on the event itself, whereas Tony is reacting to the news which he is hearing for the first time. The relevant part of the data is as follows (Schegloff, 1997, p. 173):

```
35   Tony:            What's he gonna do go down and pick it up later? Er
36          →         somethin like (    ) [well that's aw]:ful
37   Marsha:                           [H i s friend ]
38   Marsha:   →     Yehh[is friend Stee-  ]
39   Tony:      →         [That really makes] me ma:d,
40                         (0.2)
41   Marsha:    →     ·hhh Oh it's disgusti[ng as a matter a'f]a:ct
42   Tony:                              [P o o r J o e y,]
```

This can easily be read in gendered terms as displaying classical male interactional behaviour with a female, that is, marked by overlaps and interruptions on the part of the male, and so might be cited as an example of gendered discourse in which the patriarchal structure is evident. Schegloff instead chooses to focus on how the couple deal interactionally with Tony's response to the news of the vandalism, which involves what is called an 'assessment' ('Well that's awful') (Pomerantz, 1984). Assessments are evaluations of the quality or the character of an event or a piece of behaviour and interactionally display a recurring preference structure, as follows: when an assessment has been issued by one party in a conversation, there is a strong normative expectation for the recipient to then issue a second assessment. If the second speaker wishes to communicate *agreement* with the first assessment, then the second assessment follows directly, is upgraded and is simple, as in the following example (Pomerantz, 1984, p. 62), in which A and B are both assessing a bridge party they have attended:

```
01   B:      Well, it was fun Cla[ire,
02   A:   →                      [Yeah, I enjoyed every minute of it.
```

In this example, A overlaps B's assessment and upgrades it. In this next example of this canonical preference structure in assessments J upgrades K's 'really funny' to 'hilarious' (Ogden, 2006, p. 1760):

```
01   K:    I find that guy (.) really funny no:w=
02   J:                                 =that Iris[h one
03   K:                                          [Irish guy
04   J:  → he's hila:riou[s
```

As these examples show, there is a preference for strong agreement with assessments, which is typically achieved, as in the above examples, using a matching assessment plus an upgrade. A second assessment which indicates *disagreement*, in contrast, is not usually communicated through explicit statements; typically it is communicated only indirectly, via a *weak* agreement, that is, an agreement lacking an upgrade. Such weak agreement, heard as disagreement, may in turn be followed by a repeated attempt by the first speaker to elicit the required upgrade from the second speaker, as in the following example (Pomerantz, 1984, p. 69):

```
01  G:        That's fantastic
02  B:   →    Isn't that good
03  G:   →    That's marvellous
```

On the basis of what is known about the preference structure for agreements and disagreements, then, Schegloff argues that what is going on in the interaction is that following Tony's assessment ('Well that's awful'), Marsha responds with 'Yeh', which constitutes weak agreement, effectively disagreement; to which Tony, in turn, responds with the canonical upgrade seeking agreement again: 'That really makes me mad.' Marsha is preoccupied with her son's plans to retrieve his car and, in neglecting Tony's assessment, runs the risk of appearing to disagree with it, an interpretation which Tony adopts. In other words, according to Schegloff, something other than the performativity of gender is going on here; we can make better sense of the data by examining the interactional micro-structure, and avoid jumping to conclusions about the interaction as exemplifying gendered discourse.

The fact that Conversation Analysis focuses on the interaction order does not mean, as is sometimes suggested, that it has nothing to offer studies of the larger social context of discourses of gender. In fact, the contrary is the case, as we shall see. In a well-known study entitled 'Just Say No? The Use of Conversation Analysis in Developing a Feminist Perspective on Sexual Refusal', Kitzinger and Frith (1999), as the title suggests, use the findings of CA on how refusal is normally done to inform their feminist analysis of 'date rape', an issue that has recently emerged in a different form with the passage of a law affecting educational institutions in California requiring both parties to explicitly consent to intimacy, and more recently still with the #MeToo movement. The California bill supersedes the 'No Means No' campaign of the 1990s, in which women were encouraged to be explicit in their refusal of intimacy rather than leaving it implicit, which might be misread as consent. Kitzinger and Frith are critical of the requirement in this campaign for 'bald, on record' refusals (Brown & Levinson, 1978), which studies of refusals in ordinary everyday interaction have shown are dispreferred interactionally (Atkinson & Heritage, 1984; Davidson, 1984; Drew, 1984; Pomerantz, 1984). While acceptances involve simple acceptances, without delay, as in:

```
01   A:        Why don't you come up and see me some[time
02   B:   →                                        [I would like to
```
                                                   (Atkinson & Drew, 1979, p. 58)

or

```
01   A:        We:ll, will you help me [ou:t.
02   B:   →                            [I certainly wi:ll.
```
                                                   (Davidson, 1984, p. 116)

Refusals are far more elaborate, marked by delays (brief pauses), prefaces or hedges such as 'Well', palliatives (expressions of appreciation, apology, etc.) and accounts (explanations, justifications or excuses), as in the following examples:

```
01   Mark:     We were wondering if you wanted to come over Saturday,
02             f 'r dinner.
03        →    (0.4)
04   Jane:  →  Well (.) .hh it'd be great but we promised Carol
              already.
```
                                                   (Potter and Wetherell, 1987, p. 86)

```
01   A:        Uh if you'd care to come and visit a little while this
02             morning I'll give you a cup of coffee.
03   B:   →    hehh Well that's awfully sweet of you, I don't think I
04             can make it this morning. .hh uhm I'm running an ad in
05             the paper and-and uh I have to stay near the phone.
```
                                                   (Atkinson & Drew, 1979, p. 58)

The fact that refusals are, as Kitzinger and Frith put it, an 'elegantly crafted interactional activity' (1999, p. 302) means that advice to women to 'just say no' involves a strategy that is routinely perceived as rude or hostile (Heritage, 1984, p. 268). What is more, men's familiarity with the normal way of refusing means that they can be in no doubt about the woman's attitude, and putting the onus on women to be direct and explicit, rather than expecting men to use their normal interpretive judgement, is a case of putting the responsibility on the victim rather than on the offender. Here, then, is an example of where the insights of CA can be used to further a feminist agenda. Kitzinger and Frith go on to interview young women about their experience of unwelcome sexual overtures, and they indeed show familiarity with the normal cultural conventions of refusal. Kitzinger and Frith were, for obvious reasons, unable to get actual data of refusals in such situations, so it will be helpful now to look at some other data where a Conversation Analysis of the actual data demonstrates the performativity of gender interactionally. We turn to this now.

7.3   GENDER AND PERFORMATIVITY: A DISCUSSION IN A UNIVERSITY SETTING

In this part of the chapter, an extended analysis will be presented of features of interaction in a multi-party setting in order to explore in detail the potential for Conversation Analysis to reveal the reality and the detail of gender performativity, so routine that it goes unnoticed by the participants, even (ironically) when they are discussing the notion of gender performativity itself. The setting is a tutorial (discussion section) in the first semester of a first-year Bachelor of Arts course called 'Self and Other' at an Australian university. The students in the tutorial are all around 17 to 19 years old; there are eight female students and a single male student ('Mikey'). The tutor, Carol, is an experienced teacher of undergraduate students. The tutorial follows lectures in this part of the course on gender and sexuality, in which the performed character of gender, and the link between discourses of gender and sexuality, have been extensively discussed. The tutorial occurs in the sixth week of the course, so that the members of the tutorial group are by now relatively familiar with one another, and with the tutor. After a general rather stilted discussion lasting a few minutes in response to Carol's question 'So what about masculinity and femininity, how are they performed? Do you think that part of the performance of masculinity is a performance of heterosexuality?', Carol livens things up by asking 'What's a man hug? Is a man hug actually an expression of ... ?' By 'man hug' she means not a full embrace, but a particular form of physical greeting between two men: each with a single arm raised parallel to his body clasps the hand of the other; each man then pulls the other towards him, and, after a brief contact (what one of the students calls 'a body bump'), the men release and pull apart again. A pat or rapid series of pats with the free hand on the other's back when their bodies are close together is an optional additional move.

In Extract 7.1, Carol requests a demonstration of the hug, which involves two male roles. Unfortunately, and ironically, Mikey, the only male in the class, claims not to know what a 'man hug' is, unlike several of the female students, who seem to know immediately what the tutor means. Gina, who is sitting next to him, teases him about his lack of familiarity – Mikey initially misunderstands the term as referring to a full embrace ('hugging a man') and takes some time before he manages to shake off this belief and understand what the tutor is referring to. A further difficulty in arranging the demonstration of the man hug called for by Carol is that Mikey is the only male in the room, apart from the cameraman videorecording the session; Carol briefly entertains the possibility of using him, but then decides to leave him alone. One of the female students appears to be on the point of nominating Jane for this role.

Extract 7.1

```
        Carol:   uh so (3.0) what what is the man (.) what's a man hug? Is a
                 man hug actually an expression of (.)
40      Mikey:   What's a?
        Carol:   a man hug we're we're
        Gina:    come on you know about man hugs= (.)
                 ((laughs))
        Carol:   =You don't know about man [hugs?]
45      Mikey:                            [What]=
        FS3:     =the man in the room
        Carol:   [You don't know what a man hug is?]
        Gina:    [You hug a man]
        Mikey:   oh, huggin' a man?!
50      Gina:    That's literally what it [is] a [man hug]
        Carol:   ((laughs))
        Mikey:                                   [Oh ok.]
                 ((class laughs))
        Mikey:   ok ok
55      Carol:   So we need a demonstration of a man hug
                 (1.0)
        S1:      We don't have another [man]
        S3:                            [We've only got]
        S:                             [Jane we need]
60      S:       ehh
                 ((class laughs and sighs))
        Carol:   so (.) [no we'll leave you alone] ((points to cameraman))
                 (.) we'll leave
        S6?:            [mm]
65               ((class laughs))
                 oh ok
        Carol:   so we [can have] [xxx]
```

This interaction is intended to engage the students in the question of discourses of gender and the notion of performativity of gender, topics which had been dealt with in detail in lectures the previous week, and appears to be succeeding. In Extract 7.2, the relativity and arbitrariness of gender as a performed, social phenomenon is emphasized: the tutor teases Jane, who is initially reluctant to demonstrate the 'man hug' ('I'm **not** a **man**'), that she needs to perform her 'inner masculinity', ironizing the essentialism of this notion; Jane in the end agrees, and, conveniently and somewhat appropriately in the light of the role she is to perform, it turns out that she has only the night before played a male role in an amateur theatre performance:

Extract 7.2

```
120   Carol:   Alright [um man hug] (.) demonstration.
      S:              [weird]
               ((laughter))
      Jane:    I'm not a man ((closed fist gesture))
               ((class laughs))
125   Carol:   no you actually you have to perform (.) uh your inner
               [masculinity]
      Jane:    [oh I have performed] [a man before
      S7:                            [She has performed as a man (.) [so it's
               all been
130   Jane:                                                         [I was
               a man in our college play last ni- last
      Carol:   Ok
      Jane:    [night] ((stands up))
               ((laughter))
```

In Extract 7.3, it turns out that Mikey, in contrast, still does not really understand what is required, so that he needs to be coached through his performance of the 'man hug' by Jane, and only at the end of the performance finally understands what it is.

Extract 7.3

```
136   Carol:   [all right Mikey] and and Jane=
      Mikey:   =I don't know, I haven't been practising [my man hug]
                                                        [((class laughs))]
      S6:      whereas [Jane has]
140   Mikey:           [Does it have to be] really quite manly? [Does it have
               to be manly?
      S:                                                        [get your
               pimp out]
      Jane:                                                     [I don't] (.)
      Jane:    It doesn't have to be really manly,
145   Mikey:   What are we doing though?=
      Jane:    =(just) you do this thing ((raises hand))
               ((laughter))
      Mikey:   oh yeah this ((pulls Jane towards him))
      Jane:    that one
150   Mikey:   and then ((bumps)) oh: yeah
               ((laughter))
      Carol:   [Oh]↑ ((rising and falling intonation in falsetto range))
      Jane:    [and then this around the back]
               ((steps away with waving hand gestures))
155   Mikey:   [Ok:]
      Jane:    I don't know what that is
      S2:                              [that's] ((makes thumbs up gesture))
      Carol:                           [that was] [great]
      Jane:                                       [it's like yeah] you're
160            a man ((repeats back patting gesture))
      S:       bash (?)
      Carol:   That was great
      Mikey:   She's [better than me at it] yeah ((pointing thumb towards
               Jane))
165   S6:            [yeah] ((laughs))
      Carol:         [That was good]
      S7:      I think Jane did it better than [Mikey did] (.)
      Mikey:                                   [yeah I know] (.)
               ((class laughs))
```

The students are clearly demonstrating an awareness of discourses of gender and that the performance of gender involves visible, culturally determined behaviours signifying a gendered subjectivity. The mocking tone of the episode suggests also a perspective on such discourses, perhaps suggesting the instability of gender roles and the ease with which they can be disrupted. But can the performed character of gender be so easily recognized, parodied and subverted? A micro-interactional analysis provides a different kind of perspective.

As we have seen, this performance by Jane and Mikey takes a while for the tutor to set up: the delay in organizing the demonstration of the 'man hug' is because of the absence of another man (the cameraman being briefly considered and rejected) and is compounded by Mikey's lack of understanding of the role. In Extract 7.4, in the interlude while the tutor tries to sort things out, Jane initiates exchanges with the other students at the table (all female apart from Mikey) involving characterizations of and attitudes to variations on the 'man hug'. In the following passage, Jane offers an assessment – 'stupid', 'one I hate' (line 67) of a particular variant of the man hug which she proceeds to characterize, partly verbally, and partly in gestures.

Extract 7.4

```
      Jane:   →   (It's) [stupid] (.) you know what one I hate (.) is when
                  they like (.) clasp like opposing hands ((gestures to
                  show clasping)) and do that sort of like (.)
70    Jane:       [half body like]        ((right shoulder forward))
      Mikey:      [ah yeah yeah] I get it ((brings right arm across body to chest))
      Carol:      [yeah]
      Gina:       [oh it's like a] (.)
      S:          [then why do you]
75    Gina:       [it's like a] [body bump] ((hits right forearm to
                  chest))
      S:          they slam    [each other down]
      S:          doof ((imitating noise of body bump)) [it's like the]
      Gina:                                              [oooh] ((noise
                  of body bump)) (.) and then they just walk away=
80    Jane:       =I eh I feel like that's a strong sort of display of
                  masculinity, the sort of like the grabbing and like the
                  going like this ((gestures of pulling toward))
      S:          [yeah]
85    Carol:      [ok] (.)
      S:              [yeah]
      Anne:           [Two gorillas]
      Jane:   →           [Stupid
```

Jane begins with a part description ('they like (.) clasp like opposing hands') accompanied by a gestural display (ll. 68–69) (Figure 7.1).

Figure 7.1   Jane: 'clasp like opposing hands'

Figure 7.2   Jane: 'half body like'

This is followed by a further characterization of the movement which relies more heavily on gesture and less on verbal description: 'and do that sort of like/half body like' (ll. 69–70), accompanied by a forward movement of her right shoulder (Figure 7.2).

Her formulation of the men as 'they' seems to define the women in the group as her audience. In fact, however, she is facing both Mikey and Gina across the long table at which they are all sitting, and he is attending closely to her description of the phenomenon (the 'man hug') that he has so far failed to recognize. He is the first to respond (l. 71) – 'ah yeah yeah I get it', accompanying the words with a gesture of

Figure 7.3   Mikey: 'ah yeah, I get it'

Figure 7.4   Gina: 'oh it's like a'

bringing his right arm and fist to his left breast, which he repeats, the second time with the sound of contact, in an alignment with her demonstration (Figure 7.3).

Gina, who is sitting next to Mikey, and thus also facing Jane, displays her understanding of the gestural account, and her affiliation with the assessment, with a mixture of gesture (she hits her right forearm to her chest) and verbal description ('it's like a body bump' – note that in this phrase the word 'body' echoes 'half body thing' in Jane's turn, and her body alignment, with an open stance ready for physical contact, mirrors Jane's) (Figures 7.4 and 7.5).

Figure 7.5 Gina: 'body bump'

Gina's contribution is verbally and sonically mirrored and upgraded by one of the female students sitting next to Jane ('they <u>slam</u> each other down') with accompanying sound effects ('doof'), imitating the noise of the body bump. Gina in turn acknowledges with her own vocalization the sound of the body contact ('oooh') and then describes the closing move of the sequence of moves constituting the 'man hug' ('and then they just walk away'). Jane now provides a different kind of assessment, more academic in character ('I eh I feel like that's a strong sort of display of masculinity'), reflecting in its formulation the academic character of the tutor's earlier incomplete question ('Is a man hug actually an expression of ... ?', itself an echo of the question that initiated the original discussion: 'So what about masculinity and femininity, how are they performed? Do you think that part of the performance of masculinity is a performance of heterosexuality?'). Jane further characterizes the physical gestures involved in the man hug, returning to the initial step of each man pulling the other man towards themselves: 'the sort of like the ... ', with a further, intensified verbal description, ('grabbing'), the characterization being completed non-verbally ('and like the ... going like this', accompanied by a gesture of pulling toward). Another student, Anne, offers an upgraded assessment: ('Two gorillas'). The sequence is brought to a conclusion by Jane's partly overlapping coda ('Stupid'), repeating the same phrase she had used to initiate the sequence in the first place. The word thus acts as a verbal framing for the whole episode.

What is striking in this episode is the collaborative and affiliative character of the responses of three of the other female students to Jane's verbal and gestural account of the variant of the 'man hug' that she thinks is 'stupid' and 'hates'. In the Conversation Analysis research tradition, 'the term affiliation [can be] used to describe actions with which a recipient displays that s/he supports the affective stance expressed by the speaker' (Lindström & Sorjonen, 2013, p. 351). This is echoed by Stivers (2008, p. 35): 'with the term affiliation I mean that the hearer displays support of and endorses the teller's conveyed stance'; by 'stance', Stivers means 'the teller's affective treatment of the events he or she is describing' (2008, p. 37). (Note that in our case, the 'events' are accounts of practices.) Affiliation can be achieved in a number of ways (Lindström & Sorjonen, 2013): laughter; response cries; prosodic matching and upgrading; and multimodal means: 'verbal and vocal resources, gaze, gestures and body orientation in making relevant and displaying (dis)affiliation' (p. 359). Stivers adds assessments, which 'are generally agreed to display affiliation ... with the speakers' (2008, p. 36).

We can see evidence of this affiliation among the other participants in multiple ways. Jane's audience demonstrate their hearing (and viewing) of her account, and their affiliation with her stance, in various readable ways. Sacks, in his *Lectures on Conversation* (1992), refers to a number of techniques for 'tying' the contribution of successive speakers to earlier speakers as ways of demonstrating how the first speaker has been heard. We have a number of these tying techniques here. First, given the prominence of gestures in Jane's account, the two audience members facing her – Mikey and Gina – demonstrate their uptake of her account using gestural means themselves. They emphasize the physicality of the contact between the two male participants: both collaboratively complete (Lerner, 2004) the trajectory of the gesture initiated by Jane by themselves, bringing the arm into contact with the chest, Gina more forcefully than Mikey. This gestural demonstration is elaborated verbally by naming the gesture ('body bump') and it is characterized verbally by an unnamed female participant: 'they slam each other down'; it is also elaborated sonically by utterances imitating the sound of the physical contact: 'doof', 'oooh'. In terms of affiliative assessments, Jane announces her stance clearly in her introductory remark: '(It's) stupid. You know what one I hate.' Several of these responses to her account can be read as second pair parts to this assessment. Such second pair parts typically involve upgrades when agreement is indicated (see earlier in this chapter for detailed discussion of the preference structure of assessments, with agreement preferred, indicated by an upgrade). The upgrading occurs in a suite of intensifications gesturally, sonically and verbally ('slam', 'doof', 'two gorillas'). Moreover, affiliation is achieved as well in the othering of men through deictic references, 'they' three times, from three different female participants. Jane indicates that her stance has been understood by her auditors by her closing repetition of the opening assessment ('stupid').

A further means of affiliation is through what are known as 'second stories' (Stivers, 2008). 'Second stories' are extensively discussed by Sacks (1992) in his *Lectures on Conversation*. He demonstrates that story-telling is a social practice, both in the way in which the initial story is designed to be heard by the speaker's audience, and by the way in which listeners demonstrate that it has been so heard. The hearer is implicated in the initial telling; and the function of the second story is to demonstrate to the first teller that their story has been heard in the way that the second speaker understands the first story to have been intended to be heard. Thus, the first storyteller will announce the point or moral of the story before telling the story, so that the story is to be heard as illustrating that point, and also thereby indicating when the story will have reached its conclusion.

We have an example of a second story as affiliation in Extract 7.5, which follows the episode of Jane's demonstration of 'what one I hate'. During Carol's further attempts, at l. 80, to get Mikey and Jane to demonstrate the 'man hug', complicated by Mikey's claimed lack of familiarity with the sequence of gestures involved and Jane's general reluctance to take the role of a man, Anne takes the floor and playfully demonstrates a further variant of the man hug and shares her amusement with the other students.

Extract 7.5

```
80   Carol:  →   [so Jane and Mikey we need a] (.) a man hug
     S:           [You know what one I]
     Anne:  →   [I don't understand (.) so they go in for the bump]
                 ((fist bump gesture)) How do they always
                 ((laughter))
85   Anne:  →              [know (.) ((fists coming together in
                 front of chest gesture)) that they're gonna do]
     Jane:        ((laughs)) [Why me?]
     Gina:                   [What are you gonna do, a man hug.]
                 ((laughter))
90   Anne:  →   [do something else]
     Gina:        [just go for it]
```

```
      Anne:    →  [they always know] what to do=
                     ((laughter))
      Mikey:      =I don't know
95    Anne:    →  when they go in [for the bump]
      S:                          [There/Yeah]=
      Anne:    →  =but I'm like  [there are so many different things]
      Gina:                      [I dunno what a man hug is]
      Mikey:                     [I haven't practised] my man hug
100                [recently]
                     ((laughter))
      Gina:       [a man hug is just like]=
      Carol:      [what was that?]
      Anne:    →  =[mate??] you know how they go in for like the the fist
105                bump ((indicating with hand))
      Anne:    →  and then they do (.) [like cool things with like]
      Carol:                           [Oh is it called a fist bump?]
      Anne:    →  they do a hand shake then they go in the
      Anne:    →  bump and then they do like ((makes explosive sound,
110                hands wide apart))
      Carol:                                       [oh the bump]
      Anne:    →  and then ... how do they know what [to do 'cause they
                     always do it]
                     ((laughter))
```

Here is Anne's contribution, represented simply as content, not interaction – it may be helpful to understand the trajectory of her point,
given how broken up it is with other people's turns:

> I don't understand … so they go in for the bump [fist bump
> gesture]. How do they always know [fists coming together in front
> of chest gesture] that they're gonna do something else? They
> always know what to do when they go in for the bump. But I'm
> like there are so many different things, you know how they go in
> for like the fist bump [indicating with hand] and then they do
> like cool things with like they do a hand shake then they go in
> the bump and then they do like [makes explosive sound, hands
> wide apart] and then … how do they know what to do? 'cause
> they always do it.

There are a number of features of the interactional construction of
this contribution which constitutes itself as a second story. Anne
aligns herself with what has gone before, in several ways. She does
so lexically, first by again positioning the men whose behaviour she is
describing as 'they', and secondly by her echoing of the word 'bump'.
Further, Anne's detailed account of the choreography of the men's
joint action, accompanied by a series of gestures and sonic representation of the action, affiliates not only with Jane's gestural account but
also with the earlier contributions of the other female students
(Figures 7.6 and 7.7).

Figure 7.6   Anne: 'they go in for the fist bump'

Figure 7.7   Anne: 'and then they do like [makes explosive sound, hands wide apart]'

Anne's ironic appreciation of the coordination required in the joint execution of these rituals by the men focuses on the participants' dependency on signals from the interactional partner, and the possible confusion that may be involved. She invites further contributions from the other participants, as her expression of wonder at the men's ability to coordinate is framed as a (mock) question. What follows in Extract 7.6 are two further second stories, second to Anne's account, from Gina, and then Holly, who each give mocking accounts of mistiming in the coordination:

Extract 7.6

```
        Gina:                           [and the best is when] the other
115                     person doesn't know what they're doing and someone
                        tries to do it and the other person is like uhhhm
                        ((indicates awkward clash with hands))
                        [nup got no idea]=
        S:              [yeah I d-]=
120     Holly:          =You know what's good is like when they go for like
                        like the horizontal but you're sitting there going
                        for like the vertical ((makes horizontal and
                        vertical fist gestures))
                        ((class laughs))
        Holly:          [and then...]
        Gina:           [or (like) the High five]
125     Holly:          [oh]
        Gina:           ((laughs))
        Carol:      →   Alright [um man hug] (.)demonstration.
        S:                      [weird]
                        ((laughter))
130     Jane:           I'm not a man ((closed fist gesture))
```

Again the shape of the contributions aligns with the earlier ones. Gina's 'and the best is when' is both an echo of the mock admiration in Anne's phrasing, but also an echo of Jane's 'You know what one I hate', as indicating a series ... 'one', 'the best'. (Much earlier, in l. 81, an unidentified female student, possibly Holly, makes an unsuccessful bid for an account, 'You know what one I', which exactly mirrors Jane's 'You know what one I hate'.) Gina's gestural accompaniment to her account also mirrors the gestures of the previous speakers (Figure 7.8).

When Holly's turn comes, its phrasing ('You know what's good is like when') further mirrors Jane's phrasing. 'You know' echoes Anne's earlier formulation, 'you know how they go in for like the fist bump', with its appeal to shared knowledge among the audience. Holly echoes earlier contributions in referring to men as 'they' but replaces this subsequently by impersonal 'you' as she imaginatively and humorously engages with the confusion ensuing. She also, like the previous speakers, extensively uses gestures to demonstrate the variants of the man hug that she is mocking (Figures 7.9 and 7.10).

The episode ends in affiliative laughter, and Gina congratulates Holly by 'high fiving' her – using this joint gesture as a sign of

Figure 7.8   Gina: 'the other person is like uhhhm [indicates awkward clash with hands]'

Figure 7.9   Holly: 'they go for like like the horizontal'

the successful coordination of the joint storytelling, perhaps in ironic counterpoint to the uncoordinated confusion of the hapless males.

Figure 7.10   Holly: 'but you're sitting there going for like the vertical'

The series of accounts of variations on the man hug by the four female students is an example of what Ryave (1978) calls 'a series of stories', although here we have examples not of narratives, but of accounts of practices. Ryave draws attention to two features of series of stories of the type found here. First, the stories or accounts illustrate a moral point, which is rendered explicit, usually by the provider of the first account; this is precisely what Jane does by labelling the practice she describes as 'It's stupid' at the beginning and end of her account ('stupid'), as was noted above. Second, the relationship of the series of accounts is a relationship not only of topic and the organization of the account but of the significance of the accounts. Ryave distinguishes two types of procedure for establishing the significance of a series of stories or accounts. In the first, each successive story 'utiliz[es] the very same significance statement of a preceding story in order to construct its own recounting' (p. 127). This is illustrated in the successive turns of Anne, Gina and Holly, where the point of Gina's and Holly's stories, as series of stories following Anne's, is the problem of coordination in the achievement of the man hug, the point raised by Anne as a rhetorical question, leading to absurd effects when the coordination misfires, as it does in Gina's and Holly's accounts. Ryave describes the effect of the series of stories of this first type of procedure as follows: 'A succeeding story-teller can show, in and through his story, that and how they understand, support, sympathize and agree with the preceding story' (p. 128). In the second type of procedure, the significance of the first story is reinterpreted: this is what Anne does in relation to Jane's earlier story, focusing not on the stupidity of the practice but on the wonder that it can be brought off at all, given how absurdly complex it is. The continuity is thus a continuity of significance, this time the absurdity of the details of the male behaviour; note that all three accounts are accompanied by laughter. And relevantly for the argument of this chapter, Ryave has demonstrated, as these examples themselves show, that 'The meaning and relevance of a description ... is not a pre-given matter to be analytically determined solely by inspecting the particulars of some recounting, but is itself best conceived as a social activity that is interactionally negotiated and managed in and through the emerging particulars of a situation' (p. 130) – that is, it is a phenomenon of the interaction order.

The mock rehearsal by the women of behaviours deriving from discourses of masculinity presents a dilemma for the only male present, Mikey. As the tutor and other class members look to him for a demonstration of the masculine ritual which is the subject of this discussion, they do not find what the discourse of masculinity would lead one to expect. Mikey feels obviously uncomfortable with the ascribed performance role; it is clear that this behaviour is not part of his repertoire as a man; his masculinity is not constructed or performed in this way. We have seen how his initial complete lack of understanding slowly gives way to a recognition of the behaviours being described, but it is one thing to recognize this in the behaviour of other men, and another to enact it in his own. In Extract 7.7, an awkward demonstration of the 'man hug' by Jane and Mikey finally ensues: they rise from the table and approach each other while the rest of the class watches.

Extract 7.7

```
136  Carol:     [all right Mikey] and and Jane=
     Mikey:  →  =I don't know, I haven't been practising [my man hug]
                                                 [((class laughs))]
     Gina:      whereas [Jane has]
```

```
140  Mikey:   →         [Does it have to be] really quite manly?
                        [Does it have to be manly?
     S:                 [get your pimp out]
     Jane:              [I don't] (.)
     Jane:              It doesn't have to be really manly,
145  Mikey:   →  What are we doing though?=
     Jane:              =(just) you do this thing ((raises hand))
                        ((laughter))
     Mikey:             oh yeah this ((pulls Jane towards him))
     Jane:              that one
150  Mikey:             and then ((bumps)) oh: yeah
                        ((laughter))
     Carol:             [Oh]↑ ((rising and falling intonation in falsetto
                        range))
     Jane:              [and then this (around the back)]
                        ((steps away with waving hand gestures))
155  Mikey:             [Ok:]
     Jane:              I don't know what that is
     Mikey:                                   [that's] ((makes thumbs up
                        gesture))
     Carol:                                   [that was] [great]
     Jane:                                              [it's like yeah]
160                     you're a man ((repeats back patting gesture))
     S:                 bash (?)
     Carol:             That was great
     Mikey:   →  She's [better than me at it] yeah ((pointing thumb
                        towards Jane))
165  Gina:              [yeah] ((laughs))
     Carol:             [That was good]
     Holly:             I think Jane did it better than [Mikey did] (.)
     Mikey:   →                                         [yeah I know] (.)
                        ((class laughs))
```

Mikey repeatedly indicates his lack of identification with the 'manly' discourse being represented by the man hug. He explicitly states his hesitation ('I don't know'), humorously apologizes for his lack of competence ('I haven't been practising my man hug') and seeks instruction on the style of the performance required ('Does it have to be really quite manly? Does it have to be manly?'); and finally explicitly asks for instruction on the moves to be rehearsed ('What are we doing though?') (Figure 7.11)

Through these questions he constructs himself as a novice, an apprentice; and ironically it is Jane who adopts the role of expert and simultaneously the provider of reassurance in relation to his lack of confidence in the role. She answers his question with reassurance ('It doesn't have to be really manly') and then begins the demonstration of the sequence of gestures required ('Just you do this thing', accompanying the first gesture of raising the hand). This triggers recognition in Mikey via a twice-repeated change of state token ('oh yeah'), once ('oh yeah this') as he follows Jane's lead and again as he

Figure 7.11   Mikey: 'What are we doing though?'

completes the gesture, thus framing his actions. Jane confirms that he has identified what needs to be done ('that one'). The class laughs and Carol signals mock surprise with an exaggerated change of state token; but it is not over yet. Jane reminds Mikey of a further gesture, the back pat followed by release, which Mikey acknowledges ('OK') as they perform it. Evaluative commentary on the quality of the performance follows from the tutor, who repeats 'That was great' twice, but Mikey disparages the quality of his own performance, pointing out that Jane's was superior: 'She's better than me at it.' Despite the tutor's insistence that 'That was good', both Gina and Holly endorse Mikey's self-deprecating evaluation, Holly explicitly: 'I think Jane did it better than Mikey did', an evaluation which Mikey apologetically accepts ('Yeah I know').

The position of Mikey is in interesting contrast to the roles enacted by the women as they characterize the male behaviour that they recognize as informed by discourses of masculinity. Mikey's lack of immediate recognition of and identification with the masculinity embodied in the man hug ritual puts him in something other than the space created by the masculinist discourse with which the female students demonstrate they are thoroughly familiar. Moreover, as we have seen, in the earlier episode (Extract 7.4) he responds to Jane's account, even as she is characterizing it as 'stupid' and 'the one I hate': he affiliates with her account, both verbally and gesturally, and with laughter, in a way that is similar to that of the female students. The response, while certainly to Jane's description, as his 'ah yeah yeah, I get it' indicates, is still perhaps not to her assessment 'stupid'.

In summary, as the female students constitute themselves as experts on this kind of male behaviour, and as critics of it, they display a consciousness of gender as performed and show familiarity with that aspect of the discourse of masculinity – ironically, in contrast with the sole male student in the group. They do so jointly and cooperatively. In this interaction work, they can be said to be performatively producing their gendered identities, in the very act of mocking the gendered behaviour of men, and as part of an academic discussion of the performative nature of gender. And the performativity is not only in the substantive *content* of their turns but in the *interactional structuring*, through the collaborative orchestration and displays of affiliation that the structure of their turns communicates.

The female students display themselves as 'experts' on men's stereotypical performance of masculinity in the 'man hug'. While mocking it, they acknowledge and underline the reality of masculinity *as discourse* – for example, it is not clear that the women are reporting on their actual observation of male behaviour, or of their understanding of representations of that behaviour, for example in television or film. And we may also ask for whom these male performances are intended, performances that are reported in such detail by the women? For other men, certainly, to make themselves recognizable as (heterosexual) men, but it is also surely significant that the displays are attended to by women, for whom the men are rendered 'Other' – we have noted the recurrence of a distancing 'they' throughout the women's accounts. In this carefully coordinated and orchestrated joint activity among the women students, we can clearly observe the performativity of gender within the interaction order. The performativity is achieved interactionally; it is through the coordinated interaction that the action of affiliation is observably accomplished. The performativity of gender in Mikey's interactional behaviour is at odds with the performativity of gender which is the subject of his female fellow students' mocking accounts; in this particular iteration, we observe 'slippage', the lack of instantiation of the expected discourse, a space in which we can see the (temporary) possibility of agency, even of resistance to discourse norms. But it is clear that this resistance comes at some cost, of embarrassment and caricature. Significantly, a few moments later (Extract 7.8), Mikey achieves a more typically masculinist role as he holds the floor over a number of turns in exclusive interaction with the tutor and offers an authoritative analytical account of the male behaviour being discussed:

Extract 7.8

```
Mikey:                                    [but I] feel also
        like if a man went up and like hugged another man like
        properly= ((accompanies with gestures))
Carol:  =yeah=
```

```
     Mikey:   =it would stand out more (.) than if a woman went up and
              hugged another woman
220  Carol:   Why does it stand out?
     Mikey:   Wh- because of the whole idea (.) that= (.)
     Carol:   =yeah
     Mikey:   um= (.)
     Carol:   =Sorry I'm just [pushing the]
     Mikey:                   [men yeah] men (.) are uh like the (.)
              neutral (.)
     Carol:   mm yep
     Mikey:   [and]
     Gina:    [yeah]
     Mikey:   and the positive and women are the negative↑ so it's more
              obvious↑ like if a woman (.) wears a suit it's less
              obvious than if a man wears a dress, (.)
230  Carol:   Mm
     Mikey:   if [uh...]
     Carol:      [because] the man is the marker of what's [normal]
     Mikey:                                               [exactly]
              so (.) if yeah=
     Carol:   =yeah=
     Mikey:   =yeah=
     Carol:   =yeah
```

To sum up: what is interesting in these extracts is that while the participants in the discussion are clearly able to achieve a perspective on the performative character of gender intellectually, and to recognize masculine discourses and to evaluate them critically, at the very same time they continue to enact the performativity of gender, as is revealed through attention to what is going on in the interaction order. While the students at one level easily orient to the concepts that have been presented in the lectures preceding this tutorial, and in the tutorial itself, at another level they persist in their gendered performativity, presumably quite unconsciously. The performativity of gender is so deeply naturalized that it is difficult to become conscious of it, even at the very moment when at the conscious level it is the actual topic of conversation. And yet although the performativity of feminine gender is seamlessly coordinated among the contributions of the women, there is a temporary failure of performativity in line with discourse norms on the part of Mikey, illustrating the slippage that can occur in any particular iteration. This instability in the operation of discourse is precisely the point that Butler seizes on as being the locus for possible resistance, and change.

7.4 CONCLUSION

Much more could be said of the data in the extracts from the university tutorial, and the analysis offered here is by no means exhaustive. A number of concepts from the literature of Conversation Analysis on face-to-face interaction, including assessments, affiliation, tying, colla-borative completion, second stories and series of stories have been used to establish the way in which gendered performativity can be studied at the micro level. The analysis reveals the iterative displays of gendered action visible in the structure of minute-by-minute interaction among the participants in this tutorial group. What is remarkable is that struc-turing of these displays is at one level being attended to by the partici-pants as they contribute to the seamless patterning which mutually enacts their affiliation as women but is never consciously foregrounded. Instead, and ironically, the overt character of the women's reports is intended to mock and debunk men's gendered ways of behaving in interaction. This chapter has shown the potential of Conversation Analysis to reveal the operation of social structure, the discourse of gender, in the filigree of interactional behaviour. It thus reveals itself as a promising candidate for poststructuralist discourse analysis. We will go on in the following chapter to consider the potential for another aspect of the work of Harvey Sacks, membership categorization, to contribute to this kind of analysis.

7.5 SUGGESTIONS FOR FURTHER READING

The relationship of Conversation Analysis to feminist scholarship is controversial, but much original and important work is being done. Key papers in the argument about the acceptability of Conversation Analysis as a methodology for doing feminist research include Kitzinger (2000, 2006, 2007), Wilkinson and Kitzinger (2007) and par-ticularly Speer (2012). A number of feminist scholars have explored the possibility of reconciling Conversation Analysis and poststructur-alism more generally, including Wetherell (1998), Speer and Stokoe (2011) and in particular the book by Speer (2005), who has an extended and very helpful discussion of the topic. Speer there and elsewhere (2002; 2012) addresses epistemological concerns about marrying Conversation Analysis with feminist research.

8 Categorizing Others in Casual Conversation

In what terms do we refer to people's identities in casual conversation? I recently asked my friend Claire to tell me about her son-in-law Mike, whom I had met briefly at a party but otherwise did not know. Mike and his wife Catherine have a young daughter, not yet two years old. She replied in the following terms: 'He's a good person. He's ethical, sets high standards for himself. He's very intelligent. He worships Catherine. And I say this a lot, but if he could breast feed his daughter he would – he's totally involved in her upbringing – a modern father, you could say.' Notice that Claire uses category terms as a way of characterizing Mike: 'a good person', 'a modern father', and goes on to elaborate in her further remarks ('he's totally involved in her upbringing') what she means by her use of these categories.

Casual conversation is full of such examples. Think of how people respond when you ask them to describe someone important in their world but whom you have not met. You might ask, 'What's your new boss like?' or 'What's your son's girlfriend like?' and you will notice that people often use social category terms to characterize the person – 'He's French', 'She's a real intellectual' and so on. These everyday practices provide potential evidence of the terms in which we categorize others, terms dictated by the discourses that circulate in our social worlds; the evidence is abundant in the material of everyday conversation.

In Chapter 4, we looked at how racist discourses are visible, often fleetingly but unmistakably, in everyday language use, both written and spoken. In this chapter, we examine a specific feature of conversation, the way people characterize others in terms of social categories and what are seen as their associated behaviours and characteristics. This feature was noted in the early work of Harvey Sacks on what he called Membership Categorization. Sacks was interested in how identity categories were deployed and oriented to by conversational participants, as part of his exploration of the interaction order. While Sacks ultimately did not pursue this line of research, for reasons that are discussed by Schegloff (1992b), it continues to be influential in studies of subjectivity – although it remains controversial, as it again raises the issue of the relationship between the macro- and micro-orders of sociality that we explored in the previous chapter. In this chapter we will consider further that debate and the potential for Membership Categorization Analysis as a tool to analyze the operation of discourses of subjectivity in the language of everyday interaction.

8.2   WHAT IS MEMBERSHIP CATEGORIZATION ANALYSIS?

Membership Categorization Analysis (MCA) (Hester & Eglin, 1997; Day, 2013; Fitzgerald, 2015; Housley & Fitzgerald, 2015) is an approach to the analysis of the use of category terms and their deployment in casual conversation which was developed in the early work of the sociologist Harvey Sacks (1992) and has become a substantial research field since. It addresses the question of the extent to which, and the way in which, participants in everyday conversational interaction categorize the identity of individuals who are the subject of talk. It deals with the way in which people are seen and see each other as members of categories with stereotypical characteristics. It is thus potentially a powerful tool for studying the operation of racist, sexist and other kinds of discourse in ordinary conversational settings.

Central to the analysis proposed by Sacks is what he calls a 'Membership Categorization Device' (MCD), consisting of *categories* and *rules* for using them. Sacks observes that such categories typically come in what Sacks calls *collections* or groupings, meaning categories that naturally go together, for example family categories such as 'son', 'daughter', 'father', 'mother', 'husband', 'wife' and so on. Schegloff (2007a, p. 467) provides further examples:

> [male/female]
> [Buddhist/Catholic/Jew/Muslim/Protestant ...]
> [American/Canadian/Dane/French ...]

BUT NOT
[male/female/technician]

MCDs involve rules for drawing inferences from the categories. Sacks famously gives a simple example: when we read in a child's story 'The baby cried. The mommy picked it up', we hear the 'mommy' as the mother of the child. This is because of what Sacks calls a 'consistency rule': if a person in a story such as this is categorized as a member of the collection 'family', 'then other persons in the setting may be referred to or identified ... by reference to the same or other categories from the same collection' (Schegloff 2007a, p. 471).

A crucial feature of categories in Sacks's account is that they are what Sacks calls 'inference-rich': 'A great deal of the knowledge that members of a society have about the society is stored in terms of these categories' (1992, Vol. I, p. 40). In other words, the categories are the subjects of discourses in which the characteristics of category members are specified in some detail. Categories have associated with them what Sacks calls 'category-bound activities', 'conventional expectations about what constitutes a category's normal behaviour, such that absences are accountable' (Stokoe, 2010a, p. 63). For Schegloff (2007a, p. 469), 'The membership categories ... are the store house and the filing system for the common-sense knowledge that ordinary people have ... about what people are like, how they behave, etc.' The link created in discourse between membership categories and category-bound activities is such that mention or viewing of category-bound activities can lead to identification of membership of the category to which the activity is bound. A poignant example of this is given by Sacks in his data from telephone calls to a Suicide Prevention Centre. The following exchange occurs in the course of a call by a man to the Centre:

A: Is there anything you can stay interested in?
B: No, not really.
A: What interests did you have before?
B: I was a hair stylist at one time, I did some fashions now and then, things like that. (Sacks, 1992, Vol. I, p. 46)

A few minutes later the listed activities are spelled out as category-bound activities (bound to the category 'homosexual male'):

A: Have you been having some sexual problems?
B: All my life.
A: Uh huh. Yeah.

B: Naturally. You probably suspect, as far as the hair stylist and, uh, either
        one way or the other, they're straight or homosexual, something like
        that.   (Sacks, 1992, Vol. I, p. 46)

This last example, involving category-bound activities (in this case
occupations) conventionally associated with homosexual males, can
be reinterpreted as a citation of discourses of homosexuality. In fact,
key features of the MCD can be better understood in terms of the
poststructuralist approaches to subjectivity advocated in this book.
For example, the fact that categories come in collections is because
discourses are coherent and offer accounts of particular subject
positions within the discourse; they do not identify categories at
random but group certain categories of subject as having a relation
to others. Gail Jefferson provides an example of a collection of categories informed by discourses of race:

ROGER: *That* was a vicious school there – it was about forty percent Negro,
          bout twenny percent Japanese, the rest were rich Jews, heh hhh
                                                          (Jefferson, 1990, p. 64)

Second, the fact that category-bound behaviour is the subject of discourses and therefore unchallenged by a lack of fit between the category and an individual explains some further features of membership
categorization pointed out by Schegloff (2007a). For example, category
knowledge does not change because of evidence to the contrary:

> If an ostensible member of a category appears to contravene what is
> 'known' about members of the category, then people do not revise
> that knowledge, but see the person as 'an exception', 'different', or
> even a defective member of the category. (Schegloff, 2007a, p. 469)

Schegloff goes on to point out that people who are objectively members of categories but lack the competence to carry out the behaviours
associated with that category may see themselves or be seen as 'pho-
nies'. On the other hand, people who are not recognizable as members
of that category, but who in fact display such behaviours, may be seen
as merely 'imitating' the behaviour associated with categories they
don't belong to. These things reflect the fact that discourses construct
categories and specify category-bound activities, and subjects are seen
and see themselves in terms of those discourses; they are unrecogniz-
able otherwise. This has a further implication: that any member of
a category may be seen as a *representative* of that category. Sacks points
out that at the time of the assassination of President Kennedy in 1963,
before the identity of the assassin was known, people were afraid that

it might have been carried out by a member of a category to which they themselves belonged. Sacks (1992, Vol. I, p. 42) writes:

> [In] the hours between the assassination of President Kennedy and the determination of who it was, and thus what category it was that performed the act ... you can see persons reporting themselves as going through 'Was it one of us right-wing Republicans?', 'Was it one of us Negroes?', 'Was it a Jew?' etc. That is, 'Was it me?' in that sense.

It is clear, then, that discourses construct membership categories and define category-bound activities. This aspect tends to be ignored or downplayed by many practitioners of MCA, because of its local, situated focus on members' practices in interaction. For example, in discussing the MCDs 'family' and 'stage of life' in Sacks's famous discussion of the interpretation of the sequence 'The baby cried. The mommy picked it up', Hester and Eglin (1997, p. 19) state:

> In neither case [MCDs 'family' and 'stage of life'] does he [Sacks] subscribe to the view that these devices have transcendental relevance. That such devices are made and found relevant by members across a variety of social occasions speaks only to their relevance for members, not to any cultural pre-programming regarding usage.

Given the ethnomethodological focus of MCA, that is, on the relevance for members in the particular occasions of the use of categorization devices, rather than on the categorizations as it were in their own right, this comment makes sense. Nevertheless, the categories themselves don't come from nowhere, and their existence potentially provides empirical evidence of the discourses circulating in social groups at any particular moment, and the subjectivity choices they entail.

Sacks (1992) gives some classic examples of the uses members make of categories. These include defining and policing group membership. For example, in a study of teenagers in the 1960s attending group therapy sessions, the members used the term 'hotrodder' to describe themselves, as a way of drawing boundaries around who did and did not count as legitimate members of that category. The category was contrasted with the category term 'teenager', which was seen as an adults', outsiders', term. In the following example using data from the same group therapy session, the choice of category terms serves another purpose, of disguising personal feelings to the other members of the group. One of the participants asks about the absence of another member, Louise, the only female in the group. In doing so, he uses the generalized gender categories 'opposite sex' and 'chick' to forestall any inference that his concern might have been personal ('he wasn't going to say he likes her or anything like that' – Sacks, 1992, Vol. I, p. 60):

KEN: So did Louise call or anything this morning?
DAN: Why, didju expect her t'call?
KEN: No, I was just kinda hoping that she might be able to figure out some
        way t-to come to the meetings and still be able t'work. C'z she did
        seem like she d-wanted to come back, but uh she didn't think she
        could.
DAN: D'you miss her?
KEN: Well in some ways yes, it's- it was uh nice having-having the oppo-
        site sex in-in room, you know, havin' a chick in here.
                                            (Sacks, 1992, Vol. I, p. 597)

Sacks also points out that Ken's use of such categorizations as a way of referring to Louise is a safe compliment categorization in that it attends to the possible perceptions of other group members, who are all male – in contrast to a remark such as 'it was nice having someone smart in the room', smartness being one of 'a whole range of categories which also *can* apply to any other person in the room' (p. 60).

Studies of membership categorization seem to be of two broad types. In the first, studies ask of the data, 'In what terms are individuals categorized? What activities and qualities are associated with such categorizations?' This focus on the 'what' of members' categorization practices in some ways resembles that of Critical Discourse Analysis but instead is based on participants' rather than analysts' understandings of the categories, and their immediate contextual relevance. This kind of analysis can be done with non-interactional material, including written material (as in the famous example 'The baby cried, the mommy picked it up', which comes from a book of stories told by children). Studies of the second type focus more, or additionally, on the work the membership categorization does in the unfolding sequential interaction and is thus very close to the focus of Conversation Analysis.

An example of the first approach to analysis can be found in a paper by Nguyen and Nguyen (2017), who studied how children in two Singapore families are socialized into understanding the category-bound activities of the membership category 'good boy/

girl', and hence of the salience of that category in interaction with parents. While the data are interactional (between the child and the parent), the focus is not on the interaction order as such, in terms of turn-taking, for example. In the following example from their data (Nguyen & Nguyen, 2017, p. 31), the father is trying to persuade Alex, four years and zero months, to take a shower, which he is reluctant to do.

```
1    Dad: TAKE↑SHOW↓ER:.
2    Ale: I don't want to take shower:.
3    Dad: why:.
4         (0.4)
5    Ale: cau:[se
6  → Dad:     [are you a good boy:?
7         (2.5)
8    Dad: are you a good boy:?
9    Ale: ↑°nuh:::::°
10   Dad: you're a good boy:.
11        good boy:. take shower f[irst.
12 → Ale:                         [I not good boy.
13        (0.3)
14 → Dad: ↑THEN ↓you're naughty boy:.
15        (1.5)
16   Dad: are you a naughty boy?
17        (0.2)
18   Dad: ((hiccups)) HICK
19        (2.5)
20   Dad: ↓are you a >naughty< boy?
21        (3.0)
22   Dad: ↑good boy take shower first.
23 → Ale: I don't want to-
24   Dad: ((hiccups)) HI[CK
25   Ale:              [I don't want to take shower.
26   Dad: but. (.) ((gently)) ↑what (.) ↓are you going to do::
27        (0.4)
28   Ale: I want to play my toy:.
```

In this extract, the category 'good boy' is contrasted with its opposite, 'naughty boy' – these are the two subject positions presented to Alex. The parent is socializing Alex into an understanding of what being in the category 'good boy' entails: 'good boy take shower first' (Alex wants to 'play my toy').

In the following example (Nguyen & Nguyen, 2017, p. 29), the parent is socializing Jayden (three years and nine months) into an understanding of the category 'good boy' and its category-bound activities, this time with a heavily religious overtone:

```
208  Jay:  I like <transformers>.
209  Dad:  <transforme:rs>. yes. =so we thank Jesus
210        for:? having: for giving us tee vee:
211        (0.2)
212  Dad:  and at the same time we ask Jesu:s? please:?
213  →     help Jayden to be a good boy:? so that when
214        mommy switches off the tee vee::?
215        (0.2)
216  Dad:  or anybody  switches  off the tee vee?
217        that you will not be angry, and will not do
218        anything wro:ng.
219        (0.2)
220  Dad:  mhm? so we ask Jesus for: good things like that
221  →     or to help you to be a: (0.2) a good boy,
222        Jesus will give it to you:.
223        (0.4)
224  Dad:  'kay?
225        (0.2)
226  Dad:  so you ask Jesus Jayden? so Jesus- Jesus
227        is hearing your prayers, Jesus (.) ↓okay I'll help
228  →     J- Jayden to be a? (0.2) <good boy:.> ↑thank you
229        Jesus, then? <↑good ↓ni:ght.> ↑a::↓men.
230        (0.4)
231  Dad:  father [son holy spirit.
232  Jay:         [why Jesus say(.) okay:
```

Here, the category-bound activities in focus include accepting the authority of the parent in deciding the limits of television watching and refraining from anger or retaliation when the child's wishes are not fulfilled.

A further example of a study of the 'what' of membership categorization practices can be found in an interview study by Stirling and Manderson (2011) of women who have had a mastectomy as a consequence of breast cancer. Here again the analysis does not focus on turn-taking, but on how the use of membership category terms and category-bound activities variously positions the informant in relation to the interviewer. In Example 5 in their data, below, Glenda (G) has had a mastectomy as part of her treatment for breast cancer, and R is the researcher. The category term here is the generalized pronoun 'you', referring to the group of breast cancer survivors who have experienced mastectomy, which excludes the researcher:

```
G:  [you] go for six weeks-
    is- is the-
    (0.8)
R:  mm=
G:     =time that they give everybody,
    you know six weeks-
    (0.5)
    or if have- if your cancer's worse you might go on for a bit longer,
```

```
(0.8)
you can go on for however long your doctor wants you to but,
(1.5)
```
(Stirling & Manderson, 2011, p. 1588)

In Example 8 in their data, given below, the generalized 'you' refers to the membership category of 'mothers', to which the researcher does belong:

```
G:   You know when you've got babies you-
     (0.5)
     it's mother and baby you know?
R:   [yes]
G:   [you] want to hold them close to your body and your chest and,
     k-
     (0.6)
     kiss them and cuddle them and,
     (0.4)
     all those things I couldn't do with her?
```
(Stirling & Manderson, 2011, p. 1589–90)

Stirling and Manderson (2011, p. 1590) comment:

> In all the examples discussed in this section, Glenda uses generalized you to invoke a 'membership category' to which she belongs. The specific category at issue in each case is discernable in some cases from direct mention ('*it's mother and baby you know?*'), but more usually from the 'category-bound activities' expressed by the predicates and other lexical items in the clauses containing *you*, including nominals in construction with possessive generalized *you* (*your babies, your cancer*) (Sacks, 1992). Furthermore, the context of participation in a sociological interview in a study targeting women who had had breast cancer arguably makes always relevant the membership category of '(breast) cancer patient/survivor'. In examples (3)–(5), Glenda situates herself as a member of a group – of people who have been diagnosed with and treated for breast cancer – which excludes the addressee. In contrast, in examples (6)–(9), Glenda positions herself and the interviewer as within an in-group of women – mothers – who share knowledge, understanding and experience of matters of childbirth and mothering.

Further examples of the analyses of MCA focusing on the 'what' of members' practices can be found in Baker (2000), who gives a number of examples in schooling contexts involving both written texts and spoken interaction.

We have seen so far that many of the categories and category-bound activities available to members derive from prevailing discourses and provide evidence of orientation to those discourses in the lives of speakers. But it is important to emphasize that MCA is less interested in the categories themselves and their origin in and reflection of social discourses than in the practices of members as they deploy membership categories. In other words, the specifics of the local interactional level, as ever, complicate the relationship to the macro-order of discourse.

What motivates a speaker to choose a particular social category to characterize an individual? This is the issue of *selection*. Sacks (1992, Vol. I, Lecture 6) points out that each person being talked about could be categorized in terms of any one of the sets of categories that people use in conversation – sex, age, race, religion, occupation, for example – but typically only one may be chosen. Why is it chosen by the participants at this point? 'Why this, now'? Sacks asks:

> For any person being talked of, how is it that Members go about selecting the set in terms of whose categories that person is going to be talked of? ... Members ... use one set's categories for some statements and another set's categories for other statements ... we're going to have to find out how they go about choosing among the available sets of categories for grasping some event. (Sacks, 1992, Vol. I, p. 41)

Schegloff uses this fact to caution us against the 'promiscuous' use of MCA, 'which can steer analysis into dangerous, shallow waters indeed' (Schegloff, 2007a, p. 465). He writes:

> Actual membership in a category is not a sufficient basis or grounds for using it to categorize someone ... So there must be other grounds – grounds of relevance – both for interactional co-participants and for researchers ...
>
> It is because multiple [categories] are available ... that relevance is the issue, and how categories ... become relevantly oriented to becomes a key topic for inquiry ...
>
> If we want to characterize the parties to some interaction with some category terms, we need to show in principle that the parties were oriented to that categorization ... in producing and understanding – moment by moment – the conduct that composed its progressive realization. In doing so, we will need to be alert to the ways in which the parties make accessible to one another these orientations, because that is the most serious and compelling evidence of their indigenous-to-the-situation status. If we can show that, we neutralize the equivocality which otherwise subverts category-based inquiry. (Schegloff, 2007a, pp. 474–5)

For Schegloff, this is a major constraint on the usefulness of the analysis of categories and category-bound activities in conversation, which he notes Sacks ultimately abandoned:

Commonsense knowledge cannot properly be invoked as itself providing an account, rather than providing the elements of something to be accounted for. In my view, Sacks abandoned the use of 'category bound activities' because of an incipient 'promiscuous' use of them. (Schegloff, 1992b, p. xlii)

Schegloff (2007a) notes a further potential difficulty in the conduct of the social category membership: not every attribute or description reference to persons in terms of social categories is susceptible to analysis using MCA. He argues that it is necessary to distinguish between person-reference using features that conversational participants treat as attributes, and membership categorization using category terms and category-bound activities – but that this distinction is not always easy to make. He gives an example of a conversation where two students, Ava and Bee, are talking about a teacher in Bee's linguistics course who is introduced in the following way by Bee:

```
01  Bee:  nYeeah, ˙hhThis feller I have-(nn)/(iv-)'felluh'; this
02        ma:n. (0.2) t! ˙hhh He ha::(s)-uff-eh-who-who I have fer
03        Linguistics [is real]ly too much, ˙hh[h=]
```
(Schegloff, 2007a, p. 478)

Bee explains that another class member, a nurse, has pointed out to her that the lecturer has a slight physical handicap, a stiffness in his fingers. Bee now explores the implications of the fact that he is characterized for her as a 'handicapped person', a characterization she accepts:

```
22  Bee:                         [Yihknow] she
23        really eh-so she said you know, theh-ih- she's had
24        experience. ˙hh with handicap' people she said but ˙hh
25        ih-yihknow ih-theh- in the fie:ld.
26        (0.2)
27  Ava:  (Mm:.)
28  Bee:  thet they're i:n[::.=
29  Ava:  [(Uh [huh)
30  Bee:  [=Yihknow theyd- they do b- (0.2)
31        t! ˙hhhh they try even harduh then uhr-yihknow a regular
32        instructor.
33  Ava:  Righ[t.
34  Bee:      [˙hhhh to uh ins(tr)- yihknow do the class'n
35        evr[ything.] An:d,
36  Ava:     [Uh huh.]
37  Bee:  She said they're usually harder markers 'n I said wo::wuhh
38        huhh! ˙hhh I said theh go, I said there's- there's three
39        courses a'ready thet uh(hh)hh[hff
40  Ava:                               [°Yeh
41  Bee:  I'm no(h)t gunnuh do well i(h)n,
```
(Schegloff, 2007a, p. 479)

The attributes or descriptions potentially treatable as part of a Membership Categorization Device in this extract include the following: 'feller', 'man / who I have for Linguistics', 'a woman / in my class / who's a nurse', 'has a handicap', 'Handicap people' 'they try even harder', 'they're usually harder markers'. How would we determine which ones are part of such a device? Activities bound to the category of 'people with a handicap' – 'trying harder', 'marking students' work more harshly' – are treated as significant by Bee, who feels they have implications for her chances of success in the three courses she is taking that are taught by this 'handicapped person'. In this case, it is clear that Bee herself is seeing the teacher's physical stiffness in terms of the social category 'handicapped' with its category-bound implied behaviours. Not all references to personal attributes are like this; they are often simply used by a speaker to introduce or identify a person who may be unknown to the interlocutor. Schegloff is critical of work in MCA which does not make a clear distinction between the orientation to category terms of analysts on the one hand and that of members on the other. Clearly, not all studies of membership categorization are susceptible to this problem. For example, the studies by Nguyen and Nguyen (2017) and Stirling and Manderson (2011) cited above demonstrate that the participants themselves are oriented to the category terms they are deploying.

A number of researchers working in MCA have tried to respond to the various objections to membership categorization that Schegloff has raised. Butler and Fitzgerald (2010, p. 2464), for example, claim that 'The sequential and inferential orders of interaction can be examined in parallel in a way which contributes to both endeavours.' Hester and Eglin (1997, p. 9) cite an early study by Schegloff (1972), which examines 'the interrelatedness of sequential organization (. . . "insertion sequences") and categorization work ("selecting formulations")'. Watson (1997) argues for an integration of sequential analysis and categorization and cites, for example, Sacks's work on telephone calls in which the 'Caller' and 'Called' category pair in telephone calls 'appl[ies] to people in a way that has them as *categories* and not merely the person they are, somebody with a name' (Sacks, 1992, Vol. II, p. 544, emphasis in original). These categories, in turn, influence the way in which the conversation may be closed. Such categories as 'Caller'/'Called' in telephone conversations are categories internal to a specific type of interaction and may thus be less relevant to the kinds of subject positions in discourse which have been the focus of this book.

More relevantly for our purposes, and in a study which clearly demonstrates the potential for the analysis of membership categorization to be integrated into an analysis of the significance of turn-taking, Stokoe (2010) reports on the way gendered categories are deployed in police interviews. In a study of police interviews with men who have been arrested for the offence of domestic violence, but not yet charged with it, Stokoe examined whether, and if so in what way, the men's self-representation in the interview might affect the level of the charge or whether they were charged at all. She recorded 22 hours of such interviews and identified instances of the phrases 'I wouldn't hit a woman' or 'I don't hit women' by the men charged. In each case, she analyzed the location of the phrase in the ongoing interaction: specifically, the design of the turn in which the phrase appeared, the action(s) being done in that turn, and the design and action-orientation of the police officers' response. For example, she examines whether the police officers topicalized the categorization or simply responded to the 'primary action' of the turn.

Through the analysis, Stokoe identified a practice she calls 'category-based denial', whereby speakers accomplish the social action of denying by making claims about their character, disposition and category membership. Those charged deploy the categories 'men who hit women' and 'men who don't hit women', and claim to belong to the latter. The denials may occur either in response to an accusation or as part of a longer narrative account. While such denials are not topicalized by the police officers or mediators interviewing them, neither is the categorization disputed or remarked upon, but left 'naturalized' in the interaction.

The 'reflexive co-determination' (Schegloff, 2007a, p. 473) of identities, as in the Caller/Called example, involve what Butler and Fitzgerald (2010, p. 2463) call tacitly invoked membership categories:

> A much less explored domain of Sacks's work on membership categories relates to the ways in which MCDs are invoked without the use of any category terms, i.e. the relevance of category membership and devices beyond instances of description. One aspect of this involves examination of the 'reflexive co-determination' (Schegloff, 2007: 473) of action and membership – that is, how sense is made of particular actions by virtue of the locally relevant identity of the speaker, and similarly how the speaker's identity is implicated in the characterization of social action ...

An interest in the tacit aspects of membership categorization, as opposed to the use of formulations of categories and activities, has the potential to lead to what Schegloff (1992) described as a 'promiscuous' analytic application of interpretations to members' conduct that is not grounded in the details of talk in the way that is generally regarded to be essential in conversation analytic research.

There are, of course, powerful examples of this approach in classic Conversation Analytic work on institutional talk of the kind we discussed in Chapter 6. For example, we saw how *and*-prefacing in questions characterizes the work of health visitors and distinguishes it from casual conversation (Heritage & Sorjonen, 1994). Similarly, we saw how distinctive were the rules for turn-taking in news interviews (Clayman & Heritage, 2002). But it is not clear how the notion of implicit membership categorization adds to the insights of this work, other than to underline the potential for Conversation Analysis to establish the institutional character of the interaction by establishing evidence of an orientation to institutional roles among the participants. The Conversation Analysis approach is always to work from the ground up, so to speak, from the data itself, to see what practices, and hence what possible subject positions, emerge from it. It does not look in the first instance at the subject positions, that is, the membership categories.

8.3 CONCLUSION

Overall, it seems that the promise of Membership Categorization Analysis as a form of poststructuralist discourse analysis is most obviously evidenced in studies whose focus is on the actual categories that are evident in conversation and in other texts, including written texts. What distinguishes this work from related work in Critical Discourse Analysis is its attention to the context in which the categories are used, and in conversation in particular, to the orientation of the conversational participants to the categories and the uses that they make of them. But this emphasis on members' own orientations proves analytically somewhat difficult, as Schegloff points out, and runs the risk of what he calls 'promiscuous' analysis if it is not grounded in detailed contextual and interactional analysis. The second approach situates attention to membership categories within an analysis of interaction, and is methodologically rigorous, subject to the disciplined analysis demanded of Conversation Analysis. At its best, for example in work by Liz Stokoe and others, it is not open to the criticisms of Schegloff. But its promise has already been affirmed in earlier work within the CA tradition on institutional discourse, and it is unclear what can be gained from the superimposition of analytic terms such as Membership Categorization Devices and the like in this kind of work, particularly where it involves tacitly invoked membership categories. As work on MCA continues to flourish, the usefulness and coherence of the two approaches will be consolidated and clarified. Certainly, some of the most interesting work in language and subjectivity is being carried out under the umbrella of MCA, for all its theoretical and analytic difficulty.

8.4   SUGGESTIONS FOR FURTHER READING

The fundamental texts on Membership Categorization Analysis (MCA) are the discussions in Sacks's lectures (1992), and the critical discussion by Schegloff (1992b) in his introduction to that volume. Schegloff (2007a) is an invaluable resource. Classic introductions to MCA can be found in Hester and Eglin (1997) and Silverman (1998); more recent introductions are available in Day (2013), Fitzgerald (2015) and Housley and Fitzgerald (2015). Stokoe (2010) is an example of the use of MCA in a way that is compatible with the assumptions of Conversation Analysis, so meeting Schegloff's objections to its 'promiscuous' use. A special issue of *Discourse Studies* (14(3), 2012) features an excellent lead article on MCA by Stokoe (2012) with responses from a number of other scholars.

9 Technologies of Subjectivity: Language Tests and Identification

9.1 INTRODUCTION: THE SHIBBOLETH

The operation of power through discourse sometimes uses language itself to classify subjects. Language has long acted as a means for group categorization. We experience this routinely in daily life when we use someone's accent or other features of their speech to 'place' them, geographically and/or socially. The operation of language as a tool of power through identification is expressed in the biblical story of the shibboleth. A single word, *shibboleth* – a Hebrew word meaning 'an ear of wheat', or perhaps 'a stream' – functioned, with a given pronunciation, as a password at the end of a military conflict in the Bible (Judges 12:4–6). In the biblical story, knowing the 'appropriate' pronunciation of the password gave protection; not knowing the password spelled death. Single-word shibboleths are found in every age and culture, including in our own times – examples have recently been reported in Nigeria and in Assam, India (further examples are discussed in McNamara and Roever, 2006). In Nigeria in March 2010, according to a newspaper report,[1]

> Funerals began taking place for victims of the three-hour orgy of violence on Sunday in three Christian villages close to the northern city of Jos, blamed on members of the mainly Muslim Fulani ethnic group . . .
>
> Survivors said the attackers were able to separate the Fulanis from members of the rival Berom group by chanting 'nagge', the Fulani word for cattle. Those who failed to respond in the same language were hacked to death.

[1] 'Over 500 Christians slaughtered in Nigeria', *Times of Malta*, 9 March 2010, www .timesofmalta.com/articles/view/20100309/world/over-500-christians-slaugh tered-in-nigeria.297421, retrieved 10.3.2018.

In Assam, in north-east India, a linguist reports on his blog,[2]

> At the height of the 'Assam Agitation' nationalist movement from 1979 to 1985, people were often made to count from 1 to 7 to see if they were 'Assamese' or an illegal 'Bengali'. The idea is that in Assamese the number 7 is pronounced [xat] with a velar fricative [x] . . . while in Bengali/Bangla the number is pronounced [sat] . . . The instant the speaker said [sat], they were hit and taken away (or worse).

Shibboleth-like language tests can be operationalized not only by a single word, but by any use at all of language associated with the social category which is the potential target of violence. At the final, decisive battle of the English Civil War, defeated Royalist soldiers tried to escape undetected from the victorious Republican army. The Royalist Highlander soldiers, who spoke Scots Gaelic, were identified by their inability to speak English, and put to death; those who were English managed to pass as Republicans by speaking English (Manley, 1691; see McNamara & Roever, 2006).

Nor need the use of the shibboleth test be restricted to a single event or occasion of violence such as this. The more general phenomenon of the use of language knowledge as a means of social identification can assume a particular significance in contexts of violence. Stories from the Holocaust tell of Jews disguising their linguistic identity through shedding accents, pretending not to understand German when their knowledge of the related language Yiddish gave them at least a passive understanding, and disguising their bilingualism to pass as monolingual speakers of Polish, Lithuanian and so on. Bilinguals in the Khmer Rouge terror in Cambodia disguised their competence in French, as this was taken as a sign of education, and educated people were targeted. In such cases, then, we may speak of a regime of shibboleth consciousness: first, no single word or its pronunciation is involved, but speech in general; second, the relevance of the shibboleth is not limited to a particular moment but is a sustained feature of social relations; third, the threat of violence is pervasive, so that conformity with the regime must be sustained at all times, or the social and political consequences felt. As we saw in our discussion of Foucault at the beginning of this book, the notion of life being conducted in conformity with a pervasive regime of surveillance through language, where the details of language behaviour offer opportunities for assessment and interpretation, extends beyond settings of intergroup

---

[2] 'Shibboleths in North-east India', *Consonant Aspirations*, 3 February 2011, www .consonant-aspirations.com/search?updated-max=2011–02-07T02:30:00– 08:00&max-results=7&start=7&by-date=false&m=0, retrieved 10.3.2018.

violence to social relations in general. Among the specific techniques of surveillance Foucault identifies is the examination:

> The examination combines the techniques of an observing hierarchy and those of a normalizing judgment. It is a normalizing gaze, a surveillance that makes it possible to qualify, to classify and to punish. It establishes over individuals a visibility through which one differentiates and judges them. That is why, in all the mechanisms of discipline, the examination is highly ritualized. In it are combined the ceremony of power and the form of the experiment, the deployment of force and the establishment of truth. At the heart of the procedures of discipline, it manifests the subjection of those who are perceived as objects and the objectification of those who are subjected. (1977, pp. 184–5)

Formal language assessment procedures can thus be seen as potential technologies of subjectivity. They may represent the point of insertion of powerful discourses in the life of an individual, who is recognized and made visible through the procedure of assessment. In Foucault's words (1977, p. 187):

> Disciplinary power ... is exercised through its invisibility; at the same time it imposes on those whom it subjects a principle of compulsory visibility. In discipline, it is the subjects who have to be seen. Their visibility assures the hold of the power that is exercised over them ... The examination is the technique by which power ... holds [its subjects] in a mechanism of objectification.

The discourse of homophobia, for example, was made concrete in a language test designed to exclude homosexual recruits from the Royal Canadian Mounted Police in the 1950s (Kinsman, 2004). As one of a battery of psychological tests, potential recruits were hooked up to equipment designed to detect physiological responses to emotional stimuli, as in lie detection procedures, and were asked to read aloud a vocabulary list containing ordinary, familiar words with and without a secondary meaning in the (at the time) secret homosexual jargon – words such as *fruit* (= 'homosexual'), *trade* (= 'casual sexual partners') and *cruise* (= 'seek out casual sexual partners'). Any physiological response triggered by recognition of the slang meanings would alert the recruiters to a state of language knowledge in the recruit which would then identify him as a member of the category 'homosexual', an identification which was associated with harsh psychological, social and even criminal sanctions in that era.

Further examples of the way language tests are used in the service of policies of exclusion include tests used in Germany and

Finland following the collapse of the Soviet Union, designed to reduce the number of ethnic Germans and Finns from long-standing communities in the former Soviet Union wishing to exercise their legal right of return to the countries which their ancestors had left often centuries earlier. In the German case, a test of knowledge of the increasingly obsolete ethnic variety of German spoken traditionally in the community concerned was used (Schüpbach, 2009). The use of the test exploited the fact that a vigorous programme of linguistic and cultural assimilation of the community on the part of the Soviet Government in the post-war years meant that many of the younger members of the community wishing to emigrate to Germany had no competence in the variety being tested and therefore were prevented from exercising their right of return. Being linguistically incompetent, they were not recognized as 'true' ethnic Germans. In this and the Finnish case, the tests used were technically very sophisticated and well managed, and the fact that they gave no grounds for criticism in terms of technical quality helped to disarm critics of the policy.

However, shibboleths have in history also served an inclusive, protective function, with shibboleth-like passwords acting as a form of legitimate self-defence. During the Second World War, on the day that Nazi forces invaded the Netherlands in 1940, the password used in the Dutch navy was *schavuit* ('rascal'), one which potential German infiltrators would find difficult to pronounce. Czech resistance groups are said to have used the Czech word *řeřicha* ('watercress') as a password during the Nazi occupation with a similar protective intent of detecting spies. So can we distinguish between just and unjust uses of the shibboleth? This will depend on your view of the justice of the cause in which it is deployed – and in the case of a 'just' cause, the quality of the shibboleth itself. We will examine this issue by looking in depth at a latter-day shibboleth: the use of language analysis for the identification of asylum seekers as part of the substantiation of asylum claims under the refugee convention. While language analysis in this context is not a conventional language test, it shares many features with more conventional language tests, and examining this procedure in the light of validity theory in language testing illuminates the question of the justice or otherwise of its use. We will also examine how this assessment procedure is located within evolving discourses of forced migration, economic migration and the reception of migrants of both kinds in the developed world. It is thus an example of language assessment as a technology of subjectivity.

9.2 LADO: LANGUAGE ANALYSIS FOR THE DETERMINATION OF ORIGIN OF ASYLUM CLAIMANTS

War and conflict in the twenty-first century have led to a significant growth in the number of asylum seekers around the world. There were approximately 1 million pending asylum seeker applications being considered by various governments in 2009, adding to the some 15 million existing refugees in various receiving countries. This vast movement of peoples has been associated with heated, sometimes acrimonious, political debates in many countries over the administrative and political management of the flow of asylum seekers and other migrants. The transformation of the movement of peoples brought about by globalization and other social changes means that governments experience

> increasing difficulty ... in distinguishing between forced migrants and the much more numerous volume of people labelled economic migrants.
> In the minds of policy makers and immigration officials it is necessary to fragment and make clear cut labels and categories of the often complex mix of reasons why people migrate and migrate between labels – the so called asylum–migration nexus. (Zetter, 2007, p. 178)

Consider the following article, which appeared in an Australian newspaper late in 2011:[3]

Appeals Open Asylum Floodgates
Massive numbers of initially rejected refugees are winning appeals to stay in Australia.
Appeals by about three quarters of boat arrivals whose initial asylum claims were deemed to be non-genuine succeeded in the past year.
The rate of overturned appeals was 46 per cent in 2009–10, says a new Immigration Department report.
Asylum seekers whose initial claims are rejected are able to appeal to tribunals and independent experts appointed by the Federal Government.
While only 38 per cent of Afghan boat arrivals were initially judged to be refugees in 2010–11, almost 80 per cent of those rejected won visas on appeal.
Similarly, only a quarter of Iranian arrivals were at first accepted by immigration officers, but 78 per cent of those who missed out were

---

[3] John Masanauskas, 'Appeals open asylum floodgates', *Herald Sun*, 28 November 2011, www.heraldsun.com.au/ipad/appeals-open-asylum-seeker-floodgates/story-fn6bfkm6-1226208581053, retrieved 11 March 2018.

given visas on review, said the Asylum Trends Australia 2010–11 report.

Two things may strike the reader about this report. The first is the emotional and negative tone of the reporting in this conservative newspaper ('open [the] floodgates', 'massive numbers'), indicative of the inflamed character of the discourse around the issue of asylum seekers in Australia, as in many countries in Europe and elsewhere, at that time and since. The second is the extraordinary number of reversals of initial administrative decisions on appeal to the courts,[4] evidence of the difficulty that the administrative authorities are experiencing (or the inadequacy of the methods used) in determining the legitimacy of asylum claims, which governments are bound to honour by the 1951 United Nations Refugee Convention. These are distinct from the claims of those deemed to fall under other categories of 'forced' and 'economic' migrants (Castles, 2003) towards whom current discourses are increasingly unsympathetic.

The determination of asylum claims within discourses of migration involving the labelling and categorization of migrants as requiring or not requiring protection is made more difficult where, as is often the case, the asylum seeker arrives without identity papers. One of the bureaucratic procedures used to determine to which category a claimant belongs, and hence their subjectivity in this bureaucratic landscape, is known as Language Analysis for the Determination of Origin of asylum seekers, or LADO (Eades & Arends, 2004; Reath, 2004; Eades, 2005, 2009; Muyskens, Verrips & Zwaan, 2010; Patrick, Schmid & Zwaan, 2019). It involves the linguistic analysis of the speech of asylum seekers, in order to establish where possible a picture of a person's language socialization. A successful asylum claimant has to establish that they are actually from a region in which they have a well-grounded fear for their well-being and safety. Members of particular groups from one place may be subject to persecution, whereas members of the same group in a different place may not; the former have a claim to asylum under the international Refugee Convention, but not the latter. Individuals from a different area or a different group may even deliberately misrepresent themselves as belonging to a group deserving protection as a way of gaining access to desired

---

[4] In fact, this difficulty appears to be a persistent one. A study initiated by the Australian sociolinguist Diana Eades a decade earlier (Eades et al., 2003) examined appeals by Hazara asylum seekers from Afghanistan to the Australia Refugee Review Tribunal, in which it was found that of 58 cases included in the study, 44 had been overturned on appeal.

migration destinations. Language evidence – the way the person speaks – can be important in providing clues as to the person's place or places of socialization and can be used to support (or reject) a claim as to origin.

But this is not a simple matter. The boundaries of language communities do not overlap with national boundaries, and the authorities may not believe that a person's linguistic socialization took place in the area or areas claimed, but in an adjoining area where there is no threat to the safety of the groups concerned. Consider the map (Figure 9.1) of the national boundaries of Guinea-Bissau and Senegal, two of several states in West Africa which have had a recent history of political conflict, giving grounds for Convention asylum motives.

Now compare it with the map of the linguistic complexity of the area (Figure 9.2)

As can be seen at a glance, the linguistic boundaries do not coincide with the political ones, a frequent phenomenon in postcolonial settings. The language Mandinka, for example, is spoken in three countries, Senegal, The Gambia and Guinea-Bissau; it is spoken in non-contiguous areas, and some of the areas in which it is spoken cross borders. Nationality cannot simply be determined from the fact that a person is a speaker of this language.

This was the issue in the (actual) case of a Mandinka-speaking asylum seeker in Switzerland, claiming to be from Guinea-Bissau. Could an analysis of his linguistic repertoire help to lend credibility to his claim that he was from Guinea-Bissau, fleeing the civil war, and so eligible for asylum, and not from either Senegal or The Gambia, in which case he would have no claim to asylum? There were

Figure 9.1   Map of Guinea-Bissau and neighbouring countries
© Hel-Hama/WikiCommons

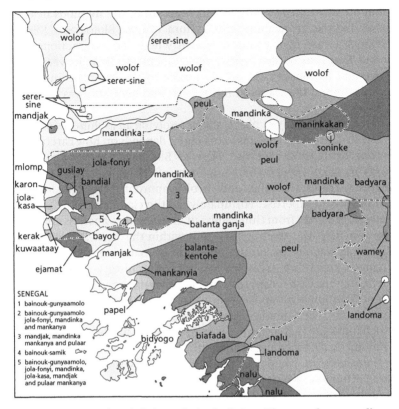

Figure 9.2 Linguistic boundaries in Guinea-Bissau and surrounding countries
© Mutuzikin.com, permission granted by the author

complications. For one thing, while his Mandinka showed the influence of Portuguese, spoken in Guinea-Bissau, it also had some French, English and Arabic influence, which you would not necessarily expect to find in a Mandinka speaker from that country. In fact, he had a very limited command of standard Portuguese, the official language of Guinea-Bissau, which he would be expected to have spoken, given that it is the medium of instruction in the education system in the country. Moreover, he had excellent competence in Arabic, and some English, neither of them typical. How could he establish that his linguistic repertoire was consistent with language socialization in a place where a real threat of persecution existed? His somewhat atypical profile was in danger of putting him at risk of refusal, an all-too-common situation in many jurisdictions using the methods of language analysis in dealing with asylum claims. Blommaert (2009) recounts a case of a young Rwandan where the assumptions the United Kingdom Border Agency made about the link between language and nationality did not do justice to the complex linguistic socialization of the claimant in the case, and his claim was unjustly refused.

Can language analysis play a role in resolving an asylum claim such as this in a just way? One answer is that it depends on how carefully it is done, with what expertise. First, as Blommaert (2009) shows, it needs to acknowledge the complexity of life trajectories and the linguistic traces resulting, and involve appropriately sophisticated sociolinguistic expertise. Fortunately for the claimant in the case of the asylum seeker from Guinea-Bissau, the language analysis commissioned by LINGUA, the linguistic unit within the Swiss Secretariat of Migration, was able to confirm his claims by matching evidence of his language repertoire with his complex life history, and thereby strengthen his case for protection. The analysis showed that the variety of Mandinka he spoke was from Guinea-Bissau and southern Senegal, not The Gambia; and it had no influence of Fula or Wolof, which indicated that it was not from Senegal. He had been educated in a Koranic Arabic-medium school rather than in a mainstream school in Guinea-Bissau, where he would otherwise have learned some standard Portuguese, which accounted for his fluent Arabic and the traces of Arabic influence in his Mandinka. The influences in it from English and French were also consistent with his history: he had spent a year studying in The Gambia, where English is spoken; both his mother and his wife were Mandinka speakers from Senegal, a country where the Mandinka speakers show the influence of French; and in any case there is interaction between the Mandinka-speaking communities of Guinea-Bissau and the neighbouring Mandinka-speaking communities of Senegal. And most convincing of all, he was a fluent speaker of Portuguese Creole.

Language analysis is a technically complex process, and much is at stake on the outcome of the analysis. The quality of the language analysis, the validity of the interpretation of the language evidence available, is thus a crucial issue. Unfortunately, the quality of the language analysis illustrated by this case is the exception internationally, rather than the rule, as the study of Australian asylum cases by Eades et al. (2003) indicates (see also Maryns, 2004; 2005; 2006). The reports of the cases gave some insight into the quality of the language analyses, which were shown to be very poor, often using a single unexpected feature of speech to form a negative judgement about the credibility of the claimed language socialization of the individual concerned. The concerns in that paper about the quality of the language analyses have been echoed by others familiar with the practice in other countries, and this has led to the formulation of professional guidelines for how language analysis should be carried out (Language and National Origin Group, 2004), guidelines which have been endorsed by a number of professional organizations internationally. While these guidelines are helpful and are gradually exerting an influence on the practices of government agencies internationally, the danger of arriving at an unjust conclusion remains. What can be done to guarantee that appropriate inferences about a person's language socialization are being drawn from language analyses? In the following section, I will argue that the literature on validity within language testing offers a useful perspective on the reasonableness and defensibility (validity) of conclusions drawn from language analysis. We shall then return to the larger question of how we may understand this practice as a technology of subjectivity.

9.3 LADO AND LANGUAGE TESTING

It may seem at first sight surprising to relate the practice of language analysis in the asylum process to language testing. Language analysis is about categorization and relies on sociolinguistic understanding of the link between proficiency in a language and language socialization, whereas language testing is typically more psycholinguistic or cognitive in focus, although it has crucial social and political functions which are less often foregrounded, an issue to which the field is slowly becoming more oriented (Shohamy, 2001; McNamara & Roever, 2006). The question to be determined in LADO is not usually 'How much of language X has this person learned? How proficient is this person in the language?', the typical issue to be addressed in language testing, but 'Who is this individual? Is he/she a member of a given speech community? What has been his/her language socialization?' Often, determining what a person does not know is as important as determining what they do know. However, despite this important difference, both language testing and language analysis are characterized by the same features. Both procedures involve observing and interpreting *evidence* from a language user's performance, *interpreting* it to form an impression of the person's language competence and making *decisions* based on this impression.

For example, in the UK, Ireland, Australia and elsewhere, a language test such as the Occupational English Test (OET)[5] (McNamara, 1996) is used as part of the procedure for admitting international medical graduates whose medical socialization has not been done in English to practise in the UK, Ireland, Australia and elsewhere. Evidence is sought from performance on tasks which simulate the communicative demands of the target situation (such as communicating with patients on clinical matters, reading case histories and so on), and this evidence is interpreted to form an impression of the candidate's readiness to undertake such tasks in the real situation. A decision to admit to the next stage of the registration process or not is then based on this impression. Similarly, language analysis is used to help decide whether the asylum seeker's application can be supported. Evidence of the applicant's language repertoire is sought, usually from an interview, and this is interpreted to form an impression of the nature of the repertoire, which is then compared with the claimant's narrative of their socialization in various contexts. A report of this impression may then be relevant to the final decision about granting or denying asylum. In fact, this chain from evidence to inference to decision is common to assessment in many other areas of life. When we use the evidence of a curriculum vitae, a professional reference and a job interview to form an impression of who among a set of candidates may be the best person for a job, we are drawing inferences about the candidate from the evidence and making decisions about which candidate to employ based on these impressions. When we meet new partners or spouses of those close to us, we use the evidence of conversation and interactions to form impressions of the personality and compatibility of the new person and may use this impression as the basis for expressing congratulations or reservations about the new relationship. In all these cases from ordinary life, it is clearly possible to get it wrong. And just so with the impressions drawn from language tests, or from language analysis, and the decisions based on these impressions: they may not be fair and reasonable. The systematic interrogation of interpretations yielded by assessments, based on a principle of scepticism, is known as *validation*. Without validation, language tests – and language analysis – are like a police force without a court system.

---

[5] www.occupationalenglishtest.org/test-information, retrieved 12.3.18.

Given the need to validate assessments, including those from language analysis, what is there to guide us? This has been the question addressed by validity theory. The still classic treatment of the subject is that of the American educational theorist Samuel Messick, who defines validity as follows (Messick, 1989, p. 13):

> Validity is an integrated evaluative judgement of the degree to which empirical evidence and theoretical rationales support the adequacy and appropriateness of inferences and actions based on test scores or other modes of assessment.

The reference to *inferences* should be clear from the preceding discussion: all assessments involve inferences from evidence – in the case of language analysis, not from 'test scores', but from 'other modes of assessment'. Once inferences have been made, *actions* will follow – in the case of asylum seekers, the granting or denial of some form of protection, depending on the inference. How *adequate* (reasonable) are such inferences (and, accordingly, how appropriate are the *actions*, such as granting or refusing asylum, which follow from them)? The *reasoning* ('theoretical rationales') forming the basis for interpreting the evidence must be examined. In addition, *empirical evidence* in support of this reasoning must be sought and *competing explanations* considered.

9.4 THE PROCESS OF VALIDATION IN LANGUAGE TESTING AND IN LADO

Because of the generality and broad scope of Messick's discussion of validity, subsequent validity theorists have tried to make the process of validation more orderly. Foremost among these is Michael Kane (e.g. Kane, 2006; 2012), who defines a series of challenges to the meaningfulness and fairness of assessments arising in relation to each of five aspects of the assessment process: designing test tasks to elicit the language sample to be evaluated; establishing procedures for judging the quality of the elicited response; determining the overall consistency of the judgement; establishing the basis for the interpretation of the performance – establishing what it says about the testee; and using the impression of the candidate derived from the assessment procedure to make a relevant decision about him/her – for example, to admit them to university study, to admit them to employment, to allow them to proceed to the next level of education or training – or, in the case of LADO, to use the language analysis in support of their claim for asylum. We can compare how these stages apply in the

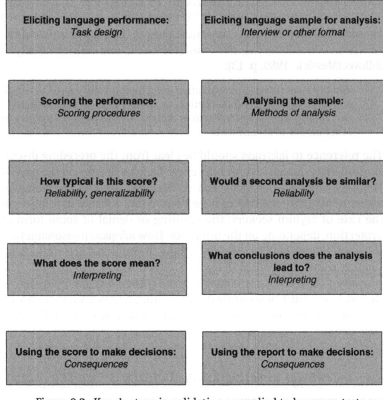

Figure 9.3 Kane's steps in validation as applied to language tests and LADO

context of language tests on the one hand (McNamara & Roever, 2006), and language analysis on the other, as set out in Figure 9.3 above.

Validation in language tests proceeds by identifying issues at each of the stages identified by Kane and investigating their impact on scores. For example, in the case of the assessment of oral proficiency, validation involves asking: would a candidate get the same score (that is, create the same impression of his/her ability, which is then coded as a score), on a different task? from a different rater? if the scoring criteria were different? and so on. Similarly, with language analysis, the impression of the claimant's language socialization may be affected by the way in which the evidence is gathered, by the methods of analysis used, by the way in which the question to be addressed is formulated and related to the evidence gathered, and the way the report is used in decisions about the claimant.

Let us consider in detail how complex the issues are in just the first of these steps, eliciting the speech sample. In language testing, in the testing of spoken language, different formats are used to elicit the candidate's speech sample. Well-known tests of proficiency in spoken English adopt different, sometimes radically different methods. In IELTS, the candidate is involved in a one-on-one interview with an examiner; in the Cambridge suite of general English tests, the candidate is engaged in an interaction with another candidate; in the OET, referred to above, the candidate undertakes his or her professional role in a role play simulating frequently encountered, professionally relevant tasks, such as informing or persuading a patient; in the Test of English as a Foreign Language Internet-Based Test (TOEFL iBT), the candidate participates in a monologic task delivered at a computer terminal; in the Pearson Test of English (Academic), the candidate responds to a set of routine digitally presented stimuli designed to elicit a highly predictable set of utterances. Imagine a candidate facing the choice of which test to take, or a set of candidates seeking admission to a particular university course who have taken a variety of these tests. The method used to elicit speech from the candidate will result in a different kind of speech sample – monologue versus dialogue versus the production of highly predictable single utterances. Will the impression the examiner or scorer has of the candidate's ability to speak English be affected depending on the kind of speech sample available to be judged and scored?

If so, this raises obvious issues about the comparability of scores from different tests, and hence of fairness. Considerable validity research has been undertaken to investigate this issue within language testing. O'Loughlin (2001), for example, compared performances of candidates using closely similar tasks under two test formats: a 'live' interaction with an examiner, and a monologic performance in response to a task stimulus. He found that for some candidates, this did result in different impressions of their spoken competence.

Similarly in the case of language analysis, there is considerable variation at present among the various agencies carrying out language analysis as to how the speech sample for the analysis is elicited. The variables involved are summarized in Table 9.1.

For each dimension of variation – participants, length, speech genre, topic, channel and code – there are a number of possibilities, any of which may affect the speech sample available for analysis, and consequently potentially alter the impression of the claimant's language socialization.

Table 9.1 *Variables in the elicitation procedure*

Participants (other than claimant)	No other participant (monologue)			
	Case officer			
	Interpreter			
	Person responsible for analysis	Native speaker status	(+NS)	(−NS)
		Training in linguistics	(+ formal academic training)	(− formal academic training)
	Interviewer, non-analyst	Training	(+ training as an interviewer)	(− training as an interviewer)
Length	Brief (5 minutes)			
	Moderate (up to 30 minutes of usable language from asylum seeker)			
	Full (up to one hour or more of usable language from asylum seeker)			
Speech genre	Interview	Structure	(+ structure)	(− structure)
	Monologue			
	Dialogue			
Topics			(+ knowledge of country)	(− knowledge of country)
Channel	Face-to-face			
	Telephone			
	Combination (e.g. case officer, + interpreter on telephone)			
Code	Asylum seeker's first language			
	Asylum seeker's second language (lingua franca)			
	Variety related to asylum seeker's first language			
	Combination (e.g. lingua franca + asylum seeker's first language)			

The *participants* in the interaction, other than the asylum claimant, vary as a function of whether the procedure for gathering the language sample is independent of the main asylum interview. Most often, there is no dedicated language analysis interview; instead, speech from an interaction with a case officer, usually through an interpreter, is used, and in that sense the material to be analyzed is a sample of convenience. Less often, for example in Switzerland, the speech sample is gathered through a separate interview. An interview may be conducted by the language expert responsible for carrying out the language analysis, who may be either a native speaker or a non-native speaker of the asylum seeker's L1 or a variety close to it, and may or may not have formal academic training in linguistics. Alternatively, for logistical reasons, the interview may be carried out by a person who will not do the analysis: this person is typically a native speaker of the asylum seeker's L1 or a variety close to it and may be trained or untrained as an interviewer. The identity of the interviewer or person interacting with the claimant may be consequential – whether the person is seen as a foreigner, and a person in authority, or is seen as a compatriot, and ideally someone of the same ethnic and social background, though this then raises issues of anonymity and issues of within-group obligation.

The *length* of the interview, and the resulting amount of usable data, varies accordingly. When a dedicated language analysis interview is available, this is usually of reasonable length, an hour or even longer, and certainly sufficiently long for an adequate speech sample to be elicited. But this is unusual; typically, the interview with the case officer offers a much-reduced length of material on which to do the analysis. This is particularly the case when an interpreter is involved, as a considerable amount of the time is taken up in translation back and forth, thus reducing the amount of usable data.

The *speech genre* is usually an interview, but it is sometimes a monologue, as in a procedure which has been used by the Norwegian government. Here, and in interactive formats involving a government official or language expert, given that the situation by definition is formal and highly consequential, it is likely that a formal register in sociolinguistic terms will be elicited and thus will provide no evidence of the speaker's informal varieties; this may have serious implications for inferences about the varieties the claimant speaks. For example, many of the asylum claimants from Afghanistan come from the stigmatized Hazara group, a (Shiite) religious minority in Afghanistan, who speak the Hazaragi ethnolect of the national language Dari. However, in a formal interview with a government official, Hazaras are more likely to speak a more standard form of Dari, particularly if, as is most likely, the interpreter is a non-Hazara and likely to use a more standard variety of Dari, to which the claimant may accommodate. If the goal of the language analysis is to determine the person's ethnicity, then the Hazara identity of the claimant is likely to be obscured by these factors. In an attempt to get a sample of a less formal variety, which might be associated with a particular region or ethnicity and hence be more relevant to the issue of the speaker's identity, evidence from more equal interactions is sometimes sought, for example a conversation with a speaker of the same variety who is not a government representative, although this usually happens only in appeals.

The *topics* dealt with also vary, for example the extent to which they include or exclude knowledge of the country and culture of the claimed region of origin. In the case of Switzerland, for example, the language analysis is supplemented by an analysis of the asylum seeker's knowledge of the surroundings and way of life of the place(s) in which he/she claims to have lived, which means that these topics form the content of the language sample which is then analyzed; this gives some consistency to the content of the sample, in terms of topics. In other cases there may be little consistency of topic, and no opportunity to deliberately explore linguistic features of interest as part of the elicitation itself.

Channel is another important variable. Increasingly, interviews other than with case officers are carried out via telephone, for logistical reasons (language experts with expertise on a particular region may not be geographically close to where the claimant is), and to preserve the anonymity of both parties.

The *code* used in the interaction varies from the asylum seeker's L1, to a variety closely associated with it, to an L2, often a lingua franca. We have seen above how this may have consequences for the nature of the language sample elicited.

From the point of view of the validity of assessments, any one of these variables, and combinations of them, may affect the chances of a certain outcome, that is, the impression of the speaker's repertoire drawn from the analysis. In order to validate the process, research needs to be carried out into the potential impact of any of the variables, either alone or in combination; this would parallel the research efforts that have gone into exploring the impact of related variables in the assessment of spoken language within language testing. McNamara van den Hazelkamp and Verrips (2016) have tried to set out the range of possibilities involved here and have extended it to consider the issues involved in each of the other stages in Kane's approach, as the basis for a research agenda to investigate the impact of variables in the language analysis procedure. For example, conclusions from multiple samples, gathered under varying elicitation conditions, from the same asylum seekers could be compared to estimate the impact of the different conditions on impressions of the claimant's repertoire. The vexed issue of the appropriate qualifications of the analyst (for example, whether the analyst needs to be a native speaker of the language concerned, and/or should be required to have formal linguistic training – see Cambier-Langeveld, 2010; Fraser, 2011; Verrips, 2011) could also be explored by analyses of the same set of speech samples by language experts with different backgrounds.

9.5 INTERPRETING THE EVIDENCE

The most difficult of Kane's stages is that of interpreting the evidence. In language testing, this involves specifying what it is that the test is intended to show about an individual ('the construct') – what they know or can do – and seeking evidence to support the interpretation of the score as an indication of the level of the person's knowledge or ability in these terms. Similarly, in language analysis, this is the most complex and difficult stage. The issues here are forensic: is the linguistic repertoire of the claimant such as would be expected given the information available to the analyst about their language socialization? (Note that this information is vital to the conduct of a defensible analysis, but in many jurisdictions it is not routinely available, so that the analyst is forced to rely on stereotypical expectations, which can lead to erroneous conclusions, as in the distressing case reported in Blommaert, 2009.)

The forensic questions to be addressed in LADO involve a potentially large range of sociolinguistic issues.[6] An idea of the range of issues, and the forensic questions with which they are associated, can be gained from Table 9.2, where the differing kinds of contexts in which the relationship of speech variation to geographical location occurs is set out, and illustrated with examples drawn from actual cases.

---

[6] The following section draws on the results of a research project carried out for the LINGUA unit within the Swiss Secretariat of Migration (McNamara & Schüpbach 2012; McNamara & Schüpbach, 2018).

Table 9.2 *Forensic questions addressed in Language Analysis for the Determination of Origin (LADO)*

Sub-category of regional variation	Sociolinguistic issue	Example	Expectation	Forensic question in this language analysis
National varieties of a 'pluricentric' language	Languages which have different national varieties	Egyptian Arabic vs Lebanese Arabic Swahili from Tanzania vs Swahili from the Democratic Republic of Congo	If the claimant is from country X, he/she may be expected to speak the associated national variety.	Does the claimant speak the expected national variety?
National variety with regional variation	Languages which have different regional varieties within a single country	Mandinka in northern Senegal vs Mandinka in the Casamance region of southern Senegal	If the claimant is from region X of the country concerned, he/she may be expected to speak the regional variety associated with region X.	Does the claimant speak the expected regional variety?
Regional variety which crosses borders	Languages where a regional language variety straddles current national borders.	Mandinka in Senegal, The Gambia and Guinea Bissau Kurmanji Kurdish in Iraq, Iran, Turkey and Syria	If the claimant is from country X, he/she may be expected to speak the regional variety associated with country X.	Does the claimant speak the regional variety associated with country X?

Local variation	Regional language variety which shows intra-regional local variation	Palestinian Arabic as spoken around Tubas in the northern part of the West Bank	If the claimant is from a specific place within region X, he/she may be expected to speak the specific sub-variety associated with that place.	Does the claimant speak the sub-variety associated with the specific place he/she claims to be from?
Ethnic variety	A language variety associated with a particular ethnicity	Fur or Zaghawa in Sudan/Darfur Hazaragi varieties of Dari	If the claimant is from a particular ethnicity, he/she may be expected to speak the associated ethnolect.	Does the claimant speak the expected ethnolect?
Discontinuous speech area	Varieties of some languages occur in speech islands (such as diasporic contexts, refugee camps, etc.)	Varieties of Arabic spoken within a particular Palestinian refugee camp Varieties of Tibetan spoken in exile, in refugee camps in India	If the claimant is from one of these speech islands, he/she may be expected to speak the associated variety.	Does the claimant speak the variety associated with this speech island?
Pidgin, creole variation	Some pidgin and creole varieties emerge in the context of language contact and show lectal variation	West African creoles and the pidgins and creoles spoken in Nigeria	The sociolinguistic features of the pidgin/creole spoken are expected to be compatible with the claimed region of socialization.	Are the sociolinguistic features of the pidgin/creole spoken compatible with the claimed region of socialization?

For example, returning again to Mandinka: it is a national language in Senegal, but with different varieties spoken in different parts of the country – the Mandinka spoken in northern Senegal is different from the variety of Mandinka spoken in the Casamance region of southern Senegal, the location of a prolonged independence struggle. Someone claiming to be from the Casamance region of Senegal would therefore be expected to speak the variety of that region. Similarly, as we have seen, Mandinka is also a language with communities of speakers not only in Senegal but also in The Gambia and Guinea-Bissau. As in the case mentioned earlier, a refugee from the conflict in Guinea-Bissau might be expected to speak the variety of Mandinka typical of that country, that is, a variety with loanwords from Portuguese, the colonial language. Complex cases may involve multiple such issues, each of which must be determined in turn.

For each issue to be determined, the preliminary question of whether the issue is potentially decidable using language analysis is considered. Often, there is simply inadequate sociolinguistic information to address the issue, and no reliable language analysis can be carried out. This applies currently to the situation in south Somalia, for example, although some governments insist on carrying out language analyses involving this region, relying on out-of-date or patchy sociolinguistic data. Where current sociolinguistic data is available to the language expert, an argument in terms of the relevant features of phonology, lexis, morphology and syntax in the language sample is then made in relation to the issue. Where the initial expectation is not confirmed, alternative explanations need to be considered; these often involve factors in the biographical trajectory of the claimant (Table 9.3).

Table 9.4 sets out in the form of a grid a procedure for evaluating the validity of inferences in LADO in those situations where it has already been established that there are sufficient relevant sociolinguistic descriptions to be drawn on in the analysis. Each of a potential series of aspects of the expected linguistic profile of the claimant is determined – for example, that if the speech sample is, as claimed, from a speaker of Mandinka from Guinea-Bissau, it will show features that are influenced by being in contact with Portuguese or Portuguese Creole. Were a sufficient number of instances of such features found in the language sample being considered? (Clearly, multiple examples in different linguistic domains will be required as the basis for confirmation or disconfirmation: a problem in many of the cases involving Hazaras studies by Eades et al. (2003) was that a

Table 9.3 *Biographical factors potentially influencing the linguistic repertoire*

Biographical factor	Sociolinguistic issue	Example	Expectation	Forensic question in this language analysis
Mixed ancestry	If a person is socialized into a household where the parents speak different languages, the person may have knowledge of a language that would otherwise be unexpected.	The Arabic of a speaker with one parent from Iraq, the other from Egypt, may indicate familiarity with both varieties of Arabic.	A claimant from such a background may have a linguistic repertoire reflecting in part that background.	Does the individual have mixed linguistic ancestry? Is the observed repertoire potentially compatible with this expectation?
Linguistically mixed marriage	A person married to a speaker of a different language or languages may reflect in his/her speech repertoire the spouse's language(s).	A Roma women who grew up speaking Albanian and learned her husband's variety of Romanes after marriage.	A claimant in such a marriage may have a linguistic repertoire reflecting features of the spouse's language(s).	Is the applicant married to a speaker of a different language or languages? Does the observed repertoire reflect exposure to the language(s) of the spouse?
Complex migration: Refugee camps	Stays in refugee camps may involve interaction with speakers of other varieties or languages also living in the camps.	Kenyan refugee camps with people from Somalia, Sudan, etc.	A claimant's linguistic repertoire may show possible linguistic traces from any such extended periods of stay in the refugee camp.	Has the individual a complex migration history which includes periods in refugee camps? Is the observed repertoire potentially explicable in terms of experience of language contact in refugee camps?

Table 9.4 *Evaluation grid for the validity of inferences in LADO*

WHAT IS EXPECTED?	SUFFICIENCY OF EVIDENCE; QUALITY OF LINGUISTIC ANALYSIS				EXPECTATION CONFIRMED?	POSSIBLE ALTERNATIVE EXPLANATION FOR FINDING IF NEGATIVE
	Syntax	Morphology	Lexis	Phonology		

single occurrence of an unexpected lexical item had been seen as
sufficient to decide against the applicant.) Does the analysis demonstrate clearly the presence of the expected features? If not, alternative explanations must be considered. For each new factor to be
considered, the process is repeated: is the issue determinable,
given our current state of sociolinguistic knowledge of the impact
of the factor concerned? Is there sufficient evidence within the
language sample to determine it? In this way, the validity of the
conclusions about the claimant's socialization are explicitly and
systematically addressed.

In the case of the asylum claimant from Guinea-Bissau, the first
issue to be determined was whether the variety of Mandinka spoken
was that expected from the claimant's region of socialization
(Guinea-Bissau). In this case, the issue was one of 'regional variation
which crosses borders', given that the Mandinka speech area
includes parts of three countries. There were sufficient descriptions
of the three varieties available to the language expert to make the
determination possible in principle, and ample evidence was available in the speech sample, with multiple examples of the expected
features observable. While the expected variety was confirmed (a
variety spoken in Senegal and Guinea-Bissau, and in this case one
showing the influence of Portuguese), there was the complicating
factor that the speech of the claimant also showed the influence of
both English and French, which would not be expected. In this case,
biographical factors (the variety spoken by the mother and the wife
of the claimant) and the claimant's residence in a third country (The
Gambia) were then investigated and were sufficient to explain this
complexity.

9.6 VALIDATION: THE SOCIAL CONTEXT

All that we have covered so far represents only one aspect of the validation of assessments, according to Messick. It represents what he terms 'construct validity'. But there are three more facets of validity, as set out in a famous matrix (Messick, 1989) (Figure 9.4).

We can elaborate the distinctions present in the matrix in a form more relevant to the context of language analysis (Figure 9.5).

We will comment briefly about each of the other cells in the matrix. The second cell, on the top line, suggests that an analysis which is valid for one context may not be valid for another. This arises most clearly when language analysis is used as part of the procedure of deporting a person whose asylum application has failed. It is one thing to determine if a person is or is not from a region they claim to be from; it is another to determine positively which region a person is from, a necessary preliminary to deportation.

The third and fourth cells introduce consideration of the broader social, political and cultural context within which the practice of language analysis is situated. The third cell raises the question of the values represented by the policies language analysis is used to support. The fourth deals with the intended and unintended social consequences of the practice of language analysis.

Although the practice is designed to assist those eligible for protection under refugee conventions to make a credible case in the absence of official papers establishing their identity, like all administrative procedures, it is subject to the pressures of time and resources typical of administrative systems, with attendant threats to the quality of the analysis. Blommaert (2009) has shown how complex the language socialization of asylum seekers may be on the trajectory of their journey to the place where they claim asylum, and how difficult it may be for bureaucracies to deal with this. There is the issue of the

	TEST INTERPRETATION	TEST USE
EVIDENTIAL BASIS	Construct validity	Construct validity + Relevance / utility
CONSEQUENTIAL BASIS	Value implications	Social consequences

Figure 9.4   Facets of validity (Messick, 1989, p. 20)

	WHAT LANGUAGE ANALYSIS REPORTS ARE ASSUMED TO MEAN	WHEN LANGUAGE ANALYSIS REPORTS ARE ACTUALLY USED
USING EVIDENCE IN SUPPORT OF CLAIMS: THE FAIRNESS OF LANGUAGE ANALYSIS REPORTS	What reasoning and empirical evidence support the claims we wish to make about individuals based on an analysis of their spoken language?	Are these interpretations meaningful, useful and fair in particular contexts?
THE SOCIAL CONTEXT OF USING LANGUAGE ANALYSIS IN THE DETERMINATION OF ORIGIN	What social and cultural values and assumptions underlie the constructs used in language analysis and the inferences we make about individuals in relation to them?	What happens in the larger social context when we use language analysis in the determination of origin?

Figure 9.5 Understanding Messick's validity matrix

political pressure on the process, too: there is often considerable political advantage to governments in reducing the extent of immigration through increasing the rate of unsuccessful asylum applications. Both of these pressures may lead to the language analysis being conducted in such a way as to result in arbitrary, typically negative decisions about the validity of the asylum claim, as revealed by the Eades et al. (2003) study. Even when the results of that study were communicated to the Australian government, the response from the minister concerned was a bland restatement of the government's confidence in the methods of the private Swedish companies who conducted the analyses on behalf of the government. The political climate of the time was such that criticism of the fairness of the procedure was less politically damaging for the government than to appear to be 'weak' on the question of asylum seekers.

The quality of the language analysis is at stake here. If the language analysis is carried out carefully and professionally, it serves to guarantee the rights of those with a legitimate claim to protection, a claim which governments are all too ready to deny if they can find a pretext – for example, the results of a shoddily conducted analysis – for doing so. The attack on the rights of the asylum seeker comes from a failure to devote administrative resources to establishing the reality of the claimant's language socialization as part of the evidence of the credibility of his/her claim. This failure may simply be a question of allocation of resources, but prioritizing resource allocation is usually the result of policy decisions which are all too easily explicable given the politicization of the refugee question in so many countries.

We have focused in this discussion mostly on one aspect of the justice of the language analysis procedure, the quality of its execution. This aspect of the justice of assessment, as it were internal to the operation of assessment, may be termed *fairness* in contrast to a broader notion of the external, contextual role of assessment, for which we may use the term *justice* (McNamara & Ryan, 2011; McNamara & Schüpbach, 2018). Fairness here refers to the technical quality of the assessment procedure, necessary for it to yield accurate and consistent results, and conclusions about individuals which are not dependent on the vagaries of the assessment process. Thus any attempt to introduce quality controls and quality standards for LADO, as represented, for example, by the guidelines recommended for its use (Language and National Origin Group, 2004), can be seen as addressing questions of the *fairness* of the procedure. The issue of ensuring quality involves an attempt to fix the meaning of the interpretation of the evidence of language analysis within the legal framework of refugee law as the basis for ensuring protection.

What the distinction between fairness and justice suggests, however, is the question of whether the *justice* of the use of LADO is greater than the technical quality of its execution. The very refugee law that language analysis seeks to implement is of course itself the product of social and political compromise at a particular historical period, the years immediately following the Holocaust, when the world's attention was on the fate of those who had been refused access to asylum and had consequently suffered the most terrible of fates. But times have changed. The social and policy context in which language analysis is carried out is rapidly changing and highly politicized. In the words of Stephen Castles (2003, p. 17),

> The distinction between forced migration and economic migration is becoming blurred ... Failed economies generally also mean weak states, predatory ruling cliques and human rights abuse. This leads

to the notion of the 'asylum-migration nexus': many migrants and asylum seekers have multiple reasons for mobility and it is impossible to separate economic and human rights motivations – which is a challenge to the neat categories that bureaucracies seek to impose.

The categories that bureaucracies impose are referred to by Wood (1985, p. 1) as 'labels': 'Labelling is a way of referring to the process by which policy agendas are established and more particularly the way in which people, conceived as objects of policy, are defined in convenient images.' Zetter (1991), in a famous paper, points out that 'Labelling is a process of designation, for it involves making judgements and distinctions; crucially, it is non-participatory' (p. 45). That is, the asylum claimant is subject to the processes of recognition that we have discussed extensively earlier in this book; it is crucial to the success of their claim that they be seen as 'legitimate', deserving of protection under the restrictive rules of the refugee convention. Zetter (1991, p. 46), discussing the distribution of food and other rights in refugee settings in the 1980s, goes on to describe the identity functions of these bureaucratic procedures:

> It is through the apparently normal, routine, apolitical, conventional procedures of programme design and delivery that identity is determined. For the instrumentality of these procedures lies in the conformity they demand from refugee clients to gain access to the resources and label.

He adds (p. 59):

> Labelling matters so fundamentally because it is an inescapable part of public policy making and its language: a non-labelled way out cannot exist. A theory of labelling provides some constructs with which to observe the way bureaucratic procedures and practices form a refugee identity ... By reinforcing actions of designation, labelling means conditionality and differentiation, inclusion and exclusion, stereotyping and control.

In a paper revisiting the argument of the earlier paper over twenty-five years later, Zetter (2007, p. 174) argues that there has been a 'transformation of the refugee label' which 'is a response to this complexity enacted by a process of bureaucratic "fractioning" in order to manage the "new" migration'.

And any attempt to tighten up a procedure so that it correctly identifies those to whom asylum must be granted has the corollary that it will more efficiently detect those whose claim is unwarranted under the strict terms of asylum law. We can best understand this paradox by considering Derrida's discussion of the shibboleth.

9.7 LANGUAGE AS SHIBBOLETH: A POSTSTRUCTURALIST PERSPECTIVE

Let us return to where we began this chapter, to reconsider the significance of the shibboleth in the light of the discussion so far. The biblical story has long been cited by writers on language testing (Lado, 1949; Spolsky, 1995; Davies, 1997; McNamara, 2005) as a reminder of the social and political functions of tests, and their misuse. *Shibboleth* is also the title of a poem of the twentieth-century German Jewish poet Paul Celan, and of the paper in which the philosopher Jacques Derrida discusses aspects of Celan's work. Derrida discusses the inherent ambiguity, the 'undecidability',[7] of the ancient notion of the shibboleth as a metaphor for the protection language affords. On the one hand, it is a means of inclusion: 'A password, a ... word transmitted like ... a handclasp, a rallying cipher, a sign of membership and a political watchword' (Derrida, 1986/2005, p. 27).

But the fact that the shibboleth necessarily acts as a two-edged sword, that inclusion always leads to exclusion, leads Derrida to speak of 'the terrifying ambiguity of the shibboleth, sign of belonging and threat of discrimination' (Derrida 1986/2005, p. 27). The work of language testers in the development and validation of language tests and other assessment procedures, and of language experts involved in LADO, can in fact be understood as involving the construction of shibboleths. And so here we encounter the indeterminacy of the shibboleth – its terrifyingly ambiguous potential.

Language testing theory in a certain, rather literal, sense recognizes the potential indeterminacy of the test score, and its response is to try to remove this ambiguity, to fix its meaning. The process of test score validation can be understood as an attempt to make the meaning of a test score determinable or definitive and is, in this sense, a classically modernist and positivist enterprise. Validity theory requires us to define the test construct in terms of which the test score is said to have meaning. This yields a 'true' reading of the score, the one sanctioned by the test construct. Various kinds of threats to this 'true' reading are also countenanced. On the one hand, test scores can potentially be misleading indicators of the construct: hence, we have

---

[7] The shibboleth forms part of a catalogue of 'undecidables' in Derrida's work; others include the pharmakon and the trace.

discussion of 'construct irrelevant variance' and 'construct under-representation' (Messick, 1989), and test validation research aims at revealing the extent of such threats, in order to improve the quality of the information yielded by the test and hence the meaningfulness of the score in terms of the construct.

There is, however, another kind of meaning, and another kind of ambiguity, in test scores, to do with the *values* embodied in test constructs. That the construct in terms of which the test score is held to have meaning will be an expression of social values is recognized in the discussion of validity by Messick (1989), who argues that one aspect of test validation is the articulation and justification of the value implications of test constructs. This area of validation is too little discussed in much language testing research, except in the area known as critical language testing (Shohamy, 2001). There, as the name suggests, the goal is to reveal the hidden values in tests, the policy agendas and ideologies (Shohamy, 2006). For example, Kubota (2011) and Park (2011) analyze the function of the Test of English for International Communication (TOEIC) in Japan and Korea respectively in terms of neo-liberal political values. It was argued in Chapter 5 of this book that the function and world-wide spread of the Common European Framework of Reference for Languages (Council of Europe, 2001) needed to be understood in terms of furthering the ideology of globalization (McNamara, 2011a). Critical readings of tests such as these often reveal a tension between the overt meaning of the test construct, for example, 'language proficiency', and its covert meaning, in terms of the values or ideologies it represents. Another way of putting this is that the interpretations of individuals encoded in test scores can be made in reference to multiple constructs; test scores are never the manifestation of a single cultural value. A test score is a sign open to various readings, and hence to dispute; tests are often sites of competition or struggle over values.

What is important about all these examples is that the impact of the test exceeds the intentions of its sponsors and developers. Tests attempt to fix, to define, to categorize, to stabilize, often summarizing complex judgements of ability based on the evidence of complex performances in a single score with a single defensible meaning: 'she is an IELTS 6'. The goal of language test validation research is usually taken as achieving a single 'correct' reading of the score, in terms represented by the overt test construct. But poststructuralism opens up not single but multiple readings: in thinking of test constructs as shibboleths, it leads us to realize that language test scores and their constructs, together with their social implications in terms of values and consequences, are *undecidables* in a Derridean sense. That is, they are texts open to interpretation, inherently unstable, and the various readings of the test scores may be socially beneficial or socially harmful, depending on the reading.

Now let us consider the parallel case of language analysis used to determine identity in refugee settings. The legal framework of existing refugee law requires that the identity of the claimant be definitively established, in terms relevant to the provisions of the law. Where was the person socialized? To what extent is the claimant's linguistic repertoire compatible with the trajectory of their lives to date? Does the language evidence suggest that the person's story of their residence is credible? That is, given that the modernist practice of fixing the meaning of the interpretation of the evidence within the legal framework of refugee law is in fact the basis for ensuring protection, it is crucial in defending the rights of asylum seekers that this be done as carefully and as professionally as possible. Hence the existence of the professional guidelines for carrying out this work; and the evidence of language analysis, professionally conducted, used in appeals by those who have been refused asylum partly on the basis of poorly conducted analyses by governments who may care little about the quality of LADO used in making decisions. So greater technical sophistication in the execution of LADO is crucial to achieving a just resolution of an asylum claim.

But there are further, more imponderable questions about language analysis which its technical quality cannot resolve. For the validity of language analysis will always remain an open question. Whose interests are we working in when we carry out LADO? On the one hand, it can, as we have seen, guarantee the human rights of asylum seekers. But it is also likely, in the current political context, that governments are motivated to carry out LADO not only to fulfil their obligations under international refugee conventions, but possibly as a way of reducing the number of successful refugee claims. That is, ironically, the very sophistication which can guarantee protection for those eligible under existing law is also likely to result in a greater capacity for the detection of 'false' claimants, resulting in the denial of the protection of asylum to those who fall outside the scope of the law as it stands. The question of the *fairness* of practices *within* the existing law leaves aside the wider question of the adequacy of current refugee law within which the interpretations about the credibility of claims based on language analysis are made; that is, the question of who should be offered protection in the first place, the *justice* of the procedure. How can we resolve the paradox? Even in the rather unlikely event of the successful renegotiation of international refugee conventions, we would still be faced with the need to administer the law. This forensic necessity may again include the devising and deployment of shibboleths, with their 'terrifying ambiguity', the promise of inclusion and the threat of exclusion.

9.8 CONCLUSION

Tests as bureaucratic procedures, as Foucault observed, play a fundamental role in modernity, as a mechanism for surveillance of the subject. Language analysis for the determination of origin in asylum cases is a classic example of such a procedure: to what category will a claimant be assigned, as having a credible claim, or as someone falling outside the protection of international asylum agreements? The work of language testers – and the sociolinguists who carry out LADO – falls within the field of law and justice, and in particular its administration. This leads to a fundamental ambiguity in the work they do, expressed most clearly in Derrida's notion of the shibboleth, at once a mechanism for inclusion, and a mechanism for exclusion. Laws can exist in the service of justice, and of injustice. In the case of LADO, and of language tests more generally, the quality of the procedures used in the administration of the law are one aspect of their justice – a poorly conducted LADO procedure can jeopardize the possibility of recognition of an asylum seeker's claim to protection as legitimate and thus lead to injustice. There is thus the need for professional expertise and integrity in the execution of the procedures used to classify people in this and other policy contexts. Looking beyond questions of the fairness (internal quality) of language tests and test-like administrative procedures involving language to the broader issue of the defensibility of their use, the outward-facing question of their justice, we are faced with the 'terrifying ambiguity' of the shibboleth, in Derrida's words. But this ethical dilemma of responsibility is not restricted to language testing; it is representative of the fundamental dilemma of applied linguistics as an applied field. In a discussion of the social and political contexts in which the work of applied linguists is carried out, Kramsch (2005) argues that procedural and methodological issues are 'sociopolitical questions that cannot be answered by researchers alone. They have to be discussed in an open forum of political ideologies and interests' (p. 560). While researchers are unlikely to be able to frame or amend policies, they can at least clarify what is at stake, and here the insights of poststructuralism make what is at stake vividly clear.

9.9 SUGGESTIONS FOR FURTHER READING

The classic treatment of values and consequences as aspects of the validity in language assessment is Messick (1989), whose argument is elaborated in McNamara and Roever (2006), which also contains an extended discussion of the shibboleth. Kane (2006) is a key text on the validation of language assessments; a more accessible version, directed at those working on language in particular, is Kane (2012). Two foundational texts on the social and political meaning of language assessments are Spolsky (1995) and Shohamy (2001), the latter introducing the term Critical Language Testing and relating her discussion to Foucault's notion of disciplinarity and its manifestation in the examination. There is an extensive literature on LADO: comprehensive article-length treatments can be found in Eades (2005; 2009), and Muyskens, Verrips and Zwaan (2010) and Patrick, Schmid and Zwaan (2019) contain collections of papers on the subject.

10 Conclusion: Discourse and Discipline

The evidence of discourse and its disciplining effect is all around us. Let me give three further examples to conclude the argument of the book.

I have been travelling to the United States more or less every year since 1990 and have noticed in that time a shift in the discourse circulating there about Australia and Australians. When I first went to the United States, Australia was not on anyone's radar. It was seen as very remote, and not relevant to the experience of the average American. In the last decade at least, however, this has changed. When ordinary people I meet in cabs, in shops or socially now hear that I am from Australia, they typically react with versions of the same response: 'I would love to go there. A friend/family member has been there and loved it. They say it reminded them of what America was like in the 1950s.' Australia clearly represents something important for Americans these days, perhaps a nostalgia for a society that was seen as less complex and less troubled, less disillusioned. What on the surface is a discourse about Australia is, more importantly, a discourse about America. What is noticeable is that the same point is made time and again, by different people all over the country. It is not as if suddenly people are independently arriving at this point of view and just happen to be voicing similar opinions. No, this is an example of a new discourse, which people ventriloquize: they endlessly, itera-tively repeat it, it circulates and serves to construct an aspect of American subjectivity, and my subjectivity as a visitor to the United States. I am recognized in the terms of the discourse in a new way – fortunately the construction of Australians in this discourse is benign so that as a result I am treated warmly rather than indifferently as a visitor to the United States. I may experience a feeling of a certain pleasure, even of pride, in being so recognized, and thus an aspect of my subjectivity as an Australian has undergone a change.

A less personal example involves a linguistic phenomenon which has in the last forty or fifty years increasingly assumed significance within discourses of British (and accordingly Australian) national identity. As I was revising the manuscript for this book, the young graduate student who was helping me sent me some comments about a draft chapter he had read and on which I had invited him to comment. Among other helpful suggestions and edits, he corrected thirty instances of words which I had spelt *-ize*, changing them to *-ise* (for example *emphasizes/emphasises, conceptualizing/conceptualising* and *theorize/theorise*). These corrections reflect a change in the conventions about spelling such words that I witnessed when I was living in London in the 1970s and 1980s. An anti-American discourse had started to identify the spelling *-ize* for these words as American and somehow unattractive, and the spelling *-ise* began to signify British identification, as against the American Other. The motivation for this was perhaps (and continues to be) a reaction to coinages of new words ending in *-ize*, such as *incentivize, alphabetize* and so on, which were seen as a particularly American phenomenon. Burchfield, the editor of the third edition of the powerful British style guide *Fowler's Modern English Usage*, refers to the 'widespread current belief that new formations of this kind are crude, overused, or unnecessary' (1998, p. 422). Gradually the objection to these new coinages transferred to the ending in *-ize* that many used, rather than to the coinages themselves.

Ironically, however, this preference for *-ise* in British usage has obscured the etymology of these words (the Greek verb from which the ending ultimately derives is in fact spelled with a 'z'). The practice of generally using *-ise* was criticized by Sir Ernest Gowers, the editor of the second edition of *Fowler's Modern English Usage*, which appeared in 1965 (Gowers, 1965, p. 314):

> In the vast majority of the verbs that end in *-ize* or *-ise* and are pronounced -īz, the ultimate source of the ending is the Greek *-izo* ... Most English printers ... follow the French practice of changing *-ize* to *-ise*. But the Oxford University Press, the Cambridge University Press, *The Times*, and American usage, in all of which *-ize* is the accepted form, carry authority enough to outweigh superior numbers. The OED's judgement may be quoted: 'In modern French the suffix has become *-iser* ... Hence, some have used the spelling *-ise* in English, as in French, for all these words [from Greek and Latin], and some prefer *-ise* in words formed in French or English from Latin elements, retaining *-ize* for those of Greek composition. But the suffix itself, whatever the element to which it is added, is in its origin the Greek *-izein*, Latin *-izare*; and, as the pronunciation is also with *z*, there is no reason why in English the special French spelling should be followed, in opposition to that which is at once etymological and phonetic.'

By the third edition (1998), edited by Robert Burchfield, the growing preference for -*ise* in British usage had been acknowledged, but was still in progress, and Burchfield remained somewhat cautious about its use. The entry reads (Burchfield, 1998, p. 422):

> Spelling. In the vast majority of the verbs that may in English be written either with -*ize* or -*ise* and are pronounced with /-aɪz/ the ultimate source is the Greek infinitival ending -ίζειν (L -*izāre*), whether the particular verb was an actual Greek one or was a Latin or French or English imitation, and whether such imitation was made by adding the termination to a Greek or another stem. A key word showing the line of descent is *baptize*, which answers to Gk βαπτίζειν and L *baptizāre*. But the French have opted for *baptiser*, and a large proportion of English writers and publishers have followed suit by writing the word as *baptise*; similarly with hundreds of other formations of this type. In Britain the Oxford University Press[1] (and, until recently, *The Times*) presents all such words with the termination spelt -*ize*. So do all American writers and publishers. It should be noted, however, that many publishing houses in Britain, including Cambridge University Press, now use -*ise* in the relevant words. The matter remains delicately balanced but unresolved. The primary rule is that all words of the type *authorize/authorise*, *civilize/civilise*, *legalize/legalise* may legitimately be spelt with either -*ize* or -*ise* throughout the English-speaking world except in America, where -*ize* is compulsory.

There are a number of things about this changing practice that are worth commenting on. First, the change itself, while appearing to be about a tiny issue of spelling, is actually explicable in terms of changes in quite other discourses, of British national identity. For a long time the influence of a classical education in Britain led to a favouring of -*ize* as being etymologically more defensible than the French preference for -*ise* in relevant cognates. The change in favour of -*ise* represents an interesting prioritization of the significant Other in British national discourse; a move away from the related Anglo-Saxon cultural tradition in favour of the previous primary Other, the French. Perhaps it is no coincidence that this change happened as Britain was exploring its connections with Europe, beginning in the 1960s and 1970s (Brexit notwithstanding). The Australian preference for the British spelling is also interesting – a combination perhaps of the remnant of a colonial attitude of looking to Britain for cultural models, and an active strain of anti-Americanism in Australian national identity.

---

[1] An entry in the Oxford Dictionaries blog entitled '-ize or -ise?' shows the current position of Oxford University Press: http://blog.oxforddictionaries.com/2011/03/ize-or-ise/. Retrieved 1.3.18.

The other interesting thing here is the way in which this spelling practice is *policed*. I have a preference for the *-ize* spelling myself: I have a degree in Latin (but alas no Greek), and thus I am sympathetic to etymological arguments. I wonder whether my preference will survive the now automatic correction procedures built into word processing programs, silently and automatically enforcing the local practice of nationalist discourse. But the policing in the case of my draft chapter was not done by linguistic authorities (both *Fowler's Guide*, and Oxford University Press, are still cautious about the use of *-ise*, despite the shift at *The Times* and at Cambridge University Press), nor done automatically by a style program, but by an individual scrutinizing another's practice, as in the case of the thirty corrections made by my student. In this case, the disciplining – the surveillance and enforcement – was done by a junior figure, my student, and a man much younger than me. And that is the nature of surveillance in discourse as Foucault sees it: we keep each other mutually under surveillance, regardless of other power differentials; we discipline each other, mutually. As a result the operation of power is complex and multifaceted, permeating social relations, not in a simple top-down fashion, and so is all the harder to detect, as it is internalized in both the viewer and the viewed.

The way in which details of linguistic practices such as this spelling practice are the subject of discourses is an example of the role of *language ideology* in the discourses informing mutual surveillance (Woolard, 1998). Hill (1998; 2008) shows how linguistic ideologies associated with racism are at play in the practice of what she calls 'mock Spanish', whereby white Americans use Spanish words in a way that makes themselves sound 'cool', at the same time as they stigmatize Hispanic Americans mixing Spanish words into English. Hill writes (1998, p. 680):

> White public space is constructed through (1) intense monitoring of the speech of racialized populations such as Chicanos and Latinos and African Americans for signs of linguistic disorder and (2) the invisibility of almost identical signs in the speech of Whites, where language mixing, required for the expression of a highly valued type of colloquial persona, takes several forms. One such form, Mock Spanish, ... presents speakers as possessing desirable personal qualities ... [and] reproduces highly negative stereotypes of Chicanos and Latinos. In addition, it indirectly indexes 'whiteness' as an unmarked normative order.

We have again here themes that have been present throughout the book: the presence of *discourse* (here, racist discourse) in the details of everyday behaviour; *policing*, or *disciplining*, required by discourse, as a practice circulating throughout a community at the 'capillary' level (Foucault, 1980, p. 96); and the way in which the focus thereby on the 'abnormal' Other inscribes the 'normal' self *invisibly*. In Foucault's words, 'Disciplinary power ... is exercised through its invisibility; at the same time it imposes on those whom it subjects a principle of compulsory visibility' (1977, p. 187).

The notion of 'compulsory visibility', and the practice of policing, became clearer to me during a recent conversation with my friends Brenda and Diane at dinner. We were talking about Stephanie, a woman we had known professionally in our earlier careers who had transitioned from a man many years previously. As part of the conversation, we discussed our initial lack of awareness that Stephanie was transsexual. Diane described an incident that had struck her the year prior to her learning about Stephanie's transition: Stephanie had come up to her and said triumphantly, 'The woman at reception said I had beautiful legs!' Two things struck Diane about this at the time: that it was unusual for a woman to compliment another woman on her legs – they might offer compliments on other aspects of their physical attractiveness, but not that; and it was unusual for a woman to report such a compliment to another woman in such a tone of triumph (and see Speer, 2011). Diane said that after she learned of Stephanie's transition, she saw this incident, and her reaction to it at the time, as 'clues' to the awareness that Stephanie was transsexual. The story struck me as a powerful example of how we routinely monitor each other's gender performativity at the micro-level of behaviour, and in so doing, police the gender boundary. Stephanie had succeeded in 'passing' with us in the period before we became aware of her transition; but not quite, in Diane's case, though no conclusions were drawn from her observation at the time. We are reminded of Heritage's remark, quoted in Chapter 2, that 'It is surprising to realize the extent to which gender differentiation consists of a filigree of small scale, socially organized behaviours which are unceasingly iterated' (Heritage, 1984, p. 197). In Chapter 7 we found evidence in the detail of patterns of interaction of the routine, unremarked re-inscription of their own gendered identity among the female students in the tutorial group discussion of gendered behaviour; in the case of Diane's 'noticing' of something odd about Stephanie, we have the 'mis-performance' of gender by another which is immediately and instinctively marked, though in this case its 'significance' – what it 'means' about Stephanie – was not immediately understood. What motivates our own gendered performativity is the fact that we are being subjected, and subject each other, to endless scrutiny in terms of the gender norms prescribed by discourse. It is extraordinary to understand the extent of social surveillance through which the disciplining power of discourse is enacted and maintained.

Language study and applied linguistics have much to offer our understanding of discourse in the construction of subjectivity, because language is a site in which the operation of discourse at the micro-level is often present and may therefore be observed, if we know how and where to look. Here we need two things: a proper theoretical understanding of the way in which discourse operates in the construction of subjectivity; and appropriate methodological tools for gathering and analysing the evidence. Let me offer some concluding remarks about each.

The theoretical basis of studies of identity and subjectivity has undergone a radical shift in recent decades with the advent of the poststructuralist theories of subjectivity that have been the subject of this book. This is not to say that older theories were useless; far from it. In the earlier work on the identity of the Israelis in Melbourne which I carried out in the mid-1980s, I drew on Tajfel's Social Identity Theory (Tajfel, 1981). This is a theory assuming conflict and competition among human groups, which in turn determines the self-perception of group membership in intergroup settings and the relative valuation of that membership. It offers powerful insights into how intergroup relations (of competition and conflict) determine social identity, and how boundaries between groups are enforced. Tajfel's interest in racism and prejudice was motivated by his personal awareness of racism in the Holocaust: a Polish Jew, he was also a French citizen and soldier. He was captured and became a prisoner of war, and although was not targeted specifically for his Jewish identity, few members of his family in Poland survived. Although Social Identity Theory was subsequently subject to an explicit critique as being essentially asocial (Henriques, 1984; Williams, 1992), dependent on an obsolete dualism of the individual and society, this critique remains misguided in my view, as the setting of the theory in intergroup relations is intrinsically social. The theory remains a valuable source of insight into many of the issues and processes dealt with in this book (McNamara, 1997).

The paradigm shift represented by poststructuralism, however, offers crucial new insights into the essentially social character of what we experience as our 'identity', and how it is constructed, and they depend on a different kind of framework of understanding. The notion of discourse proposed by Foucault, the way in which the individual is both its subject (it has things to say about individual character) and its effect (the individual subject comes into being within discourse, not prior to or outside discourse), together with the way discourse focuses on the 'abnormal' – the madman, the criminal, the sexually deviant – thereby defining by default what is seen as 'normal', though this remains outside the spotlight, so to speak – all these things have profound implications for our subjectivity, our sense of ourselves. Further, the idea that the normal-abnormal binaries proposed in discourses do not finally exclude but that the excluded is included in the definition of the self means that there is a contradiction or a paradox in subjectivity. As Butler (1999, p. 18) puts it: 'Hegel introduces the idea that self-identity is only rendered actual to the extent to which it is mediated through that which is different. ... The grammatical subject is ... never self-identical.' In many ways the subject is helpless in the face of discourse; it cannot choose how it is seen, other than by conforming its speech and its behaviour in an attempt to make it appear acceptable, unremarkable, 'normal' in the terms of the discourse. Butler stresses the helplessness of the subject: 'Bound to seek recognition of its own existence in categories, terms, and names that are not of its own making, the subject seeks the sign of its own existence outside itself, in a discourse that is at once dominant and indifferent' (Butler, 1997, p. 20). This awareness of the pain of the experience of subjectivity, emerging from inevitable engagement with social processes that may be oppressive and are arbitrary and contradictory, is one of the most profound contributions of poststructuralism. Vulnerability is constitutive of the subject in poststructuralism. It makes it particularly appropriate for understanding racism, homophobia, sexism and other discourses shaping our experience. Poststructuralism, however, does not offer a simple political platform of 'us' and 'them'. Derrida cautions us that subjectivity is not an easy or self-evident notion, or an easy platform for political organization:

> Our question is still identity. What is identity, this concept of which the transparent identity to itself is always dogmatically presupposed by so many debates on monoculturalism or multiculturalism, nationality, citizenship, and in general, belonging? (Derrida, 1998, p. 14)

There is never a self which is simply separate and autonomous, capable of freely deciding to act and if necessary to resist, as is assumed in much of the critical writing in applied linguistics. Instead, the relationship of the Self to the discourses that form it is a struggle, not a simple opposition. This is most evocatively conveyed in Derrida's relationship with French language and culture, and his engagement with the deeply poignant poetry of Celan, writing in German, the language of the perpetrators of the violence he and his family suffered, but also *his* language. This complex involvement of the Other in the Self complicates enormously the issue of agency, and of resistance.

Poststructuralism in the work of Foucault, Derrida and Butler is Nietzschean: it takes a pessimistic view of the possibilities of human 'progress' and therefore does not subscribe to the progressivist notion in Hegel of the evolution of consciousness which so heavily influenced Marx. It is thus at a tangent at least, if not at odds, with the Marxian political orthodoxy of much critical work in applied linguistics. It is, however, deeply critical, and therefore political, in alerting us to the oppressive character of all discourse, operating in the delicate filaments of social perception and interaction, and making us eternally vigilant for the way in which all discourses, even apparently progressive ones, can carry the potential for violence. In a discussion of the shibboleth (see Chapter 9), a password guaranteeing protection, Derrida writes (1986/2005, p. 30):

> The value of the shibboleth may always, and tragically, be inverted. Tragically because the inversion sometimes overtakes the initiative of subjects, the goodwill of men, their mastery of language and politics. Watchword or password in a struggle against oppression, exclusion, fascism and racism, it may also corrupt its differential value, making of it a discriminatory limit, the grillwork of policing, of normalization, and of methodical subjugation.

What are the tools that applied linguistics has available to reveal the process of subjectification and the character of subjectivity in everyday life? There are two main possibilities. One is to focus on the content of what is said, and the manner in which it is formulated, to reveal the topics and preoccupations of particular discourses. We have seen examples of this in several sections of the book: in the content of reports of everyday racism in Chapter 4, in the discussion of membership categorization in Chapter 8, in the sociolinguistic analysis of features of the speech of those claiming asylum in Chapter 9, and in the examples cited in this chapter. Here Critical Discourse Analysis, enhanced through the use of corpus-based approaches (for example in the work of Baker, 2006), plays a role. (Note, however, that its thoroughly modernist politics and preferred tools of analysis (Hallidayan functionalism) are at odds with poststructuralist perspectives.) The other possibility is to study the interaction order using the tools

of Conversation Analysis, as I have argued in Chapter 7. Here again we
have a kind of contradiction: Conversation Analysis was developed
independently of poststructuralism and is not informed by it, and its
objects of study are by no means uniquely the discourse phenomena
that are the focus of poststructuralist approaches to subjectivity.
Nevertheless, I have argued that its key assumption, the turn-by-turn
enactment of social positioning which is not pre-given and simply
'beamed down' into the interaction, closely parallels the notion of
the endlessly iterated performativity of discourse. Both admit the
possibility of slippage or misfiring, which implies that the endless re-
inscription of the power of discourse in the details of interaction,
while it may be routine, is not inevitable. In that, there is some
modicum of agency.

Language study has much to offer the study of subjectivity in discourse. It can illuminate the workings of discourse, and hence of
power. But it requires theoretical and methodological clarity; this
book has attempted to be a contribution to both.

Glossary

Agency The capacity of the individual subject to control its environment and to determine the factors that influence its life and well-being.

Anti-Semitism Negative representations of the figure of 'the Jew' as Other; prejudice against Jewishness as a cultural and/or religious phenomenon.

Archaeology of knowledge In Foucault's philosophy, tracing the emergence and evolution of systems of thought.

Binary Involving an opposition between two contrasting possibilities, for example Self : Other or Normal : Abnormal.

Camp A style of self-presentation associated with certain types of homosexual men, involving flamboyance, effeminacy and self-irony.

Discourse (1) The way an aspect of reality is conceived of or represented at a particular time in history. This is sometimes referred to as 'big D Discourse'. (2) In linguistics, stretches of language use beyond the level of the sentence, either spoken or written. This is sometimes referred to as 'small d discourse'.

Essentialism The belief that there are innate or fixed characteristics of humans, for example masculinity/femininity in gender.

Ethnomethodology A branch of sociology developed in the work of Harold Garfinkel, focusing on the social processes of everyday reasoning and understanding.

Feminist poststructuralism An approach to feminism which draws on the work of philosophers such as Foucault and Derrida to understand the positioning of woman as subject, and the psychoanalytic theorist Lacan to understand the cultural origins of the psyche. Leading figures include Judith Butler and Elizabeth Grosz, among others.

Homophobia Fear of homosexuality or homosexuals, expressed in implicitly or explicitly hostile attitudes, and even violence.

Identity A modernist term, expressing the sense of self as either a psychological or a sociological phenomenon.

Identity politics The mobilization of political action in terms of categories (such as 'woman' (feminism), 'homosexual' (gay liberation) and so on) circulating within prevailing discourses.

Illocution In the linguistic pragmatics of J. L. Austin, the functional force of an utterance; the social action performed by an utterance, for example, complaint, suggestion, advice, etc.

Interaction order An independent social order, proposed by Goffman, which concerns how individuals manage face-to-face interaction.

Interpellation In the philosophy of Althusser, the way in which subjects are called into being through ideology.

Iterability In the philosophy of Derrida and Butler, the idea that the character of an event or a phenomenon is necessarily repeated and repeatable, not unique.

Latching In Conversation Analysis, when one speaker's turn immediately follows another's without the slightest pause.

Macro-level In sociology and in studies of discourse, the operation of large-scale social categories such as class, gender, sexuality, race, ethnicity, etc.

Meta-analysis An approach to quantitative research studies which aggregate the findings of a large number of studies on a single topic, to get a firmer basis for conclusions about the impact of the factors or variables being studied.

Micro-level In contrast to **macro-level**, in sociology and in studies of discourse, social interaction in conversation and the detail of actual language use.

Notional/functionalism An approach to language curriculum design focusing on coverage of semantic domains or of pragmatic functions in discourse as the basis for a curriculum which is not specific to any one language.

Other Not-Self; in Hegel's philosophy, and in poststructuralism, a figure in discourse which leads to a sense of Self as not-Other; in the work of Foucault, the typical subject of discourse.

Panopticon A proposal by the eighteenth-century utilitarian social reformer Jeremy Bentham for the design of prisons so that the prisoners would be under constant surveillance from a central point, leading to a consciousness of their visibility to the warder. Used by Foucault as a paradigm for the role of surveillance in the process of creating subjects in modernity.

Performance The acting out of a social role.

Performativity The presentation by an individual subject of an observable subjectivity by means of language, appearance and behaviour.

Plurilingualism An ability to speak more than one language, seen as an attribute of an individual; in contrast to **multilingualism**, which is the distribution of multiple languages within a society or community.

Poststructuralism A name for the thought of a loose group of philosophers and social theorists, including Foucault, Derrida and Butler among others, who stress the social processes involved in the construction of the Self, and emphasize vulnerability as constitutive of the subject.

Pragmatics The study in linguistics of the social actions performed by utterances in context.

Queer theory A branch of feminist poststructuralism which emphasizes the need to move beyond a dependence on the binary oppositions typical of discourse. It questions the mobilization of individuals in terms of categories represented by existing discourses of gender and sexuality.

Recognition The social process of being seen in terms of social categories and subject positions defined within discourses circulating in a given social space at a given time.

Self A subject position in the binary pair Self–Other, seen in poststructuralist theory as being dependent on discourses defining the Other, and hence the Self by default.

Subject (1) (noun) A topic in discourse (2) (noun) A type of individual who is the focus of discourse (3) (adj.) subject to: under the power of.

Subject position The characterization of a type of individual within discourse.

Subjectivity The sense of Self which is the result of being the subject *of* and subject *to* discourse.

Surveillance The process by which we subject one another to scrutiny in terms made available by discourse.

Visibility The requirement of discourse that individuals be seen, and see each other, in terms suggested by the discourse.

References

Abe, H. (2004). Lesbian bar talk in Shinjuku, Tokyo. In S. Okamoto & J. S. Shibamoto Smith (Eds.), *Japanese Language, Gender, and Ideology: Cultural Models and Real People* (pp. 205–21). Oxford: Oxford University Press.

Abu-Lughod, L. (1990). The romance of resistance: Tracing transformations of power through Bedouin women. *American Ethnologist, 17*(1), 41–55.

Ahearn, L. M. (2001). Language and agency. *Annual Review of Anthropology, 30*, 109–37.

Akiyama, T. (2004). Introducing speaking tests into a Japanese Senior High School entrance examination. Unpublished PhD thesis, University of Melbourne.

Althusser, L. (1971). *Lenin and Philosophy, and Other Essays* (B. Brewster, Trans.). New York: Monthly Review Press.

Anderson, B. (1991). *Imagined Communities: Reflections on the Origin and Spread of Nationalism*. (Revised edn). London: Verso.

'The art of elocution. No. 2. Correct pronunciation'. (1912). In *Every Woman's Encyclopaedia*. Available at: http://chestofbooks.com/food/household/Woman-Encyclopaedia-3/The-Art-Of-Elocution-No-2-Correct-Pronunciation.html, accessed 22.1.2018.

Atkinson, J. M. & Drew, P. (1979). *Order in Court: The Organisation of Verbal Interaction in Judicial Settings*. London: Macmillan.

Atkinson, J. M. & Heritage, J. (Eds.) (1984). *Structures of Social Action: Studies in Conversation Analysis*. Cambridge: Cambridge University Press.

Austin, J. L. (1962). *How to Do Things with Words: The William James Lectures Delivered at Harvard University in 1955* (J. Urmson & M. Sbisá, Eds.). Harvard, MA: Harvard University Press.

Baker, C. D. (2000). Locating culture in action: Membership categorization in texts and talk. In A. Lee & C. Poynton (Eds.), *Culture and Text: Discourse and Methodology in Social Research and Cultural Studies* (pp. 99–113). London: Routledge.

Baker, P. (2002). *Polari: The Lost Language of Gay Men*. New York: Routledge.
(2006). *Using Corpora in Discourse Analysis*. London: Continuum
(2008). *Sexed Texts: Language, Gender and Sexuality*. London: Equinox.

Bakhtin, M. M. (1981). Discourse in the novel. In M. Holquist (Ed.), *The Dialogic Imagination: Four Essays* (C. Emerson & M. Holquist, Trans.) (pp. 259–422). Austin: University of Texas Press. (Original work published in 1975.)

Banki, P. (2018). *The Forgiveness to Come: The Holocaust and the Hyper-ethical*. New York: Fordham University Press.

Baron-Cohen, S. (2003). *The Essential Difference: Male and Female Brains and the Truth about Autism*. New York: Basic Books.

Bartrop, P. R. & Eisen G. (Eds.) (1990). *The Dunera Affair: A Documentary Resource Book*. South Yarra, Victoria: Schwartz & Wilkinson with the Jewish Museum of Australia.

Bauman, Z. (2004). *Identity: Conversations with Benedetto Vecchi*. Cambridge; Malden, MA: Polity Press.

Baynham, M. (2017). Intersections of necessity and desire in migration research: Queering the migration story. In S. Canagarajah (Ed.), *The Routledge Handbook of Migration and Language* (pp. 431–47). Oxford and New York: Routledge.

Bennington, G. & Derrida, J. (1993). *Jacques Derrida* (G. Bennington, Trans.). Chicago: University of Chicago Press.

Benwell, B. & Stokoe, E. (2013). *Discourse and Identity*. Edinburgh: Edinburgh University Press.

Billig, M. (1999a). Conversation analysis and the claims of naivety. *Discourse and Society*, 10(4), 572–6.

  (1999b). Whose terms? Whose ordinariness? Rhetoric and ideology in conversation analysis. *Discourse and Society*, 10(4), 543–58.

Block, D. (2007). *Second Language Identities*. London: Continuum.

Block, D. & Cameron, D. (Eds.) (2002). *Globalization and Language Teaching*. London: Routledge.

Blommaert, J. (2005). *Discourse*. Cambridge: Cambridge University Press.

  (2009. Language, asylum, and the national order. *Current Anthropology*, 50(4), 415–25.

Blum, D. (1997). *Sex on the Brain: The Biological Differences between Men and Women*. New York: Viking.

Bourdieu, P. (1977). The economics of linguistic exchanges. *Social Science Information*, 16, 645–68.

  (1991). *Language and Symbolic Power*. London: Polity Press.

Brown, A. (2003). Interviewer variation and the co-construction of speaking proficiency. *Language Testing*, 20(1), 1–25.

  (2005). *Interviewer Variability in Language Proficiency Interviews*. Frankfurt: Peter Lang.

Brown, A. & McNamara, T. (2004). 'The devil is in the detail': Researching gender issues in language assessment. *TESOL Quarterly*, 38(3), 524–38.

Brown, P. & Levinson, S. (1978). Universals in language usage: Politeness phenomena. In E. Goody (Ed.), *Questions and Politeness: Strategies in Social Interaction* (pp. 56–310). Cambridge: Cambridge University Press.

Brutt-Griffler, J. (2002). *World English: A Study of its Development*. Clevedon: Multilingual Matters.

Burchfield, R. W. (1998). *The New Fowler's Modern English Usage: Revised 3rd Edition*. Oxford: Oxford University Press.

Burck, C. (2005). *Multilingual Living: Explorations of Language and Subjectivity*. Basingstoke; New York: Palgrave Macmillan.

Butler, C. W. & Fitzgerald R. (2010). Membership-in-action: Operative identities in a family meal. *Journal of Pragmatics, 42*, 2462–74.

Butler, J. (1990). *Gender Trouble: Feminism and the Subversion of Identity*. London; New York: Routledge.

    (1997). *The Psychic Life of Power: Theories in Subjection*. Stanford, CA: Stanford University Press.

    (1999). *Subjects of Desire: Hegelian Reflections in Twentieth-Century France*. New York: Columbia University Press.

Cambier-Langeveld, T. (2010). The role of linguists and native speakers in language analysis for the determination of speaker origin. *The International Journal of Speech, Language and the Law 17*(1): 67–93.

Cameron, D. (1995). *Verbal Hygiene*. London; New York: Routledge.

    (1997). Performing gender identity: Young men's talk and the construction of heterosexual masculinity. In S. Johnson & U. H. Meinhoff (Eds.), *Language and Masculinity* (pp. 47–64). Oxford: Blackwell.

    (2007). *The Myth of Mars and Venus: Do Men and Women Really Speak Different Languages?* Oxford: Oxford University Press.

    (2010). Sex/gender, language and the new biologism. *Applied Linguistics, 31*(2), 173–92.

Cameron, D. & Kulick, D. (2003). *Language and Sexuality*. Cambridge: Cambridge University Press.

Campbell, C. P. (Ed.) (2010). *Race and News: Critical Perspectives*. New York: Routledge.

Canagarajah, S. (1999). *Resisting Linguistic Imperialism in English Teaching*. Oxford: Oxford University Press.

Carr, J. & Pauwels, A. (2005). *Boys and Foreign Language Learning: Real Boys Don't Do Languages*. Basingstoke: Palgrave Macmillan.

Castles, S. (2003). Towards a sociology of forced migration and social transformation. *Sociology, 37*(1), 13–34.

Cheshire, J. & Trudgill, P. (Eds.) (1998). *The Sociolinguistics Reader: Gender and Discourse* (Vol. II). London: Arnold.

Chomsky, N. (1965). *Aspects of the Theory of Syntax*. Cambridge, MA: MIT Press.

    (1966). Linguistic theory. In R. C. Mead (Ed.), *Reports of the Working Committee* (pp. 43–49). New York: Northeast Conference on the Teaching of Foreign Languages.

    (1972) *Language and Mind*. New York: Harcourt Brace Jovanovich.

Cicourel, A. V. (1992). The interpenetration of communicative contexts: Examples from medical encounters. In A. Duranti & C. Goodwin

(Eds.), *Rethinking Context: Language as an Interactive Phenomenon* (pp. 291–310). Cambridge: Cambridge University Press.

Clayman, S. & Heritage, J. (2002). *The News Interview: Journalists and Public Figures on the Air*. Cambridge: Cambridge University Press.

Coates, J. (1986). *Women, Men, and Language: A Sociolinguistic Account of Sex Differences in Language*. London: Longman.

(1997a). One-at-a-time: The organisation of men's talk. In S. Johnson & U. Meinhof (Eds.), *Language and Masculinity* (pp. 107–29). Oxford: Basil Blackwell.

(1997b). The construction of a collaborative floor in women's friendly talk. In T. Givón (Ed.), *Conversation: Cognitive, Communicative and Social Perspectives* (pp. 55–89). Philadelphia: John Benjamins.

(2013). *Women, Men and Everyday Talk*. Basingstoke; New York: Palgrave Macmillan.

Corder, S.P. (1967). The significance of learners' errors. *International Review of Applied Linguistics in Language Teaching* 5(4), 161–70. Repr. in S. P. Corder (1981) *Error Analysis and Interlanguage* (pp. 5–13). Oxford: Oxford University Press.

Council of Europe (2001). *Common European Framework of Reference for Languages*. Cambridge: Cambridge University Press.

Damousi, J. (2010). *Colonial Voices: A Cultural History of English in Australia, 1840–1940*. Cambridge: Cambridge University Press.

Davidson, J. (1984). Subsequent versions of invitations, offers, requests, and proposals dealing with potential or actual rejection. In J. M. Atkinson & J. Heritage (Eds.), *Structures of Social Action: Studies in Conversation Analysis* (pp. 102–28). Cambridge: Cambridge University Press.

Davies, A. 1997. Australian immigrant gatekeeping through English language tests: How important is proficiency? In A. Huhta, V. Kohonen, L. Kurki-Suonio & S. Luoma (Eds.), *Current Developments and Alternatives in Language Assessment* (pp. 71–84). Jyväskylä: University of Jyväskylä and University of Tampere.

Davies, J. (2003). Expressions of gender: An analysis of pupils' gendered discourse styles in small group classroom discussions. *Discourse and Society*, 14(2), 115–32.

Day, D. (2013). Conversation analysis and membership categories. In C. A. Chapelle (Ed.), *The Encyclopedia of Applied Linguistics* (pp. 1050–5.) Oxford: Wiley-Blackwell.

De Beauvoir, S. (2010). *The Second Sex* (C. Borde & S. Malovany-Chevallier, Trans.). London: Vintage. (Original work published in 1949.)

De Certeau, M. (1984). *The Practice of Everyday Life*. Berkeley: University of California Press.

Derrida, J. (1998). *Monolingualism of the Other, or, The Prosthesis of Origin* (P. Mensah, Trans.). Stanford, CA: Stanford University Press.

Derrida, J. (2005). Shibboleth: For Paul Celan. In T. Dutoit & O. Pasanen (Eds.), *Sovereignties in Question: The Poetics of Paul Celan* (pp. 1–64). New York: Fordham University Press. (Original work published in 1986.)

Derrida, J. & Roudinesco, E. (2004). *For What Tomorrow: A Dialogue* (J. Fort, Trans.). Stanford, CA: Stanford University Press.

Dewaele, J.-M. (2010). *Emotions in Multiple Languages*. London: Palgrave Macmillan.

Drew, P. (1984). Speakers' reportings in invitation sequences. In J. M. Atkinson and J. Heritage (Eds.), *Structures of Social Action: Studies in Conversation Analysis* (pp. 129–51). Cambridge: Cambridge University Press.

Drew, P. & Heritage, J. (1992). Analyzing talk at work: An introduction. In P. Drew & J. Heritage (Eds.), *Talk at Work: Interaction in Institutional Settings* (pp. 3–65). Cambridge: Cambridge University Press.

Eades, D. (2005). Applied linguistics and language analysis in asylum seeker cases. *Applied Linguistics, 26*(4), 503–26.

  (2009). Testing the claims of asylum seekers: The role of language analysis. *Language Assessment Quarterly, 6*(1), 30–40.

Eades, D. & Arends, J. (2004). Using language analysis in the determination of the national origin of asylum seekers. *International Journal of Speech, Language and the Law, 11*(2), 179–99.

Eades, D., Fraser, H., Siegel, J., McNamara, T. & Baker, B. (2003). Linguistic identification in the determination of nationality: A preliminary report. *Language Policy, 2*(2), 179–99.

Eckert, P. & McConnell-Ginet, S. (1992). Think practically and look locally: Language and gender as community-based practice. *Annual Review of Anthropology, 21*, 461–90.

Essed, P. (1990). *Everyday Racism: Reports from Women of Two Cultures* (C. Jaffé, Trans.). Claremont, CA: Hunter House.

Essed, P. (1991). *Understanding Everyday Racism: An Interdisciplinary Theory*. Newbury Park, CA: Sage.

Fairclough, N. (1989). *Language and Power*. London: Longman.

  (2001) *Language and Power* (2nd edn). London: Longman.

  (2013). *Critical Discourse Analysis: The Critical Study of Language*. London: Routledge.

Fairclough, N. & Wodak, R. (1997). Critical Discourse Analysis. In T. A. Van Dijk (Ed.), *Discourse as Social Interaction* (pp. 258–84). London: Sage.

Fanon, F. (1963). *The Wretched of the Earth* (C. Farrington, Trans.). New York: Grove Press. (Original work published in 1961.)

  (1967). *Black Skin, White Masks* (C. L. Markmann, Trans.). New York: Grove Press. (Original work published in 1952.)

Fichte, J. G. (1922). *Reden an die deutsche Nation* [Addresses to the German nation] (R. F. Jones and G. H. Turnbull, Trans.). Chicago; London: The Open Court Publishing Company. (Original work published in 1808.)

Fishman, J. (1972). *Language and Nationalism: Two Integrative Essays*. Rowley, MA: Newbury House.

Fishman, P. (1978). Interaction: The work women do. *Social Problems*, 25(4), 397–406.

Fitzgerald, R. (2015). Membership Categorisation Analysis. In K. Tracy, C. Ilie & T. L. Sandel (Eds.), *The International Encyclopedia of Language and Social Interaction*. Boston: John Wiley & Sons. DOI: 10.1002/9781118611463.wbielsi018.

Flannery, T. (Ed.) (2002). *The Birth of Melbourne*. Melbourne: Text Publishing.

Foucault, M. (1967). *Madness and Civilization: A History of Insanity in the Age of Reason* (R. Howard, Trans.). London: Tavistock Publications.

(1973). *The Birth of the Clinic: An Archaeology of Medical Perception* (A. M. Sheridan, Trans.). London: Tavistock Publications.

(1977). *Discipline and Punish: The Birth of the Prison* (A. M. Sheridan, Trans.). New York: Pantheon Books.

(1978). *The History of Sexuality* (R. Hurley, Trans.). New York: Pantheon Books.

(1980) Power/knowledge: Selected interviews and other writings 1972-1977 (C. Gordon, Ed., C. Gordon, L. Marshall, J. Mepham & K. Soper, Trans.). New York: Vintage Books.

(1998). *Aesthetics, Method, and Epistemology. Vol. II of Essential Works of Foucault, 1954-1984* (J. D. Faubion, Ed., R. Hurley and others, Trans.). New York: New Press.

(2003). *Abnormal. Lectures at the Collège de France 1974-1975* (G. Burchell, Trans.). London: Verso.

Fraser, H. (2011). The role of linguists and native speakers in language analysis for the determination of speaker origin: A response to Tina Cambier-Langeveld. *International Journal of Speech, Language and the Law*, 18(1), 121–30.

Freud, S. (1955). A difficulty in the path of psycho-analysis. In J. Strachey (Trans. and Ed.), *The Complete Psychological Works of Sigmund Freud* (Vol. XVII, pp. 135–44). London: Hogarth Press. (Original work published in 1917.)

Frosh, S. (2005). *Hate and the 'Jewish Science': Anti-Semitism, Nazism, and Psychoanalysis*. Basingstoke: Palgrave Macmillan.

Fulcher, G. (2004). Deluded by artifices? The Common European Framework and harmonization. *Language Assessment Quarterly*, 1(4), 253–66.

Gardner, R. C. & Lambert, W. E. (1959). Motivational variables in second-language acquisition. *Canadian Journal of Psychology*, 13, 266–2.

Garfinkel, H. (1967). *Studies in Ethnomethodology*. Englewood Cliffs, NJ: Prentice-Hall.

Gee, J. (2015). *Social Linguistics and Literacies: Ideology in Discourses* (5th edn). Hoboken, NJ: Taylor and Francis.

Goffman, E. (1959). *The Presentation of Self in Everyday Life*. New York: Doubleday.

(1963). *Stigma: Notes on the Management of Spoiled Identity*. Englewood Cliffs, NJ: Prentice-Hall.

(1964). The neglected situation. *American Anthropologist, 66*(2), 133–6.

(1983). The interaction order. *American Sociological Review, 48*, 1–17.

Gowers, Sir E. (1965). *Fowler's Modern English Usage, 2nd Edition*. Oxford: Oxford University Press.

Grosz, E. (1990). *Jacques Lacan: A Feminist Introduction*. Sydney: Allen & Unwin.

Hall, S. (1996). Introduction: Who needs 'identity'? In S. Hall & P. du Gay (Eds.), *Questions of Cultural Identity* (pp. 1–17). London: Sage.

(1997). The work of representation. In S. Hall (Ed.), *Representation: Cultural Representations and Signifying Practices* (pp. 13–64). London: Sage.

Halliday, M. (1985). *An Introduction to Functional Grammar*. London: Edward Arnold.

Hegel, G. W. F. (1977). *Phenomenology of Spirit* (A. V. Miller, Trans.). Oxford: Oxford University Press. (Original work published in 1807.)

Heggoy, A. A. (1973). Education in French Algeria: An essay on cultural conflict. *Comparative Education Review, 17*(2), 180–97.

Henriques, J. (1984). Social psychology and the politics of racism. In J. Henriques, W. Hollway, C. Urwin, C. Venn, & V. Walkerdine (Eds.), *Changing the Subject: Psychology, Social Regulation and Subjectivity* (pp. 60–89). New York: Methuen.

Heritage, J. (1984) *Garfinkel and Ethnomethodology*. Cambridge: Polity Press.

(2009). Conversation Analysis as social theory. In B. S. Turner (Ed.), *The New Blackwell Companion to Social Theory* (pp. 300–20). Oxford: Blackwell.

Heritage, J. & Sorjonen, M.-L. (1994). Constituting and maintaining activities across sequences: *And*-prefacing as a feature of question design. *Language in Society, 23*, 1–29.

Hester, S. & Eglin, P. (Eds.) (1997). *Culture in Action: Studies in Membership Categorization Analysis*. Washington, DC: University Press of America.

Hill, J. (1998). Language, race, and white public space. *American Anthropologist, 100*, 680–9.

(2008). *The Everyday Language of White Racism*. Chichester: Wiley-Blackwell.

Hoffman, E. (1989). *Lost in Translation: A Life in a New Language*. London: Heinemann.

Holmes, J. (1986). Functions of *you know* in women's and men's speech. *Language in Society, 15*(1), 1–21.

Housley, W. & Fitzgerald, R. (2015). Introduction to membership categorization analysis. In R. Fitzgerald & W. Housley (Eds.), *Advances in Membership Categorization Analysis* (pp. 1–21). Los Angeles: Sage.

Hulstijn, J. H. (2007). The shaky ground beneath the CEFR: Quantitative and qualitative dimensions of language proficiency. *The Modern Language Journal, 91*(4), 663–7.

Humboldt, W. von. (1999). *On Language: On the Diversity of Human Language Construction and its Influence on the Mental Development of the Human Species* (M. Losonsky, Ed., P. Heath, Trans.). Cambridge; New York: Cambridge University Press. (Original work published in 1836.)

Hutton, C. (1999). *Linguistics and the Third Reich: Mother-Tongue Fascism, Race, and the Science of Language.* London; New York: Routledge.

Hyde, J. (2005). The gender similarities hypothesis. *American Psychologist,* 60(6), 581–92.

Inglis, K., S. Spark, J. Winter & C. Bunyan (2018). *Dunera Lives: A Visual History.* Clayton, Victoria: Monash University Publishing.

James, H. 1999. The speech of American women. In P. A. Walker (Ed.), *Henry James on Culture: Collected Essays on Politics and the American Cultural Scene* (pp. 58–81). Lincoln: University of Nebraska Press.

Jefferson, G. (1990). List construction as a task and interactions resource. In G. Psathas (Ed.), *Interactional Competence* (pp. 63–92). New York: Lawrence Erlbaum.

Kane, M. (2006). Validation. In R. Brennan (Ed.), *Educational Measurement* (4th edn, pp. 17–64). Westport, CT: American Council on Education and Praeger.

(2012). Validating score interpretations and uses. *Language Testing,* 29(1), 3–17.

Kapuściński, R. (2008). *The Other.* London: Verso.

Kinsman, G. (2004). The Canadian Cold War on queers: Sexual regulation and resistance. In R. Cavell (Ed.), *Love, Hate and Fear in Canada's Cold War* (pp. 108–32). Toronto: University of Toronto Press.

Kissau, S. (2006). Gender differences in motivation to learn French. *The Canadian Modern Language Review,* 62(3): 401–22.

Kitzinger, C. (2000) Doing Feminist Conversation Analysis. *Feminism & Psychology,* 10, 163–93.

(2005). Speaking as a heterosexual: (How) does sexuality matter for talk-in-interaction? *Research on Language and Social Interaction,* 38(3), 221–65.

(2006) Talking sex and gender. In P. Drew, G. Raymond & D. Weinberg (Eds.), *Talk in Interaction in Social Research Methods* (pp. 155–70). London: Sage.

(Ed.) (2007). Feminist Conversation Analysis: Research by students at the University of York, UK. Special issue of *Feminism and Psychology,* 17(2).

Kitzinger, C. & Frith, H. (1999). Just say no? The use of conversation analysis in developing a feminist perspective on sexual refusal. *Discourse and Society,* 10(3), 293–316.

Klemperer, V. 2000. *The Language of the Third Reich* (M. Brady, Trans.). London: Continuum. (Originally published in 1947 as *LTI: Notizbuch eines Philologen.* Berlin: Aufbau-Verlag.)

Kramsch, C. (2005). Post 9/11: Foreign languages between knowledge and power. *Applied Linguistics,* 26(4): 545–67.

(2009). *The Multilingual Subject: What Foreign Language Learners Say about their Experience and Why It Matters.* Oxford: Oxford University Press.

Kubota, R. 2011. Questioning linguistic instrumentalism: English, neoliberalism, and language tests in Japan. *Linguistics and Education, 22,* 248–60.

Lado, R. 1949. Measurement in English as a foreign language. Unpublished PhD dissertation, University of Michigan.

Lakoff, R. T. (1975). *Language and Woman's Place.* New York: Harper & Row.

(2004). *Language and Woman's Place: Text and Commentaries* (M. Bucholtz, Ed.). New York: Oxford University Press.

Lalu, P. (2000). The grammar of domination and the subjection of agency: Colonial texts and modes of evidence. *Historical Theory, 39*(4),45–68.

Land, V. & Kitzinger, C. (2005). Speaking as a lesbian: Correcting the heterosexist assumption. *Research on Language and Social Interaction, 38*(4), 371–416.

(2008). Closet talk: The contemporary relevance of the closet in lesbian and gay interaction. In V. Clarke and E. Peel (Eds.), *Out in Psychology: Lesbian, Gay, Bisexual, Trans and Queer Perspectives* (pp. 147–71). Chichester: John Wiley.

Language and National Origin Group. 2004. Guidelines for the use of language analysis in relation to questions of national origin in refugee cases. *The International Journal of Speech, Language and the Law, 11*(2), 261–6.

Lanzmann, C. (1985). *Shoah: An Oral History of the Holocaust. The Complete Text of the Film.* New York: Pantheon Books.

Lerner, G. (2004). Collaborative turn sequences. In G. Lerner (Ed.), *Conversation Analysis: Studies from the First Generation* (pp. 225–56). Amsterdam; Philadelphia: John Benjamins.

Levinson, S. (1983). *Pragmatics.* Cambridge: Cambridge University Press.

Liddicoat, A. J. (2007). *An Introduction to Conversation Analysis.* London: Continuum.

Lindström, A. & Sorjonen, M-.L. (2013). Affiliation in conversation. In J. Sidnell & T. Stivers (Eds.), *The Handbook of Conversation Analysis* (pp. 350–69). Oxford: Blackwell.

Louw-Potgieter, J. (1989). Covert racsim: An application of Essed's analysis in a South African context. *Journal of Language & Social Psychology, 8*(5), 307–19.

Lucy, N. (2004). *A Derrida Dictionary.* Malden, MA: Blackwell.

Mahmood, S. (2005). *Politics of Piety: The Islamic Revival and the Feminist Subject.* Princeton, NJ: Princeton University Press.

Manley, R. (1691). *The History of the Rebellions: In England, Scotland and Ireland: wherein, the most material passages, sieges, battles, policies and stratagems of war, are impartially related on both sides; from the year 1640 to the beheading of the Duke of Monmouth in 1685. In three parts.* London: printed for

L. Meredith at the Angel in Amen-Corner, and T. Newborough at the Golden Ball in St. Paul's-Church-Yard.

Mansfield, N. (2000). *Subjectivity: Theories of the Self from Freud to Haraway.* Sydney: Allen & Unwin.

Maryns, K. (2004). Identifying the asylum speaker: Reflections on the pitfalls of language analysis in the determination of national origin. *International Journal of Speech, Language and the Law, 11*(2), 240–60.

(2005). Monolingual language ideologies and code choice in the Belgian asylum procedure. *Language and Communication, 25*, 299–314.

(2006). *The Asylum Speaker: Language in the Belgian Asylum Procedure.* Manchester: St Jerome Press.

McNamara, T. (1987a). Language and social identity. *Australian Review of Applied Linguistics, 10*(2), 33–58.

(1987b). Language and social identity: Israelis abroad. *Journal of Language and Social Psychology, 6*(3/4), 215–28.

(1996). *Measuring Second Language Performance.* London: Longman.

(1997). What do we mean by social identity? Competing frameworks, competing discourses. *TESOL Quarterly, 31*(3), 561–7.

(2005). 21st century Shibboleth: Language tests, identity and intergroup conflict. *Language Policy, 4*(4), 1–20.

(2010). Reading Derrida: Language, identity and violence. *Applied Linguistics Review, 1*(1), 23–44.

(2011a). Managing learning: Authority and language assessment. *Language Teaching 4*(4), 500–15.

(2011b) Measuring deficit. In C. N. Candlin & J. Crichton (Eds.), *Discourses of Deficit* (pp. 311–26). London: Palgrave Macmillan.

(2012). Poststructuralism and its challenges for Applied Linguistics. *Applied Linguistics, 33*(5), 473–82.

(2013). Crossing boundaries: Journeys into language. *Language and Intercultural Communication, 13*(3), 343–56.

(2014). 30 years on - Evolution or revolution? *Language Assessment Quarterly, 11*(2), 226–32.

McNamara, T. & Roever, C. (2006). *Language Testing: The Social Dimension.* Oxford: Blackwell.

McNamara, T. & Ryan, K. (2011). Fairness vs justice in language testing: The place of English literacy in the Australian Citizenship Test. *Language Assessment Quarterly, 8*(2): 161–78.

McNamara, T. & Schüpbach, D. (2012). *Validating Lnguage and Country Knowledge Analyses in Asylum Cases: Report on the Project 'Updating the Minimum Criteria Used by LINGUA' for the Swiss Federal Office for Migration.* Melbourne: School of Languages and Linguistics, University of Melbourne.

(2018). Fairness and justice in Language Analysis for the Determination of Origin of asylum seekers (LADO). In I. M. Nick (Ed.), *Forensic*

Linguistics: Asylum-Seekers, Refugees and Immigrants (pp. 155–74). Wilmington, DE: Vernon Press.

(2019). Quality assurance in LADO: Issues of validity. In P. Patrick, M. S. Schmid & K. M. Zwaan (Eds.), *Language Analysis for the Determination of Origin*. Dordrecht: Springer.

McNamara, T., van den Hazelkamp, C. & Verrips, M. (2016). LADO as a language test: Issues of validity. *Applied Linguistics*, 37(2), 262–83.

Messick, S. (1989). Validity. In R. L. Linn (Ed.), *Educational Measurement* (3rd edn, pp. 13–103). New York: American Council on Education & Macmillan.

Milani, T. (2018). *Queering Language, Gender and Sexuality*. London: Equinox.

Moir, A. & Jessel, D. (1992). *Brain Sex: The Real Difference between Men and Women*. New York: Dell.

Moir, A. & Moir, B. (2000). *Why Men Don't Iron: The Fascinating and Unalterable Differences between Men and Women*. New York: Birch Lane Press.

Muyskens, P., Verrips, M. & Zwaan, K. (Eds.) (2010). *Language and Origin: The Role of Language in European Asylum Procedures: A Linguistic and Legal Survey*. Nijmegen: Wolf Legal Publishers.

Myers, K. A. (2005). *Racetalk: Racism in Plain Sight*. Lanham, MD: Rowman & Littlefield.

Myers, K. A. & Williamson, P. (2001). Race talk: The perpetuation of racism through private discourse. *Race & Society*, 4, 3–26.

Nguyen, H. & Nguyen, M. (2017). 'Am I a good boy?': Explicit membership categorization in parent–child interaction. *Journal of Pragmatics*, 121, 25–39.

Nirenberg, D. (2013). *Anti-Judaism: The History of a Way of Thinking*. New York: Norton.

North, B. (2000). *The Development of a Common Framework Scale of Language Proficiency*. New York: Peter Lang.

Norton, B. (2000). *Identity and Language Learning: Gender, Ethnicity and Educational Change*. Harlow: Longman/Pearson.

(2013). *Identity and Language Learning: Extending the Conversation*. Bristol: Multilingual Matters.

Norton Peirce, B. (1995). Social identity, investment, and language learning. *TESOL Quarterly*, 29(1), 9–31.

Nunan, D. & Choi, J. (2010). *Language and Culture: Reflective Narratives and the Emergence of Identity*. New York; London: Routledge.

O'Barr, W. & Atkins, B. (1980). 'Women's language' or 'Powerless language'? In S. McConnell-Ginet, R. Borker & N. Furman (Eds.), *Women and Language in Literature and Society* (pp. 93–110): New York: Praeger.

Ogden, R. (2006). Phonetics and social action in agreements and disagreements. *Journal of Pragmatics*, 38(10), 1752–75.

O'Loughlin, K. (2001). *The Equivalence of Direct and Semi-direct Speaking Tests*. Cambridge: Cambridge University Press.

(2002). The impact of gender in oral proficiency testing. *Language Testing*, 19, 169–92.

Organization of Economic Cooperation and Development (OECD) (2008). *OECD Annual Report 2008*. Paris: OECD Publications.

Orwell (1968). Antisemitism in Britain. In S. Orwell & I. Angus (Eds.), *As I Please: 1943–1945* (pp. 332–41). Vol. III of *The Collected Essays, Journalism and Letters of George Orwell*. London: Secker and Warburg. (Original work published in 1945.)

Park, J. S.-Y. 2011. The promise of English: Linguistic capital and the neoliberal worker in the South Korean job market. *International Journal of Bilingual Education and Bilingualism*, 14(4), 443–55.

Patrick, P. L., M. Schmid & K. Zwaan (Eds.) (2019). *Language Analysis for the Determination of Origin*. Dordrecht: Springer.

Pavlenko, A. (2006). *Emotions and Multilingualism*. Cambridge: Cambridge University Press.

(2007). Autobiographic narratives as data in applied linguistics. *Applied Linguistics*, 28(2): 163–88.

Pavlenko, A. & Blackledge, A. (Eds.) (2004). *Negotiation of Identities in Multilingual Contexts*. Clevedon: Multilingual Matters.

Pavlenko, A., Blackledge, A., Piller, I. & Teutsch-Dwyer, M. (Eds.) (2001). *Multilingualism, Second Language Learning, and Gender*. Berlin: Mouton de Gruyter.

Pennycook, A. (1994). Incommensurable discourses? *Applied Linguistics*, 15 (2), 115–38.

(2001). *Critical Applied Linguistics: A Critical Introduction*. London: Routledge.

Phillipson, R. (1992). *Linguistic Imperialism*. Oxford: Oxford University Press.

Picca, L. H. & Feagin, J. R. (2007). *Two-Faced Racism: Whites in the Backstage and Frontstage*. New York: Routledge.

Pigna, F. (2005). *The Myths of Argentine History: The Construction of a Past as a Justification of the Present*. Buenos Aires: Grupo Editorial Norma.

Pinker, S. (2002). *The Blank Slate: The Modern Denial of Human Nature*. New York: Viking.

Pomerantz, A. (1984). Agreeing and disagreeing with assessments: Some features of preferred/dispreferred turn shapes. In J. M. Atkinson & J. Heritage (Eds.), *Structures of Social Action: Studies in Conversation Analysis* (pp. 57–101). Cambridge: Cambridge University Press.

Porat, R. (2015). The Ausraeli approach: The Diasporic identity of Israelis in Australia. *J-Wire*, 11 August 2015. Available at www.jwire.com.au /the-ausraeli-approach-the-diasporic-identity-of-israelis-in-australia /#more-54708, retrieved 28.2.2018.

(2018) The Ausraelis: Israelis in Australia as a test case of distinctiveness vis-à-vis the Jewish diaspora. *Israel Affairs*, 24(1), 167–90.

Potter, J. & Wetherell, M. (1987). *Discourse and Social Psychology: Beyond Attitudes and Behaviour*. Newbury Park, CA: Sage.

Price, S. (1996). Comments on Bonny Norton Peirce's 'Social identity, investment, and language learning'. *TESOL Quarterly*, 30(2), 331–7.

Reath, A. 2004. Language analysis in the context of the asylum process: Procedures, validity, and consequences. *Language Assessment Quarterly*, 1(4), 209–33.

Reisigl, M. & Wodak, R. (Eds.) (2001). *Discourse and Discrimination: Rhetorics of Racism and Antisemitism*. London: Routledge.

Reynolds, J. & Roffe, J. (Eds.) (2004). *Understanding Derrida*. London: Continuum.

Ricœur, P. (1992). *Oneself as Another* (K. Blamey, Trans.). Chicago: University of Chicago Press.

Ros i Solé, C. & Fenoulhet J. (2013a). Romanticising language learning: Beyond instrumentalism. *Language and Intercultural Communication*, 13(3), 257–65.

Ros i Solé, C. & J. Fenoulhet (Eds.) (2013b). Romanticising language learning (Special issue). *Language and Intercultural Communication*, 13(3).

Roth, J. K. (2000). What does the Holocaust have to do with Christianity? In C. Rittner, S. D. Smith & I. Steinfeldt (Eds.), *The Holocaust and the Christian World* (pp. 5–10). New York: Continuum.

Ryave, A. L. (1978). On the achievement of a series of stories. In J. Schenkein (Ed.), *Studies in the Organization of Conversational Interaction* (pp. 113–32). New York: Academic Press.

Sacks, H. (1992). *Lectures on Conversation* (Vols. I & II, G. Jefferson, Ed.). Oxford: Blackwell.

Said, E. W. (1979). *Orientalism*. New York: Vintage Books.

Saussure, F. de (2013). *Course in General Linguistics* (R. Harris, Trans.). London: Bloomsbury. (Original work published in 1916.)

Schegloff, E. A. (1972). Notes on a conversational practice: Formulating place. In D. Sudnow (Ed.), *Studies in Social Interaction* (pp. 75–119). New York: The Free Press.

(1992a). In another context. In A. Duranti & C. Goodwin (Eds.), *Rethinking Context: Language as an Interactive Phenomenon* (pp. 191–227). Cambridge: Cambridge University Press.

(1992b). Introduction. In H. Sacks, *Lectures on Conversation* (G. Jefferson, Ed.) (Vol. I, pp. ix–lxii). Oxford: Blackwell.

(1997). Whose text? Whose context? *Discourse and Society*, 8, 165–87.

(1998a). Naïveté vs sophistication or discipline vs self-indulgence: A rejoinder to Billig. *Discourse and Society*, 10(4), 577–82.

(1998b). Reply to Wetherell. *Discourse and Society*, 9(3), 413–16.

(1999). 'Schegloff's texts' as 'Billig's data': A critical reply. *Discourse and Society*, 10(4), 558–72.

(2007a). A tutorial on membership categorization. *Journal of Pragmatics*, 39(3), 462–82.

(2007b). *Sequence Organization in Interaction: A Primer in Conversation Analysis I*. Cambridge: Cambridge University Press.

Schüpbach, D. (2009). Testing language, testing ethnicity? Policies and practices surrounding the ethnic German Aussiedler. *Language Assessment Quarterly, 6*(1), 78–82.

Seedhouse, P. (2005). Conversation Analysis and language learning. *Language Teaching, 38*(4), 165–87.

Seidlhofer, B. (Ed.) (2003). *Controversies in Applied Linguistics*. Oxford: Oxford University Press.

Selinker, L. (1972). Interlanguage. *International Review of Applied Linguistics in Language Teaching, 10*(3): 209–32.

Senghor, L. S. (1948). *Anthologie de la nouvelle poésie nègre et malgache de langue française*. Paris: Presses Universitaires de France.

Sheldon, A. (1990). Pickle fights: Gendered talk in preschool disputes. *Discourse Processes, 13*, 5–31.

Shnukal, A. (1983). Torres Strait Creole: The growth of a new Torres Strait language. *Aboriginal History, 7*, 173–85.

Shohamy, E. (2001). *The Power of Tests: A Critical Perspective on the Uses of Language Tests*. London: Pearson.

2006. *Language Policy: Hidden Agendas and New Approaches*. Routledge.

Sidnell, J. (2010). *Conversation Analysis: An introduction*. New York: Wiley Blackwell.

Silverman, D. (1998). *Harvey Sacks: Social Science and Conversation Analysis*. New York: Oxford University Press.

Soyinka, W. (1963). Telephone conversation. In G. Moore & U. Beier (Eds.), *Modern Poetry from Africa* (p. 111). Harmondsworth: Penguin.

Speer, S. A. (2002). What can conversation analysis contribute to feminist methodology? Putting reflexivity into practice. *Discourse and Society, 13*, 783–803.

(2005). *Gender Talk: Feminism, Discourse and Conversation Analysis*. London: Routledge.

(2011). On the role of reported, third party compliments in passing as a 'real' woman. In S. A. Speer & E. Stokoe (Eds.), *Conversation and Gender* (pp. 155–82). Cambridge: Cambridge University Press.

(2012) Feminist Conversation Analysis: Who needs it? *Qualitative Research in Psychology, 9*(4), 292–7.

Speer, S. A. & Green, R. (2007) On passing: The interactional organization of appearance attributions in the psychiatric assessment of transsexual patients. In V. Clarke & E. Peel (Eds.), *Out in Psychology: Lesbian, Gay, Bisexual, Trans and Queer Perspectives* (pp. 335–68). Chichester: John Wiley.

Speer, S. A. & Stokoe, E. (Eds.) (2011). *Conversation and Gender*. Cambridge: Cambridge University Press.

Spolsky, B. (1995). *Measured Words*. Oxford: Oxford University Press.

Stirling, L. & Manderson, L. (2011). About *you*: Authority, objectivity and the generalised you. *Journal of Pragmatics, 43*(6), 1581–602.

Stivers, T. (2008). Stance, alignment, and affiliation during storytelling: When nodding is a token of affiliation. *Research on Language and Social Interaction*, 41(1), 31–57.

Stokoe, E (2010) 'I'm not gonna hit a lady': Conversation analysis, membership categorization and men's denials of violence towards women. *Discourse and Society*, 21(1), 1–24.

(2012). Moving forward with membership categorization analysis: Methods for systematic analysis. *Discourse Studies*, 14(3), 277–303.

Tajfel, H. (1981). *Human Groups and Social Categories: Studies in Social Psychology*. Cambridge: Cambridge University Press.

Tannen, D. (1989). Interpreting interruption in conversation. In B. Music, R. Graczyk & C. Wiltshire (Eds.), *Papers from the 25th Annual Regional Meeting of the Chicago Linguistic Society. Part Two: Parasession on Language in Context* (pp. 266–87). Chicago: Chicago Linguistic Society.

Tannen, D. (1990). *You Just Don't Understand: Women and Men in Conversation*. New York: Morrow.

Ten Have, P. (2007). *Doing Conversation Analysis* (2nd edn). Los Angeles: Sage.

Turner, L. (2002). Belonging, being friends and learning to write in a second language: The social construction of self and mind. Unpublished PhD thesis, University of Melbourne.

University of Cambridge Local Examinations Syndicate (2000). *Cambridge IELTS 2: Examination Papers from the University of Cambridge Local Examinations Syndicate*. Cambridge: Cambridge University Press.

Van Dijk, T. A. (1987). *Communicating Racism: Ethnic Prejudice in Thought and Talk*. Newbury Park, CA: Sage.

(1991). *Racism and the Press*. London: Routledge.

Van Ek, J. A. & Trim, J. L. M. (1998a). *Waystage 1990* (Revised and corrected edn). Cambridge: Cambridge University Press.

(1998b) *Threshold 1990* (Revised and corrected edn). Cambridge: Cambridge University Press.

(2001) *Vantage*. Cambridge: Cambridge University Press.

Van Lier, L. (1989) Reeling, writhing, drawling, stretching and fainting in coils: Oral proficiency interviews as conversations. *TESOL Quarterly*, 23, 480–508.

Verrips, M. (2011). LADO and the pressure to draw strong conclusions: A response to Tina Cambier-Langeveld. *International Journal of Speech, Language and the Law*, 18(1), 131–43.

Watson D. R. (1997). Some general reflections on 'categorization' and 'sequence' in the analysis of conversation. In S. Hester & P. Eglin (Eds.), *Culture in Action: Studies in Membership Categorization Analysis* (pp. 49–75). Washington, DC: University Press of America.

Wetherell, M. (1998). Positioning and interpretative repertoires: Conversation analysis and poststructuralism in dialogue. *Discourse and Society*, 9(3), 387–412.

Wilkins, D. (1973). *Notional Syllabuses*. Oxford: Oxford University Press.

Wilkinson, S. & Kitzinger, C. (2007) Conversation Analysis, gender and sexuality. In A. Wetherall, B. Watson & C. Gallois (Eds.), *Language, Discourse and Social Psychology* (pp. 206–30). Houndmills: Palgrave-Macmillan.

Williams, G. (1992). *Sociolinguistics: A Sociological Critique*. London: Routledge.

Wistrich, R. S. (2010) *A Lethal Obsession: Anti-Semitism from Antiquity to the Global Jihad*. New York: Random House.

Wolfson, N. (1989). *Perspectives: Sociolinguistics and TESOL*. Rowley, MA: Newbury House.

Wong, J. & Waring, H. Z. (2010). *Conversation Analysis and Second Language Pedagogy*. London; New York: Routledge.

Wood, G. (Ed.) (1985). *Labelling in Development Policy*. London: Sage.

Wooffitt, R. (2005). *Conversation Analysis and Discourse Analysis: A Comparative and Critical Introduction*. London; New York: Sage.

Woolard, K. (1998). Introduction: Language ideology as a field of inquiry. In B. B. Schieffelin, K. A. Wollard & P. V. Kroskrity (Eds.), *Language Ideologies: Practice and Theory* (pp. 3–47). Oxford: Oxford University Press.

Young, R. & He, A. (Eds.) (1998). *Talking and Testing: Discourse Approaches to the Assessment of Oral Proficiency*. Amsterdam: Benjamins.

Zetter, R. (1991). Labelling refugees: Forming and reforming a bureaucratic identity. *Journal of Refugee Studies*, 4(1), 39–62.

   (2007). More labels, fewer refugees: Remaking the refugee label in an era of globalization. *Journal of Refugee Studies*, 20(2), 172–92.

Index